John Hurston has been an encoura istry alongside Dr. Cho is legendary; of one of God's choice servants. I k. ...ill bless and inspire those who read it, especially those who need to press into God during challenging times.

—**Tommy Barnett**
Pastor, Phoenix First Assembly of God
Co-pastor, LA Dream Center

It has been my privilege to know John Hurston over a period of thirty years. His experiences are not only an inspiration, but his book, *Divine Desperation*, speaks to all of our hearts about what God can do through a life that is dedicated totally to Him.

—**L. John Bueno**
Executive Director, Assemblies of God World Missions

If you are looking for a story of the healing power of God, then John Hurston's book, *Divine Desperation,* is for you. Reverend Hurston has a long history of seeing God's miraculous power manifested. I encourage all to read it.

—**Bishop Keith A. Butler**
Word of Faith International Christian Center
Southfield, Mississippi

I was six years old, and I still remember the moment—Maxine Poston Hurston laid her hands on my little faith-filled head. Two hours later I came up from being "slain in the spirit" and speaking in my heavenly language. Maxine's name invokes unbelievably wonderful memories—joy...tears...love...wonder...beauty...Jesus...the precious Holy Spirit! Thank you, Maxine Hurston, for loving Jesus so much that you made a difference for me.

—**Jan Crouch**
Co-founder, Trinity Broadcast Network

John Hurston has identified a key ingredient to living victoriously. His insights into Scripture and personal accounts of ministry reveal the power of divine desperation. This book will ignite you with the Spirit's fire of holy desire and will change you forever.

—**Billy Joe Daugherty**
Pastor, Victory Christian Center
Tulsa, Oklahoma

John Hurston is not the kind of man who merely writes about a subject. He lives it! This book is alive with the excitement of John's adventures and God's faithfulness. In *Divine Desperation,* God's promises become God's performances. You are going to receive a challenge, and you are going to love reading this book.

—**Charles Green**
Founder, Faith Church of New Orleans
Chairman, Oral Roberts University Board of Regents

John Hurston's memoir should be required reading for every Christian who is committed to evangelism and prayer. His stories are revelatory and exciting, but that's not all. He also instructs us very carefully on interpreting each story, constantly leading us back into Scripture and reminding us why we believe what we believe. This book is a tour de force.

—**Ted Haggard**
Pastor, New Life Church
Colorado Springs, Colorado

From the spellbinding vision of heaven to the life-changing closing chapter, this book will have you on the edge of your seat…and perhaps on your knees. Don't miss *your* opportunity to gain insight from the man who mentored the pastor of the world's largest church!

—**Marilyn Hickey**
President, Marilyn Hickey Ministries

Thirty-five years ago I was a young man when I first heard John Hurston speak. I was so moved that I could tell what he was feeling and could see what he was seeing. He is truly a Joshua and a Caleb to this generation. *Divine Desperation* will cause you to become desperate for the Divine!

—**John A. Kilpatrick**
Pastor, Brownsville Assembly of God
Pensacola, Florida

I am thrilled that the Father has inspired John Hurston to write *Divine Desperation.* The very essence of the cell church movement is embodied in his chapters. I trust all who read this will find great guidance in its pages!

—**Ralph W. Neighbour, Jr.**
Author and Cell Church Pioneer

Like Barnabas, my friend John made possible the ministry of a modern day "Paul," who was later catapulted into world prominence. Now, for the first time, we can view the story from the eyes of a man who was closer to the foundation of the church in Korea than anyone else in the world.

—**TOMMY REID**
SENIOR PASTOR, THE TABERNACLE
ORCHARD PARK, NEW YORK

This inspiring book is a *must read* for those who want to understand what it means to stay in the flow of God's move around our world today. If you are interested in what it takes to effectively grow a great church, I strongly suggest you read the powerful wisdom woven into this book!

—**BOB RODGERS**
EVANGEL WORLD PRAYER CENTER
LOUISVILLE, KENTUCKY

Dr. Hurston's life has encouraged tens of thousands worldwide. May this book build a fire in you for a holy desperation for God. Prayer brings revival and cells contain revival. Dr. Hurston has been a leader in both.

—**LARRY STOCKSTILL**
PASTOR, BETHANY WORLD PRAYER CENTER
BATON ROUGE AND BAKER, LOUISIANA

John Hurston is a hero, and his book would be a good gift for anyone! Not only it is historically valuable to the Body of Christ, it is also challenging and inspirational. My wife Joyce and I plan to read this book as part of our devotions.

—**KARL STRADER**
PASTOR, CARPENTER'S HOME CHURCH
LAKELAND, FLORIDA

Jeffery

May God bless
you as you continue
to build His Kingdom!

John Hairston

Luke 18:1-8

DR. JOHN HURSTON
with
MAXINE & KAREN HURSTON

DIVINE DESPERATION

12 POWERFUL INSIGHTS TO HELP YOU FULFILL GOD'S DESTINY FOR YOUR LIFE

Divine Desperation by John Hurston with Maxine and Karen Hurston
Published by Creation House Press
A part of Strang Communications Company
600 Rinehart Road
Lake Mary, Florida 32746
www.creationhouse.com

This book or parts thereof may not be reproduced in any form, stored in a retrieval system or transmitted in any form by any means—electronic, mechanical, photocopy, recording or otherwise—without prior written permission of the publisher, except as provided by United States copyright law.

All Scripture quotations, unless otherwise indicated, are taken from New King James Version of the Bible. Copyright © 1979, 1980, 1982 by Thomas Nelson, Inc., publishers. Used by permission.

Scripture quotations marked NIV are from the Holy Bible, New International Version. Copyright © 1973, 1978, 1984, International Bible Society. Used by permission.

Cover design by Rachel Campbell
Interior design by Sallie Traynor

Copyright © 2003 by John Hurston
All rights reserved.

Library of Congress Control Number: 2003100267
International Standard Book Number: 0-59185-171-8

Printed in the United States of America.
03 04 05 06 07 8 7 6 5 4 3 2 1

To contact the author:
Office: (850) 934-9504
Fax: (850) 932-3882
www.hurstonministries.org
hurstonm@bellsouth.net

ACKNOWLEDGMENTS

SPACE WILL NOT allow me to recognize the many people I would like to thank, including family members, friends, coworkers and fellow ministers who have blessed my life in so many ways. Here are but a few:

Dr. Cho—Thank you for your kind encouragement that I write this book. I am deeply proud of you and the way you and Grace have allowed God to mightily use your lives.

Easter Hurston—You were a godly wife to Dad and a dedicated mother to me and my sisters Leta, Aimee and Ann. Even though you have passed through "the veil," I will always be grateful that you wisely led me to the Lord and a deeper commitment to our Jesus.

Maxine—My darling wife, you have been the most excellent helpmate a man could have. Thank you for journeying with me through this exciting life and for helping me remember significant details for this book.

Karen, my daughter—I am grateful for the endless hours you have spent interviewing me and doing the actual writing of this book. Through this process we both better understood the incredible legacy God has given us. I have again realized why you are better to me than seven sons.

John Hicks and Rob Siedenburg—Thank you for your editing skills in the earlier stages of this book. Bill Langlitz, thanks for being such an efficient administrative assistant.

Allen Quain—You are a gift in your own right. Many thanks to you, your assistant, Amy Condiff, and your Creation House staff for believing in this book enough to publish it.

Paul Ai, Charles Butterfield, Terry Jones, Nam Soo Kim, Tommy Reid, Rob Robinson, Aaron Rothganger, Irvin Rutherford, Arthur Sholtis,

Glenn Stafford, John Stetz, Jim and Jean Thompson, Bob Tilton, Clyde Wasdin, Ralph Wilkerson (a few of the fine ministers and missionaries with whom I have worked)—I will ever be grateful for the wonderful opportunity to co-labor with you. You often encouraged me.

D'etta Butler, Ralph Byrd, Henry Garlock, Glenn Horst, Glen Hurst, Maynard Ketcham, Mary Martin, Manne Paulson, Lou Richards, Florence Steidal, Henry Swain—You have gone on ahead of me, and are now with our Lord in heaven. I have learned and been blessed so much by each of you.

Those who called, wrote and visited me when I was sick in the hospital (including Dr. Cho, Jim and Jean Thompson, LM Thorne, Bob Tilton, Ken Sumrall, John Kilpatrick and many others who will go nameless)—Thank you. It is only because of your prayers that I am now alive to write this book.

Jesus—Most of all, I am grateful to you. You lived and died so every good thing that happened in this book would be possible. I ask that You empower each of us, by Your Spirit, with all the boldness and wisdom we will ever need to fulfill God's unique purposes for our lives!

Table of Contents

FOREWORD

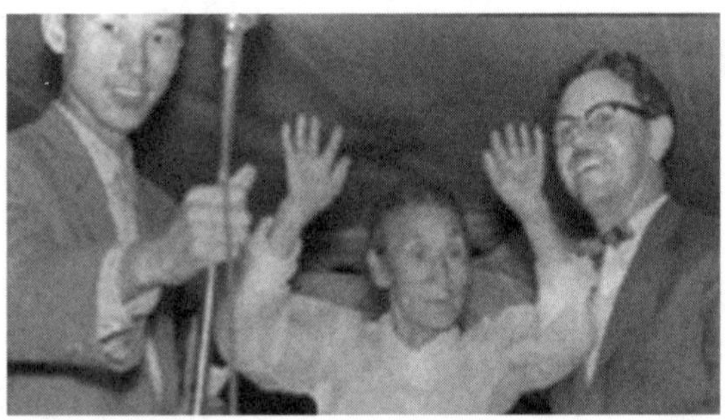

A young Dr. Cho and John Hurston during a 1958 tent revival. The older woman in the center had just been healed.

THIS BOOK WAS MY IDEA. John Hurston is one of two people to whom I owe my ministry. Jashil Choi, my deceased mother-in-law, taught me about prayer. She startled me out of sound sleep many a cold, early morning to pray. I resented her then, but what I learned from her about prayer has been crucial to my ministry.

John Hurston was my mentor. Since 1958, John and I have ministered together, worked together, laughed together and cried together. He taught me many truths about life and ministry, but especially about the Holy Spirit.

When I served as his interpreter in my earlier days, his every sermon was on the Holy Spirit and how vital it was to depend on Him. I grew irritated at John's repeated mention of the Holy Spirit, but that focus later became the bedrock of my ministry.

I have many cherished memories of John. When I was drafted into the Korean military in 1960, I left John in charge of my struggling, yet growing, tent congregation. Not only did my congregation double under his leadership, but when I returned, John was also constructing a large sanctuary much closer to Seoul's downtown. At first I refused John's request to make the move with him; it would be like starting over, because less than a handful in my tent congregation could afford the bus ride there.

But God and John prevailed, and we made the move by 1961. Because I was not yet ordained, John served for one year as the founder of that second stage of the church. When I was ordained in 1962, John stepped down and became "missionary advisor," and I became senior pastor. We then started a pattern that continued until 1970: I preached salvation and healing in multiple services on Sunday morning; John preached on the Holy Spirit in two evening services, and during many weeks he went into rural areas to plant churches.

John's wife, Maxine, was his faithful partner. Maxine was lovely both in form and in spirit, gentle in her ways and sharp in her discernment. She was ever an encouragement to me and to all those around her.

Karen, their daughter, was the child who often sat in my lap when church photographs were taken. Once, when I was quite ill and still single, she patted me on the forehead and told me not to worry. "When I grow up," she insisted, "I'll become a nurse and take care of you. If you wait, I'll marry you."

John left in 1970 to head a mission in Vietnam for five years. After Saigon fell, I asked him to return to Seoul with his family. By 1976, John helped me start Church Growth International, our church's outreach to pastors and church leaders. In five years we held 115 seminars that trained nearly 50,000 pastors and church leaders in countries around the world.

In our earlier days of overseas travel, John and I often shared a hotel room to reduce expenses. I remember our many outstanding times of fellowship and ministry together. We also had some humorous incidents, such as the time in Germany when we went out jogging, only to be chased by some aggressive dogs. We ran especially fast that time.

When God thrust me into the limelight, John never once resented my growing prominence, but instead stood behind me, encouraging me in all I felt God calling me to do. My church grew from 40,000 to 200,000 during the last five years that John officially served with me. We have stayed in contact ever since, with John always rejoicing at every new way that God used me.

John helped to transform my ministry, and I grew to fulfill my destiny in God. The church we started has become the largest church in history, now with a membership of 830,000. Learn well and apply the truths in this book, and your life will also be transformed for God's glory!

—DR. DAVID YONGGI CHO
SEOUL, SOUTH KOREA
OCTOBER 15, 2001

INTRODUCTION

ON THE NIGHT of September 20, 2001, a nurse told my family that I would soon die. Since my open-heart surgery the previous June, I had experienced a series of complications and had been in and out of the hospital several times. I had grown so weak that the doctor had me put on a respirator, a type of artificial life support that breathes for those too weak to breathe on their own.

My wife, Maxine, and daughter, Karen, cried desperately to the Lord in prayer, knowing both from Scripture and from experience that we serve a healing God. Karen was so badly shaken that she even contacted Dr. Cho's office in Korea and asked whether he would come to the States to preach my funeral.

Many people came to pray for me over the next few days, including some precious friends powerful in prayer. Jim and Jean Thompson, dear friends and pastors of a church in Maryland who have an anointing for healing similar to that of Smith Wigglesworth, flew to Florida to pray for me. As a result of their prayers, I could finally eat again. They were like John the Baptist, paving the way; but I still needed a complete breakthrough.

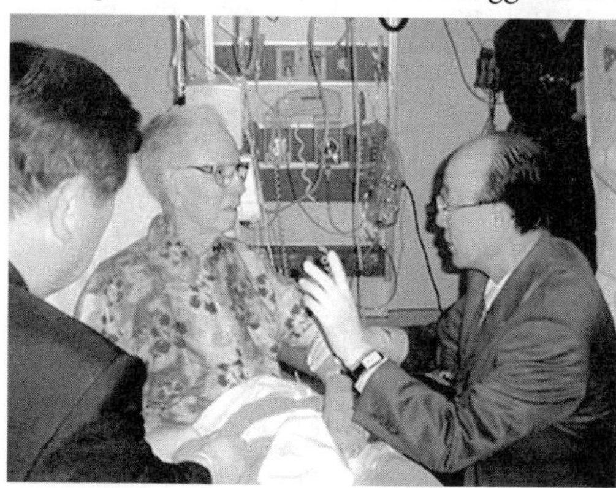

I was in the ICU when Dr. Cho came to pray for me.

When he heard the news that I was dying, Dr. Cho didn't just sit at his desk and pray for me—and he didn't prepare a funeral sermon either.

Instead he arrived in Florida on September 29, flying more than 7,000 miles from Korea. When Dr. Cho came into my room in the intensive care unit, a tangible sense of God's power entered with him. He told me that he had *not* come to preach a funeral, but rather to pray for a resurrection. Then he added, "I bring you the prayers of the 800,000 members of my congregation."

I had never been happier to see my old friend! Dr. Cho laid hands on me and prayed for my full restoration.

Following Dr. Cho's visit and prayer, I improved so rapidly that I was soon home from the hospital. Today I am in good health. God used the man I had once mentored to speak life to me.

God also used him to prompt me to write this book. The following morning, before he left to fly back to Korea, Dr. Cho told Karen that I should write a book about my life.

Even though this book was Dr. Cho's idea—and I respect him immensely—I was hesitant at first. You see, I'd rather sit across a table from you so we could talk face-to-face. I'd like you to tell me all about your own God-given dream and calling. And I'd love to encourage you by sharing some of what God has taught me.

But I've faced reality. Although I am healthy now and still travel some, I am eighty years old and we may never meet face-to-face. You may be too busy or too far away to travel to me. But you *can* read this book. Once again, the pastor of the world's largest church was right. So I'm taking Dr. Cho's advice and putting down my story in this book so I can share it with you.

I want you to succeed. I want you to know personal fulfillment as you fulfill God's unique purposes and destiny for *your* life. You are more important to Him than you know. That's why I write this book.

If you're at all like me, you enjoy a good story. In this book I tell my own story to illustrate the truths God has taught me—insights that I know will benefit you, too. It took many years of God's work in me before He could use me to mentor Dr. Cho; for that reason I use most of the chapters in this book to tell the story of those earlier years, for they were foundational to what was to follow.

So read on, my friend. Join me in the jungles of Africa, the cities of Korea and the ravages of Vietnam to uncover insights that can also help you fulfill God's divine destiny for your life.

You see, ultimately, this book is really about you. Whatever you do in life, know this: God has even greater plans for you, plans to use you even more mightily to make a difference in this world. Your desire to please Him is no accident. It's a God-given yearning, designed by the Lord Himself to lead you on to higher ground.

My role with Dr. Cho was never to direct him, but rather to encourage him in what God called him to do. May this book also encourage you to do what God has called you to do. You are worth it. After all, you are the very "apple of His eye." [1]

How to Benefit From This Book

I WROTE THIS BOOK to bring you maximum benefit. That can happen in any of three ways:

Your Personal Growth

You will find stories and principles in each chapter that are great as teaching and preaching illustrations. Each chapter also has lists and sidebars with helpful information or ideas for application. One pastor told Karen that he could preach a year of sermons from that information alone—and he was serious! Each chapter ends with an "About You" section, in which I share my heart about that insight and how it might apply to you and benefit your life.

Your Couple or Family Devotions

If you and your spouse are currently in any type of service or ministry (or plan to be), this would be a great book to read together, one chapter a week, either as a couple or as a family. Take time to discuss the questions at the end of every chapter. I believe it will enrich your relationships as well as your service for the Lord!

Your Small Group or Cell Group

There are three types of questions at the end of each chapter that were designed for two or more people to discuss, in order to better understand and apply the primary truth that chapter contains:

1. One *sharing question*, to encourage each person to tell a little about himself or herself;
2. Four or five *discussion questions*, to help all involved dig a bit deeper in that specific insight; and
3. Two to four *application* items, to challenge each of us to apply an aspect of that insight in our daily lives.

If you use the questions either in devotions or in a small group, do not feel that you have to answer each one before the devotions or group meeting is complete. Sometimes a single question will trigger a long discussion or point to a time of needed ministry. Allow the Holy Spirit to use these questions in whatever way He deems best to minister to and through you.

Insight One

DIVINE DESPERATION

Desperation helps us make God's priorities our own

COOL OCTOBER WINDS blew gently outside our small cement-block church. Inside, eight of us knelt on the bare cement floor, fervently praying around a simple wooden altar.

We had fasted that Tuesday, and we all prayed aloud that night. My wife Maxine, six church members and I were few in number around that altar, but desperation drove us. Unless God brought a breakthrough in our personal lives and in our little church in Georgia, we had no hope. Years later I would have the privilege of mentoring the man whom God would raise up to be pastor of the world's largest church, but at this point in my life, I felt like a frustrated failure. Our little church needed a breakthrough.

Suddenly, without any warning, Maxine fell onto her side. At first I was alarmed, so I looked at her face to see if she was having difficulty breathing. Her eyes were closed, but she was breathing normally. I was surprised that her face glowed with greater happiness than I had ever seen. We faced our greatest crisis since we married, and it was strange to see her smile.

I stopped praying for a few minutes and just watched Maxine. As I listened, I heard her speak in tongues, but it sounded as if she were conversing with someone. I gently put Maxine's head in my lap, hoping to make her more comfortable, yet not wanting to disturb her.

NO SHALLOW BEAUTY

For the first twenty minutes, Maxine was joyous. I have never before or since seen anyone radiate so much peace. As I watched Maxine, and others prayed, my thoughts drifted back to the past.

I was attracted from the moment I first saw Maxine. She was a strikingly beautiful young woman, with deep brown eyes that radiated a gentle kindness and matching hair that softly framed her lovely face. She exuded a godly innocence and a warm smile that captured my heart.

Hers was no shallow beauty. When Maxine was only eight years old, she sensed God's call to be a missionary in Africa. From that young age onward, she focused her entire life on that one goal. By the time I met her, Maxine was not only a delight be around, but she was also an able student at her Bible school. She helped start the school library, coordinated the weekly Friday night chapel service and spent her summers speaking in evangelistic crusades with her minister mother—looking forward to the day when she would serve in Africa. Her yearbook picture displayed her beauty, while the caption described Maxine best: "Her personality is as sweet as a rose, spreading its fragrance wherever she goes."

I knew even then that Maxine was God's perfect partner for me. God had called me to Africa as well, when I was attending a different Bible school. For such a young man, I was already experienced in ministry. I had been pastor of two churches, and had served as the assistant to the head of the denominational youth program throughout Georgia.

The more time Maxine and I spent together, the more our love for each other grew. We married in 1946, when Maxine was twenty and I was twenty-four.

NOTHING HAD PREPARED US

The outside winds grew stronger and started to whip against our building, drawing my attention back to the prayer meeting. On my right at the altar that night, Sister Sanders (we called nearly everyone in our congregation "Sister" or "Brother") prayed with diligent persistence. She was a sweet widow in her forties, a sister of the former pastor and one of our most faithful members. Sister Sanders was one of the few original members who had remained after her brother left, and now she was by my side, praying with desperation that God would work in our church.

Sister Mitchell was also in our circle of intercessors. Sister Mitchell came to every church service we held, faithful to bring her teenage daughter Joanne to play our old piano, the only instrumental music we had in our services.

Sincere Efforts are not Enough

The winds began to howl as I watched Maxine's joyous expression, and I thought back to the past months. Maxine and I were both part of a denomination whose missions department required that each potential missionary couple first pastor in the States before going overseas. Their logic was sound: if a couple could pastor successfully for a year in their own country, they would probably have a positive ministry in another country as well.

Nine months earlier, in our zeal to get to Africa as missionaries as quickly as we could, we had accepted the first church that needed a pastor. We should have prayed, asked questions of those who made the offer, and waited on God. Instead, we decided that the quickest way was the best. We thought we already knew a lot about ministry, but nothing had prepared us for this pastorate.

Upon our arrival, we discovered that our new church was much smaller and even more problem-ridden than we had been told. The wooden floor in the church building was wavy and unstable, and it needed to be replaced if services were to continue. The adjacent parsonage was incomplete and sparsely furnished, with no interior walls. The bedroom, living room and kitchen were just one large room, with a simple sheet hung around the toilet.

Worse yet, before we arrived, a relative of the previous pastor had been caught stealing money from the church. Most members were related to him and did not object, but instead simply moved on to other churches in the same city. The former pastor found another church to pastor in a different city.

On a typical Sunday only twenty to thirty people attended, with a total of $25 to $35 in the weekly offering. Our monthly salary was only $30, supplemented by occasional personal gifts. We didn't even have enough money to buy a radio, so we often ran down our battery as we sat in the car listening to the news. In our zeal we had acted so quickly that we had inherited more problems than we could have imagined.

We tried everything we could think of to help that little church grow. We held a chicken fry to raise money to replace the wooden church floor with concrete. We hung makeshift curtains around the parsonage living room and bedroom for privacy. To supplement our meager salary, Maxine worked as a nurse's aide in a local hospital.

We held a fried fish give-away on our church grounds, hoping to attract people from the neighborhood. A few took the free fish, but no one returned to church.

We tried to motivate church members to invite unbelievers by engaging in contests with other churches. The winner was to be the church or Sunday School with the largest percentage of growth within a specific period of time. We always lost those contests.

We held a ten-day revival featuring a piano-playing singer and evangelist. Curious visitors made our small building fuller than before. A few of the former pastor's relatives returned to our church, but there were no genuine conversions.

I wrote and distributed a monthly community newspaper, setting my own type at a local print shop. I thought the newspaper might draw some in our area to our church. A few came, but none stayed.

We went door to door, visiting all the homes in our community, inviting neighbors to our church. Not one came. I especially remember one woman we visited; she was proud to be an atheist. When she said that she would never come to church, we talked to her about her need for a personal relationship with Jesus. "But I'm a good person," she remarked, "I don't need Jesus." Not long after our visit, she died a peaceful death, and her relatives assumed that she had gone to heaven. We knew otherwise.

The only time our little church was completely full was when we held services with a well-known Gospel quartet. Our funds were limited, so we slept in the kitchen while the quartet took our "drape-divided" bedroom and living room. We were thrilled each night over the next two weeks, because people thronged into our building. But most who responded to the altar calls were already members of other churches. Those meetings resulted in few lasting additions to our church.

Desperation Brings Death

After months of sincere effort, we had become desperate. We had tried to do God's work our own way, copying what we had seen others do, speaking what we had heard them say. What others did in their situations might have been right for them, but their models and approach were faulty for our little church. In our desperation we learned that Jesus must be Lord of all, even of our choices in how to do His work.

We knew an evangelist named Mayme Williams, who was known for her deep spirituality and effective revivals in other churches. We asked Williams if she would hold a revival at our church. Williams prayed and finally accepted, and we clung to the promise of the upcoming revival the way a drowning man clings to a life raft.

Desperation usually brings a death—whether the death of a dream, a way of thinking, or even of a habit or action. For us, desperation meant an end to our usual flurry of activity. We instead focused on prayer and fasting the month before Williams was to hold a revival. If we were to see breakthrough, we knew we must be forceful in the realm of the Spirit.

We had invited the congregation to join us for prayer at the church every morning and every night, and to fast one meal a day. Only a few responded. About four or five faithfully joined us for prayer around the church altar at eight o'clock in the morning, and about six or seven came at seven o'clock in the evening.

Now, on this wind blown Tuesday evening, eight of us had gathered for prayer.

"God Spoke to My Heart"

The winds surged again, pulling my attention back to the present. By now others had stopped praying just to watch Maxine. I tried to direct our attention back to prayer, so most prayed with eyes open; we all wanted to catch an occasional glimpse of Maxine.

Then, abruptly, Maxine's expression changed. For the next ten minutes, as her eyes stayed closed, she stopped smiling. A frown etched her face and her body started to writhe. It was clear that she was resistant to whatever she was then experiencing.

As the wind outside grew calm, Maxine suddenly opened her eyes, looked in the direction of the pulpit and then closed her eyes again. In just a few minutes, she opened her eyes fully, and I helped her kneel at the altar.

"Maxine," I asked with great curiosity, "what happened to you?" The others stopped praying and gathered around her, anxious to hear her reply. Perhaps what had happened to Maxine was part of the breakthrough we so urgently needed.

"When we were praying earlier tonight," Maxine began, "God spoke to my heart and told me that He wanted to show me some things. I doubted that it was really the Lord, for I was unworthy; who was I that our heavenly Father would speak to me?

"Then He spoke to me again, insisting, 'I want to show you some things that I am showing to other people.' Then I said, 'Well, Lord, whatever You want. I am willing.'"

THE HOPE OF HEAVEN

Maxine had the full attention of each person around that altar. She was a godly, practical woman, not given to vague impressions or spiritual tangents. We all wanted to know what God had said and showed to her.

"I felt my spirit leave my body," Maxine continued, "and thought that I was dying. Then four winged angels lifted me toward heaven. The closer we came to heaven, the more clearly I could hear the words of the hymn: 'Must Jesus bear the cross alone and all the world go free? No, there's a cross for ev'ryone, and there's a cross for me.'"[2]

All those gathered had sung the words to that old hymn many times. But they never seemed as vital or as important as when Maxine told us that those same words had been sung on her journey to heaven.

"Then the angels and I came to the gates of heaven." Maxine paused, thrilled with what she had seen. "Those great gates of pearl are even more beautiful than the Bible describes them.

"When the gates opened," Maxine continued, "I walked inside, and there were what looked like thousands upon thousands of children, playing by a large stream lined by lush green trees. It seemed like dozens of those children came rushing toward me to welcome me there, like playful children welcoming a guest coming into their home.

"It was wonderful to be surrounded by those loving children. I stooped down, and one little girl sweetly embraced me. I immediately knew she was my mother's sister Annette—a little girl who had been burned to death. Then a little boy also came near and put his arms around me. Instantly I knew him to be Daniel, John's younger brother, who died from an infection when he was almost three. I hadn't known either of these children before, but in heaven I instantly recognized them. Paul wrote that we would one day know just as we are also known.[3] That is how it is in heaven: we recognize people immediately."

As Maxine paused, each person gathered in that small church listened in rapt attention. Each of us knew at least one relative or friend who had died as a child or as an adult believer. The thought that we would one day see them in heaven was overwhelming. The hope of heaven began to grow in me as never before.

Beautiful Jesus

Maxine persisted in telling her vision. "Then I looked up and watched beautiful Jesus come towards me. There are no words to adequately describe Him. What impressed me most about Christ was the look of love in His eyes. Dressed in a flowing robe, Jesus had long dark hair and wore sandals on His feet.

"Christ came to me, took my right hand and led me through the heavenly city. Heaven was filled with music. As I walked with Jesus, on my left shoulder hung a harp, which I played with my left hand. I don't play any instrument on earth," Maxine said, shaking her head, "but in heaven I was a harpist.

"An air of expectancy filled heaven. There was light in the heavenly city unlike any light I have ever seen on earth. There was no need for sun or moon, for Jesus was the light. As I looked outward, I could see neither the far boundary nor the end of the height of the city. It was larger than any city I've ever seen. Beauty was everywhere, and an atmosphere of boundless peace and joy permeated it."

ALL THINGS ARE READY

SCRIPTURES DESCRIBING HEAVEN

The Bible allows us glimpses of heaven's glory–

- **Heaven's angels:** Matthew 18:10; 22:30; 24:36; 28:2; Mark 13:32; Luke 2:8–14; 22:43; 2 Thessalonians 1:7; Revelation 5:11; 8:2
- **Heaven's beauty:** Revelation 21:1-2, 10–27; 22:1-5
- **Heaven's foundations and measurements:** Revelation 21:14-20
- **Heaven's gates:** Revelation 21:12–13, 21a, 25
- **Heaven's joy:** Luke 15:7
- **Heaven's marriage supper:** Revelation 19:9
- **Heaven's mansions:** John 14:2–3
- **Heaven's rest:** 2 Thessalonians 1:6–7; Revelation 14:13; 21:3-5
- **Heaven's river:** Revelation 22:1
- **Heaven's safety and blessing:** Matthew 6:20; Revelation 22:3
- **Heaven's streets of gold:** Revelation 21:21b
- **Heaven's tree of life:** Revelation 22:2
- **Heaven as a place of mysteries:** Matthew 13:11; 2 Corinthians 12:3–4; Revelation 1:20
- **Heaven as a source of reward and treasure:** Matthew 5:12; 6:1; 19:21; Mark 10:21; Matthew 6:33; 18:22; Hebrews 10:34; 1 Peter 1:3-4
- **Heaven as the location of God's throne:** Isaiah 66:1–2; Matthew 5:34; 23:22; Mark 16:19; Acts 7:49; Revelation 4:2–11; 14:3
- **Heaven as the place where the believer's name is written in the Book of Life:** Luke 10:20; Revelation 3:5; 21:27; 22:19

Maxine recounted her vision with a sense of marvel in her voice: "Jesus led me down a golden boulevard of the city. Then, from the side of a mansion, I saw Danny Flanders."

We recognized Flanders's name. He was a middle-aged minister who had unexpectedly died while constructing a new building for his church. Flanders was best known as the man who praised God with his hands raised, loudly proclaiming, "Loooooord God!"

Maxine continued, "When Danny Flanders saw me with Jesus, he raised his hands and jubilantly said, 'Loooooord God!' I smiled and then looked at the wide boulevard beneath me. I saw translucent gold; gold so pure I could see my own reflection as I gazed downward.

"As Jesus and I walked along the boulevard, I

found that I instantly recognized people I had only read about. One man especially interested me, for a light shone around his face. When Jesus saw my interest, He walked me toward him. As we grew closer, I realized that he was Stephen, the first martyr of the early church.

- **Heaven as the source of the believer's citizenship:** Philippians 3:20
- **Our crowns in heaven:** Revelation 2:10c
- **The source of heaven's light:** Revelation 21:23; 22:5
- **Heaven's entry requirements:** Matthew 7:13-14, 21; 10:32; Revelation 21:27; 22:14

"Stephen spoke to me, 'People think I was hurting when I was being stoned. At first it did hurt, but then I looked up and saw Jesus standing at the right hand of the Father.[4] After I saw Jesus, it did not hurt any more.'"

Maxine added her own thoughts, "Perhaps that's the way death is. We might be in pain when we are dying, but when we look up and see Jesus, our pain will end.

"Then I saw Peter and an angel laughing and talking together," Maxine said, returning to what she had seen in her vision. "This was the angel who had been with Peter the night the Lord released him from prison. Peter said, 'We were just laughing about the time we went to the house and the people didn't believe I was there—even though they had been praying that the Lord would release me.'[5]

"I also saw Hudson Taylor with thousands of Chinese around him," Maxine added, "and David Livingstone surrounded by Africans. As Jesus and I continued walking, I saw King David in a purple robe with a crown on his head. David was talking with Jesus about the coming millennial reign on earth.[6]

"Then I saw the young lad who gave his fish and loaves for Christ to feed the multitude.[7] He told me, 'We may have little, but what little we do have, we need to give to Jesus. Jesus will then multiply the little we have and give it to others.'

"Then Christ told me that all things in heaven are ready for His return. Jesus said, 'Only my Father knows when I will return,[8] but I am longing for my Bride. Everything is ready.' Then Jesus showed me thousands of saints who stood waiting. He explained that they were waiting to sing the song of the redeemed with all the other saints yet to come. Once again He told me that all things are ready."

By this time, we were in tears. Heaven never before seemed so real. Jesus never before seemed so wonderful.

THE ESSENCE OF HEAVEN

"Christ took me farther down the boulevard of gold," Maxine continued excitedly, "and showed me mansion after mansion. Then He stopped in front of one huge gold mansion and said, 'This mansion is yours and John's.'"

Maxine was awestruck. She explained to those gathered that we had wanted to buy a used house trailer before we left as missionaries. That way we wouldn't have to live with other people when we came back from the mission field. We had then discovered that we couldn't even afford the down payment on a used house trailer. "But," Maxine interrupted herself, "when I saw this huge gold mansion that belonged to us in heaven, those house trailers seemed like garbage.

"I held tightly to Christ's loving hand. The real essence of heaven is the ever-present Christ. There is nothing that compares to Him."

"I LONG FOR MY BRIDE"

We were all still, some with tears in our eyes, others in quiet wonder at what Maxine was saying. A silent sense of awe filled the small church building as Maxine's telling of her vision progressed: "Jesus then turned around and led me back the same way we had come. We stopped at an entrance on the left where there was a massive banquet hall. That one hall stretched out for many miles; it was so long that I could not see its end.

"A large table covered by an intricate white lace tablecloth stretched out the length of the banquet hall. On the table sat beautiful fine china, crystal glasses and gleaming silverware. I watched as breathtakingly beautiful angels, dressed in white flowing robes, walked back and forth on both sides of the table, as if waiting for guests to come so they could serve them.

"Christ said to me, 'This is the marriage supper of the Lamb. It is already prepared for My Bride. It is ready.' Christ then showed me millions of crowns, reminding me again that the marriage supper is complete and ready. Then He added, 'Every crown is finished. I long for My Bride.'"

By now a quiet astonishment rested on us. Each of us wanted to draw closer to Christ, but none of us had realized that His preparations for us in heaven were so thorough, or that He longed for us with such passion.

"Then Christ stepped to the side of the banquet hall's entrance," Maxine continued, "and slowly stopped. He turned to face me and held out His hands, His palms upward. For the first time, I clearly saw the scars in His hands. Without speaking, Jesus pulled open a portion of His robe and showed me the scar in His side. [9]

"I was amazed to see how deep each of His scars was. In that moment," Maxine said, shaking her head in disbelief, "I was struck with the depth of Jesus' love for me. I stood there, my head bowed in shame. Jesus showed me His scars of love for me, but I had no scars to show my love for Him."

To Search Out a Bride

As Maxine described the scars Jesus carried for us, many wept openly. But Maxine was not finished: "At that point I realized that I was not dead, but was instead having a vision. Jesus again took my hand in His and led me back to the gates of pearl. I realized that I was to return to earth, but I wanted so badly to stay in heaven."

Maxine paused and a holy hush fell into that little church sanctuary. Each one felt the reality of heaven and, for a moment, we sensed perfect peace in our souls.

"More than anything else," Maxine explained, "I did not want to leave Christ. So I looked around for an excuse to stay. When we almost reached the gate, I saw three people on our right running toward us. Inwardly I thought, *This is wonderful. They have something to tell me so I can stay a little longer.*

"As they approached I recognized them as Isaac, his wife Rebecca and Abraham's servant Eleazar. Isaac spoke with a sense of urgency, 'Just as Abraham, my father, sent his servant to search for a bride for me, [10] so our heavenly Father has sent the Holy Spirit to earth to search out a bride for Christ.'

"Then I knew it was time for me to return. As the gates of pearl swung open, I could see the earth below. Christ knelt at the gates' threshold and turned His scarred palms upward. Blood freely flowed from the scars in His hands and covered the whole earth below. In that moment I knew that His blood truly is enough to cover all the sins of those who repent and come to Him in faith.

"In the background I again heard the words of the song, 'Must Jesus bear the cross alone and all the world go free? No, there's a cross for ev'ryone, and there's a cross for me.'"

A different quality of quiet fell in our sanctuary. No one wanted to move. We had our eyes fixed on Maxine. She breathed deeply and continued, "Those four winged angels then gently lowered me to earth. I stood there, thinking how dark and bleak earth looked when compared to heaven. Even though it was light on earth, it was drab when compared with heaven's light."

"I Must Take You to Hell"

Maxine had been animated and joyful when she spoke of heaven. As the cool winds continued to blow outside, she seemed drained and leaned against me as she talked. "Then a different angel, strong and robust, firmly grabbed my arm. He announced his mission, saying, 'I must take you to hell.'"

At first Maxine argued, refusing to go. But the robust angel insisted. "The angel's grasp grew firmer on my arm," Maxine frowned as she talked. "He led me over the earth. As we journeyed, we saw millions of people complacently walking to what I instantly knew to be hell's entrance."

Maxine trembled and paused, seeming to gather her thoughts before she would continue.

People Journeying to Hell

After a minute of silence, Maxine went on: "Among the people journeying to hell…" Maxine paused briefly and swallowed, "I saw Mrs. Hall. I also saw our Sunday School superintendent with his hands in his pockets, as if he did not care that he was hell bound."

Deacon Hall, our faithful church treasurer, usually would have been with us but was not there that night. His wife had made it clear that she did not believe in Jesus or in church, and she sometimes kept him from coming to our prayer meetings. We knew that Mrs. Hall was not born again, and we were not surprised that Maxine saw her in the streams of people walking toward hell.

But we were stunned when Maxine mentioned our Sunday School superintendent. He had served for years as the head of the Sunday School in this small church. Although he never joined us in our prayer meetings, he was always present on Sunday mornings, and he always said the right things at the right time. If what Maxine said was true, we were harboring a hypocrite in our midst.

Maxine's words drew us back to the telling of her vision: "The angel continued to firmly guide me to hell's entrance. I can't fully explain to you what I saw next." Maxine paused again. "A large white cross stood over hell's mouth. But those complacent people ignored the cross, pushing past it into hell. As we walked and watched, a steady stream of people continued to go in."

Maxine looked each of us in the eye. "As I watched people literally push past the cross to go into hell, I finally realized that people choose to go to hell. Even if a person is on his deathbed, if he repents of his sins and receives Jesus, he will be accepted into heaven. But if a person does not receive Jesus, that person is pushing past the cross to enter hell."

A Dread of Hell

As we thought of unbelievers we knew, the atmosphere in our little church turned grim. Maxine breathed deeply once more, for the joy of heaven had quickly changed to a dread of hell. "I wanted to turn back, but the angel was firm. He pushed a crowd of people aside and made an open path to lead me past hell's mouth. As we stepped inside hell, I was astounded by darkness more vile than anything I had ever seen. That darkness covered each person like a thick shroud, like an unwelcome blanket of hopelessness.

"Even though the darkness was thick, I could still see through it. As I looked around, I saw a massive pit. I realized that the darkness was black smoke that billowed from that foul pit and that even the fire in the pit cast awful shadows as it burned. I stood on the rim of that pit and heard the horrible screams of millions of people who cried out, 'Lost! Lost! Lost!'

SCRIPTURES DESCRIBING HELL

The Bible uses many terms for hell: *Sheol, Destruction, the Pit, Hades, lake of fire and brimstone, Gehenna.* The Bible also allows us a few glimpses into hell's reality:

- **Hell as a place of judgment:** Matthew 11:22-23; Luke 10:13-16
- **Hell as the destiny of the wicked:** Job 31:2-3; Psalm 9:17; 55:15, 23; Proverbs 1:10-12; 5:1-5; 9:13-18; 21:15; Isaiah 1:28; Matthew 5:29-30; Philippians 3:18-19; 1 Timothy 6:9
- **Hell's finality:** Luke 16:19-31; Hebrews 9:26-27
- **Hell's fire:** Deuteronomy 32:22; Matthew 5:22; 18:9; Mark 9:43-48; Luke 16:24; 2 Thessalonians 1:8-9; Revelation 20:10, 14
- **Hell's mouth:** Isaiah 5:14
- **Hell's original purpose—the destiny prepared for Satan and his hordes:** Isaiah 14:12-15; Matthew 25:41; Revelation 20:1-3, 10
- **Hell's pit:** Proverbs 1:10-12; Isaiah 14:15; Ezekiel 31:16; Revelation 9:1; 20:1, 3
- **Hell's smoke:** Revelation 9:2
- **Hell's sorrows:** 2 Samuel 22:6; Psalm 18:5; 116:3
- **Hell's torment:** Luke 16:23-24; Revelation 14:10b-11; 20:10b
- **Hell's entry requirements:** 1 Corinthians 6:9-10; Revelation 20:12-15; 21:8; 22:14-15

"Around the pit was a huge ledge where people sat. Each person was hopeless and despondent, and every face had a haggard look. Each one seemed so alone, never talking to the others."

I felt a shudder go through my body. We knew the Bible described hell as a terrible place, but hearing Maxine's vision brought its horror closer than ever before.

"The angel silently led me among the people who sat on that ledge, grasping my arm as he took me toward one man. The first man I met was the rich man Christ talked about,[11] the one at whose gate the beggar Lazarus sat. In a comment riddled with unending agony, the rich man began, 'I have been here these many years, yet no one has put even one drop of water on my tongue.'

"A group of preachers then approached us, their eyes filled with hopeless regret. One explained, 'We're here because we preached the Gospel of Christ, but did not live according to the Gospel.'

"Although I saw thousands of children playing joyfully in heaven, I did not see any children in hell. But I did see one group of young people, their faces contorted with remorse, running about aimlessly. They held broken, empty whiskey bottles in their hands, shattered symbols of their former gods."

Maxine hesitated and looked down at the cement floor, "Then I saw my father, who is still alive. He accepted Christ at one point, but then turned away from the Lord. Dad was in hell like I was, just looking. When his eyes met mine, he said, 'I have seen hell, and I am not coming back.'"

"This Awful Place"

"The angel said, 'Come with me. There is one more person I must show you before we go.' I could not tell whether this person was a man or woman, for the face was marred and twisted by suffering, and it was enveloped in smoke darker than that which cloaked most. This person was ringing his or her hands and with anguish wailed over and over again, 'I was a good person on earth. I gave to many people in need. I am here because I refused the blood of Jesus which could have saved me from this awful place.'

"The angel finally started taking me out of hell. On our way back, I saw our neighbor who had recently died, the one who said she was an atheist. She stared about, in utter shock and agonizing disbelief. She had had many opportunities to receive Jesus, but had rejected Him instead."

The horror of hell now seemed so real. It was almost as if each person there could feel the thick, dark smoke. "Believe me," Maxine instructed us, "hell is more terrible than I can convey. You would not want even your worst enemy to taste such despair.

"The angel then led me back to hell's opening and once more pushed a crowd aside to let us through. I was so grateful when the angel led me back to earth. As I stood on earth again, it seemed such a beautiful place compared to hell.

"When the vision came to an end," Maxine continued, "I realized my head was resting in John's lap. As I opened my eyes, I looked at the pulpit and briefly saw Christ standing there. I closed my eyes a final time, then looked up and finally saw all of you."

Maxine smiled and then bowed in prayer. We quickly joined her. During the rest of our meeting that night, we prayed more fervently than ever before. We prayed not only for the upcoming revival, but also for Mrs. Hall, for our Sunday School superintendent, for Maxine's father and for many others to be saved. We ended by rejoicing in the hope of heaven.

THE WEEKS THAT FOLLOWED

When revival meetings started that following Sunday, our little church was filled; the divine excitement we prayed for had finally arrived. I went to Mrs. Hall's house and told her how Maxine had seen her walking complacently in hell's direction. She later came to church. When the invitation was given, she ran to the altar to give her life to Jesus. Mrs. Hall later became one of the most ardent Christians I have ever known.

When I began to tell our Sunday School superintendent how Maxine had seen him walking toward hell, he grew so angry I could not even finish. Sometimes all one can do is speak the truth in love and leave the rest to the Holy Spirit.

Soon after, Maxine's father gave his heart back to the Lord. Years later he died of lung cancer as he lay in his bed at home. Amazingly, before they removed his body, he opened his eyes, much to the surprise of Maxine's mother, brother, two sisters and friends. Weeping, Maxine's father said, "I have been to heaven. It is so beautiful. I have been with Christ. I want to go back to heaven." With these words he closed his eyes and died one last time.

In the weeks that followed, we discovered that several others had reported visions similar to Maxine's. I was also invited to speak at a national banquet for our denominational youth leaders, and I told a little of the struggle in our church. Our story so impressed one denominational executive that he arranged for us to have an early interview with the mission board. As a result, we received official appointment as missionaries much earlier than we'd expected. We were soon ready to go to Africa, equipped with all the funding we would need, a fresh perspective of heaven and a new understanding of how deeply Christ longs for us and for the lost.

The Most Important Kind

Of all the stories I told Dr. Cho through the years, Maxine's vision of heaven was his favorite. Many years later Maxine told our daughter, Karen, about her vision. Karen's main question was, "Mom, what do you remember best about heaven?" Maxine paused thoughtfully then responded, "All heaven is filled with Christ's longing for His Bride to come to Him."

In my life I've seen two kinds of divine desperation. The most important kind is similar to the distress Maxine felt when she saw people casually walking to hell's entrance. It is like the desperation Jesus felt when He looked at the city of Jerusalem and proclaimed, "O Jerusalem, Jerusalem, you who kill the prophets and stone those sent to you, how often I have longed to gather your children together, as a hen gathers her chicks under her wings, but you were not willing."[12]

A Word About Visions

God sometimes uses a vision as His tool to give us a clearer picture of what it is that He wants us to understand. Abraham had a vision of a covenant interaction with God (Genesis 15). God gave visions to prophets (Numbers 12:6), including Isaiah (Isaiah 1:1; 21:2; 22:1), Ezekiel (Ezekiel 8:4; 11:24; 43:3) and Daniel (Daniel 2:19; 8:1-26; 10:1-14). In the New Testament, God gave visions to Zechariah (Luke 1:8-22), Ananias (Acts 9:10-16), Cornelius (Acts 10:3-6), Peter (Acts 11:5-10), Paul (Acts 18:9-10) and John (Revelation 9:17).

But visions can also be false (Jeremiah 14:14; 23:16; Ezekiel 13:7). Like prophecy, visions must be weighed and tested (1 Corinthians 14:29-33; 1 John 4:1). I use four criteria to determine whether a vision is valid.

- **First and foremost,** is it true to the integrity of Scripture? If not, dismiss it. If yes, pause to consider the vision.
- **Second,** what about the character of the person reporting the vision? Beware the wandering believer who drifts from church to church, sharing his latest vision. God can let a donkey speak (Numbers 22:22-31), but tends to bring forth a faithful word from a faithful person.
- **Third,** does it cause truth to ring more clearly in my own soul?
- **Fourth,** what fruit does the vision bring?

On all four counts, Maxine's vision fit the criteria. Hers was a valid vision.

LEADING AN UNBELIEVER IN A PRAYER OF SALVATION

Leading an unbeliever in a prayer of salvation may take less than a minute. However, the process by which that person decides to pray for salvation may have taken several months or years. During that sometimes lengthy process, be prayerful, caring and sensitive to the Holy Spirit. At an appropriate time or times, consider sharing not only your personal story of how you came to the Lord and what Jesus means to you, but also one or more of these verses: Luke 19:10; John 1:12; 3:16; Romans 3:23; 10:9-10, 13; 1 Peter 2:24; 1 John 1:9; Revelation 3:20.

When an unbeliever is ready to pray for salvation, lead him in a prayer that does four things:

- **Admits his spiritual need**—Scripture is clear that "all have sinned" (Romans 3:23; 5:12); that person's starting point is to admit that he is a sinner.
- **Declares that he believes that Jesus Christ died on the cross for him**—Jesus is the only way to be restored into right relationship with God (John 14:6), and He died on the cross because He was "not willing that any should perish but that all should come to repentance" (2 Peter 3:9).
- **Reflects that he clearly repents of his sins**—It is not enough, however, to admit that one has sinned or even to believe that Jesus died on the cross for him. That person must also decide to repent and forsake his sins (Acts 3:19; for lukewarm Christians—Revelation 2:21-22; 3:3, 19-22).
- **Welcomes Jesus Christ into his heart and makes Him Lord of his life**—John wrote, "yet to all who received him, to those who believed in his name, he gave the right to become children of God" (John 1:12, NIV).

Because of this divine desperation, our heavenly Father was willing to send Jesus to earth to die for our sins. "For God so loved the world that He gave His only begotten Son, that whoever believes in Him should not perish but have everlasting life. For God did not send His Son into the world to condemn the world, but that the world through Him might be saved."[13]

With God's kind of divine desperation in our lives, our view of the lost changes. We no longer look at our unsaved neighbors, relatives and acquaintances as spiritually ignorant, but as precious people Jesus longs for us to reach in His name. We stop thinking of ourselves and our own problems and challenges, but instead make a priority of others' eternal needs.

ABOUT YOU

If we are to fulfill God's destiny for our lives, you

> Be sure to rejoice with your new brother or sister in Christ. Encourage him to now: 1) tell others about his decision; 2) daily read and study God's Word; 3) spend daily time in prayer; and 4) participate in a Bible-believing church for worship, fellowship and service.

and I need God's divine desperation to burn deeply in our hearts and souls. Like Paul, may we come to the place where we can declare with confidence, "I have become all things to all men, that I might by all means save some."[14]

But there is a second type of divine desperation—a personal kind. You might be like us that Tuesday night around the altar—desperate, maybe even at this moment. If you are, then it is time to cry out to Jesus; not just once, but until your plea reaches heaven and you have heard from Him. When you cry out in this way, you focus your desperation on our divine Lord. In that sense, your human desperation then becomes *divine* desperation, for you instead focus on Him as your sole source.

I've had many points of divine desperation through my years of ministry: when we were not reaching people with the Gospel in that first small church; when revival was not spreading in Liberia; when Dr. Cho had a physical collapse; and when Saigon was about to fall near the end of the war in Vietnam.

It's interesting. When everything is going well, we go about our lives and thank God for our blessings. Yet in times of prosperity and ease, we tend not to have a heart-felt dependency on Him. It is really for our spiritual good that life comes with problems, for it is often those very problems that drive us to the Master Problem-Solver. When we fully turn to Him, our problems become gateways to greatness, and our stumbling blocks become stepping-stones to new insights and opportunities in God's plan for our destiny.

You might be in a spot similar to mine right now. Your motives might seem right, and you might be working as hard as you know how, but little seems to be happening in the spiritual realm. You might be as desperate as I was. Be encouraged. Cry out to our Master Problem-Solver.

Consider Moses. He and the Israelites stood before the impassable Red Sea as Pharaoh's chariots grew ever closer behind them. [15]

Consider David. Even though he had been anointed king, he was in the "prison" of a cave, hiding as his father-in-law, Saul, pursued him. [16]

FOUR WAYS TO SHARE GOD'S DIVINE DESPERATION

I can best fulfill God's destiny for my life when I share God's divine desperation that the lost be saved, for He is "not willing that any should perish but that all should come to repentance" (2 Peter 3:9b). Four practical ways I do this:

- **My time in God's Word**—I often read passages that show the reality of hell and of God's love for the lost: Mark 9:43-48; Luke 15:11-32; 16:19-31; John 3:14-18; Revelation 9:2; 20:10, 14-15; 22:14-15.
- **My prayer life**—I pray daily for the salvation of specific unbelievers, both unsaved family members and those unbelievers in my circle of acquaintances.
- **My relationships with believers**—When I am with Christian friends, we pray together for the salvation of targeted unbelievers, and we talk about ways we can better reach out to them.
- **My relationships with unbelievers**—I try to spend time weekly with at least one unbeliever for whom I have been praying, both developing relationship and sharing Christ's love in relevant and meaningful ways.

Consider the early church. Herod had already beheaded James and then imprisoned Peter. [17]

Whatever problem you face, learn from Moses, David and the early church. They cried out until God heard their plea. Moses and the Israelites walked on dry ground, the walls of the Red Sea on either side, soon to see their enemies destroyed by those same waters. David went on to become the greatest king Israel ever had. The chains fell off Peter's wrists, and an angel guided him past prison guards to the very home where, though it was the middle of the night, people were in desperate and persistent prayer for his release.

Consider Jesus' words at the end of the parable of the widow and the unjust judge: "Will not God bring about justice for his chosen ones, who cry out to him day and night? Will he keep putting them off? I tell you, he will see that they get justice, and quickly." [18]

For you, crying out to Him day and night might mean spending more time in prayer, or even joining in prayer meetings at your church, no matter how few others attend. It could also mean finding a prayer partner who will join you in storming heaven. Through whatever channel or in whatever ways you express your persistent cry to God, let your problems drive you to the Problem-Solver.

But once He responds and breaks through on your behalf, don't stop there. Let your heart and soul burn brightest with His desperation to see His lost children come to Him. Christ longs for His Bride. Even now, Christ longs for you and for His lost children. If only we longed for Him as He longs for us, our lives would be much different.

Three Guidelines When in Personal Desperation

I have learned three guidelines to follow when I am in a time of personal desperation:

- **STOP trying to manipulate a solution**—God's ways and thoughts are higher than my own (Isaiah 55:9), and my attempts to bring about a solution can often worsen the situation.
- **PERSIST in crying out to God in prayer**—I want to pray once and have God immediately respond. While that sometimes happens, God also develops strength and faith in me when answers are delayed and I persistently cry out to Him.
- **WAIT for God's solution and breakthrough**—Isaiah put it best: "Those who wait on the Lord shall renew their strength; they shall mount up with wings like eagles, they shall run and not be weary, they shall walk and not faint" (40:31).

DIVINE DESPERATION: DEVOTIONAL AND DISCUSSION QUESTIONS

Sharing Question

What is one past incident when you were desperate and cried out to God, and how did that situation change?

> *Be brief. There are three guidelines to a sharing question: 1) no one is to take more than one minute in response; 2) go around the circle—if in a small group—and give each person an opportunity to respond; and 3) don't ask other questions at this point, for that stretches out the minute.*

Discussion Questions

1. What one incident or encounter in Maxine's vision of heaven and hell stood out to you? Why?
2. The longest single Bible passage on heaven is Revelation 21:10–22:5. Take turns reading verses until your group has read this entire passage. What two specific things do you notice about the beauty and reality of heaven in this passage?
3. Read Isaiah 14:12–15; Matthew 25:41 and Revelation 20:1–3, 10. What seemed to be God's original purpose for hell? Consider and read Jesus' parable in Luke 16:19–31. What can one learn about hell from this parable?
4. Give your own definition of "divine desperation," and share one way that desperation has impacted your life.

Application

1. If a believer's most important thought each day was of Christ in heaven, longing for us to come to Him, how might he or she live differently? Turn to your spouse, or another person of the same gender, and share one specific thing you

could do to make this perspective part of your daily life.

2. Pair with your spouse, or another person of the same gender. Reread "Leading an Unbeliever in a Prayer of Salvation" on pages 18–19. Let one of you take the role of an unbeliever who wants to be saved and the other person lead him or her in a prayer that does the four things listed. Switch roles and go through the process again.
3. Consider "Four Ways to Share God's Divine Desperation" (page 20). Which of these four ways do you think is the most important for a Christian to apply? Share with your spouse, or another person of the same gender, which of these four ways you now practice most often. Share one specific thing you could do to more fully share God's desire for His lost children to turn to Him.
4. Conclude by praying for each other and for the salvation of one lost person in your area.

Maxine and I on our joyous wedding day.

Maxine and I board the Ambassador *to fly from New York to Monrovia.*

Insight Two

WORD WASH

When your attitudes need cleanin', use God's Word to do the washin'

ICEBERGS SEEMED TO DANCE in the cold Greenland waters surrounding the narrow peninsula. Even though it was ten o'clock at night there was enough light at this arctic latitude to see the blue and yellow flowers lining the airstrip. Although it was August, it was cold enough for us to wear the Eskimo jackets the Air Force men had loaned us. We had finally ended our second day of flight aboard the *Ambassador,* and Maxine and I were weary.

We had been so excited several months earlier when Henry Garlock, our denomination's missions secretary for Africa, had given us our first missionary assignment. We were to oversee the young men's Bible school in Feloke, Liberia—a country in West Africa. We told all our friends, raised our needed funds and were anxious to begin. Maxine and I had gleaned much from our years of Bible training, and we wanted to help others do the same.

Because air travel cost so much in those days, our missions department had purchased a large, silver army-surplus plane—and renamed it the *Ambassador*—to transport missionaries. On a fine summer day in 1948, with Maxine's vision freshly in our minds, she and I became two of eleven passengers on the maiden voyage of the *Ambassador*.

The fuselage of a seaplane had been strapped to one side of the interior of the *Ambassador;* travel in Africa's jungle bush was often best on small planes that could also land on lakes and large rivers. We positioned our eleven seats on the other side of the seaplane fuselage. In the compartment below were the seaplane's wings and the passengers' luggage, including the mattress we were taking to Africa, with all our other earthly possessions in two sealed metal drums.

We had spent our first night in the plane on the runway in Gander, Newfoundland, sleeping in uncomfortable seats. But even with the discomfort of our travel, Maxine and I had been happy. We would soon be at the men's Bible school in Feloke, Liberia.

Our plane then flew through dangerous mountainous areas and, on our second night, we had landed on this military airstrip built on a thin coastal peninsula in Greenland. Henry Garlock was also a passenger. After we ate, Garlock asked Maxine and me to walk with him down the empty runway.

THE KEEN EDGE OF DISAPPOINTMENT

As the icebergs continued their slow waltz in the cold Greenland waters around us, the three of us stood on the empty airstrip. Garlock frowned, cleared his throat and swallowed hard, hesitant to begin. I was inwardly shaken by Garlock's frown; our past interchanges had been so pleasant. I looked at Maxine, glad that she was by my side. Garlock frowned again as he finally spoke: "We said that your first assignment was to replace a missionary who formerly headed a men's Bible school in Feloke, Liberia. However, things have changed. You will no longer be needed there."

The keen edge of disappointment pierced my soul. I could hardly believe what Garlock had said. What about our plans, our friends, our first chance to prove ourselves on the mission field? We had been planning and telling others about the men's Bible school for several months. How dare he disregard our plans and cancel our assignment so easily! Did they need us in Africa at all? My distress deepened as Garlock paused.

In that moment I realized that I might have heaven's perspective and understand Christ's longing, yet still have wrong attitudes. Our heavenly

Father continues to send His Holy Spirit to search for a bride for Christ, but when He finds us, we're far from perfect. The "garment" of our attitudes is soiled and dirtied with sin, wrong thinking and worldly standards. Maybe that's why Paul wrote about the "washing of water by the word."[19]

In the midst of my disappointment, I remembered that God's Word is the only thing that stands the test of time. Even as a boy I had read the Bible and memorized several verses. Now I understood that it was more important to apply the truth of Scripture than to know or even to memorize it.

As the ache of disappointment deepened in my heart, one scripture whirled in my thoughts: "We know that all things work together for good to those who love God, to those who are called according to His purpose."[20] I knew I loved God, and I knew He had called me. I breathed deeply and began again to trust Him to guide my steps.

Garlock broke the long silence with his explanation: "One of the men on our flight is the missionary you were to replace. He decided to return early." At least now we could understand the reason he had cancelled our assignment.

"But we can still use you in Africa," Garlock continued. "You now have several options. You could stay in Liberia and make your own assignment there, or we have specific openings in Nigeria and in South Africa. What would you like to do?"

I was startled; one minute I had felt discarded, and now I felt valued. It was highly unusual for first-term missionaries to be asked what they would like to do. I glanced at Maxine, thought about her vision of heaven and hell and remembered a verse I had memorized many years ago: "The Lord is not slack concerning His promises, as some count slackness, but is longsuffering toward us, not willing that any should perish but that all should come to repentance."[21]

I knew immediately what I should say. "Sir," I responded to the tall, stately Garlock, "we would still like to go to Liberia. We would like to preach the Gospel to villages and tribes who have never before heard the name of Jesus."

Maxine nodded her head and Garlock smiled. I was learning that, regardless of my unmet expectations, my attitude must be right. Only the washing by God's Word through God's Holy Spirit can turn our human disappointments into His divine appointments.

AN ATTITUDE OF ADVENTURE WITH GOD'S SPIRIT

Three days and four stops later, the *Ambassador* landed on an American-built airstrip fifty miles north of Monrovia, Liberia. In the 1820s, freed American slaves returned to settle in what was then known to some as Africa's "Grain Coast," and to others as the "Slave Coast." By 1847, the new country became the first independent black republic in Africa, named "Liberia," based on a Latin phrase meaning "land of the free."

Wedged between the West African countries of Sierra Leone and the Ivory Coast, Liberia then had a population of about a million, with a landmass a bit larger than that of our state of Tennessee. Liberia's flat plains along the coast gave way to rolling plateaus with tropical rain forests farther inland and then rose to low mountains in the northeast. Liberia's capital was Monrovia, named after President James Monroe.

KEY FACTS ABOUT GOD'S WORD

Its source: Inspired by the Holy Spirit (2 Peter 1:20–21)

Its effectiveness: "Alive and powerful, and sharper than any two-edged sword" (Hebrews 4:12)

It does many things:

- **Brings promise and hope:** Psalm 119:114–116; Romans 9:9; Colossians 1:5
- **Cleanses:** Psalm 119:9
- **Comforts:** Psalm 119:76
- **Delivers:** Psalm 119:170
- **Discerns:** Hebrews 4:12c
- **Endures:** Psalm 119:160; 1 Peter 1:25
- **Gives joy:** Jeremiah 15:16
- **Gives peace:** Psalm 119:165
- **Grants new life:** 1 Peter 1:23; 1 John 1:1
- **Guides:** Psalm 119:133
- **Hinders sin:** Psalm 119:11
- **Illuminates:** Psalm 119:105, 130
- **Informs and gives wisdom:** Psalm 119:98–104, 130
- **Revives:** Psalm 119:25
- **Saves:** James 1:21
- **Sustains:** Psalm 119:92–93; Luke 4:4
- **Teaches:** Psalm 119:66

During our bumpy ride over an unpaved road, Maxine and I looked intently at the surrounding countryside. We watched rural Liberians travel on foot on either side of the road to Monrovia. Most were poor, illiterate farmers whose families used old-fashioned methods to raise crops such as cassava, rice and sugar cane. They also bred sheep, goats, pigs and other livestock. With its tropical foliage and scantily clad natives, Liberia was all we expected it to be.

As our bumpy ride continued, I remembered how God sent Abraham on a journey from his homeland[22] and later sent millions of Israelites on a journey through the wilderness to a land of promise.[23] Jesus sent His disciples into the towns and villages in Israel,[24] and later told us that we were to "go...and make disciples of all the nations."[25] God is in the sending business, thrusting His children into adventures with His Holy Spirit.

When the large jeep finally stopped at the mission house in Monrovia, we were again excited. This was more than a long ride over an unpaved road in a developing nation. God was shaping our attitudes. We were in an adventure with His Holy Spirit, and we were finally missionaries in our beloved Africa.

Attitude Toward Spiritual Authority

Three days later we were on a small mission plane. Our first stop was to be Liberia's interior town of Newake. Without highways or roads, our only way to get there was to take this mission plane, so small that there was only one passenger seat. So Maxine sat on my knees, with our one suitcase on her lap. After takeoff, we looked below us at the lush green jungle forests that stretched out in several directions.

The airplane engine was too loud to allow casual conversation. As I held Maxine, I recalled Garlock's last directive: "You will later be able to preach the Gospel in areas that have never before heard of Jesus. Now, however, I want you to visit four of our mission stations in the interior and hold meetings in each place. I want you to first help strengthen what we've already established."

Once again we were disappointed. Once again I needed God's Word to wash my attitude. Then Paul's words to Titus rang in my thoughts, reminding us to "be subject to rulers and authorities."[26] Garlock was our superior. It was not our place to disagree with his decision, but rather to trust the Holy Spirit to work out His timing. Wondering what God would teach us through this situation, we left our mattress and most of our belongings in the mission home in Monrovia and packed one suitcase for the trip.

When the buzz of the plane engine grew even louder, my attention turned to the small airstrip below. We landed safely and were greeted by two missionary couples from our first stop, the young women's Bible school in the town of Newake.

There were no roads in the area, so we walked down a wide dirt path, carrying our suitcase. The missionaries first stopped at a nearby cemetery. "Thirteen of these graves," one man pointed out, "are filled with missionaries and with their family members who died in Liberia. Many grew sick as they walked through the jungle bush and picked up deadly tropical diseases. But even though these missionaries were Spirit-filled and gave their lives, there has never been a nationwide revival in this country. Many here are resistant to the Holy Spirit."

How We Are to Respond to God's Word

- **Properly receive it:** Mark 4:14-20; Luke 8:11-15; 1 Thessalonians 2:13
- **Obey it:** Psalm 199:2-8, 55-56; Luke 11:28; Revelation 3:8
- **Delight in it:** Psalm 119:16, 24, 35, 47, 77, 174
- **Practice it:** James 1:22-23

We pondered his words as we looked at those graves. Jesus said it best, "Unless a grain of wheat falls into the ground and dies, it remains alone; but if it dies, it produces much grain."[27]

Maxine and I picked flowers, then reverently laid them on two graves. We were deeply touched by the scene before us. We knelt in the middle of that cemetery and began our earnest prayer, "God, please don't let us die until we see a sweeping national revival in this country."

We were young, but we were serious. We knew that God wanted more increase in Liberia, and we wanted God to use us to accomplish great things for His kingdom.

Attitudes and Early Experiences

During the rest of our somber walk to the mission station, the missionaries shared their concerns about the nearly fifty young women in the Bible school. As we ate a late supper, they told us that we would need to use an interpreter for the upcoming two weeks of planned meetings. Although English was the official language spoken in Liberia's large coastal cities, various tribes spoke nearly twenty different languages in the jungle "bush."

I did not sleep well that night. I had never before spoken through an interpreter, but that was not the main reason for my discomfort. As a chimpanzee squealed in the distance and Maxine slept soundly on the other side of our bed, I gazed at the mosquito net that hung above us and felt the tropical night. The troubling resistance in my soul almost suffocated me.

Two Attitudes That Need Word Wash

I have two types of attitudes that often need the washing of God's Word:

1. **Attitude toward disappointment**—Life often contains many disappointments and unmet expectations. Some Word wash verses for disappointment: Jeremiah 29:11; Romans 5:3-5; 8:28; 2 Corinthians 1:3-4; 4:8-18.
2. **Attitude toward others, especially people in authority**—Sometimes people, especially authority figures, seem unfair or uncaring. Some Word wash verses when authority seems unfair: Romans 13:1-3; 1 Timothy 2:1-3; Titus 3:1-2; Hebrews 13:17; 1 Peter 2:13-20.

Two themes dominated the missionaries' concerns. First, although their purpose in this Bible school was to train future pastors' wives, they were not sure that all were born again; others seemed uncertain in their dedication to the Lord. That posed no problem to me. I was eager to preach on salvation. God's Word and Maxine's vision had made heaven and hell clear realities to me.

Their second concern was that most had not received the baptism of the Holy Spirit. As I thought about that, I began to be uncomfortable. I remembered how they had talked about Liberians being resistant to the Holy Spirit.

ATTITUDE TOWARD THE HOLY SPIRIT

THREE TYPES OF WORD WASH

Since God's Word is compared to water (Ephesians 5:26), we frequently need to wash in it. I use three basic types of Word wash:

1. **General Word wash**—Just as I take a daily bath, I also need to daily read God's Word to nourish my soul and spirit. To do this I systematically read through the Bible each year.
2. **Concentrated Word wash**—When my "Word battery" grows weak, I need to "jump start" it. I have done this by listening to Scripture tapes as I drive to work; by fasting for a day and reading a book of the Bible; and by fasting for ten days and reading through the New Testament.
3. **Specific Word wash**—When I find I have a harmful or negative attitude, I need to wash that with specific scriptures by reading, memorizing and/or meditating on them until my attitude lines up with His Word.

As our room filled with night jungle sounds, my thoughts roamed to younger days. I grew up in a Pentecostal home. Our church services were usually long, so during evening meetings I slept on a pallet underneath the front pew while my mother sat on the pew behind me. I often woke up in the middle of the altar call, startled by people speaking in tongues, shouting and dancing "in the Spirit" around me.

Sister Tullis had caused me special concern. She was especially expressive and, when she shouted and danced "in the Spirit," I was afraid that she would step on me and hurt me. I was careful to get as far back under the pew as I could. As a young boy, I decided that the Holy Spirit gave just passing emotional experiences, nothing that would ever interest me.

By the time I turned thirteen, Sister Tullis and her family lived across the street from our house. I was tossing a ball in our yard one day when it rolled into the street, then into Sister Tullis's yard. Since she said our family could play there, I felt the freedom to play with that same ball in her yard.

Suddenly I heard a loud noise coming from one of Sister Tullis's rooms. Being a curious boy, I found a box to stand on and peaked into the window of their bedroom.

What I saw rocked me to the core of my being. Her husband, who we knew did not believe in Jesus or go to church, had a belt in his right hand and was repeatedly beating Sister Tullis. Instead of leaving that abusive situation, she had decided to stay and rely on the Holy Spirit. Instead of running or trying to block him, she knelt by their bed, raised her hands in praise to God and spoke in tongues. Instead of a look of distress on her face, there was joy and peace. Her belief in the Holy Spirit made a profound difference in her reactions to a harsh situation.

In that moment I became convinced that "this Holy Spirit and speaking in tongues stuff" was a genuine experience that helped people through life's daily difficulties. For the first time in my life, I also wanted more of the Holy Spirit. What I had before dismissed, I then wanted to have.

Years later, I met Mr. Tullis. His wife's reliance on the Holy Spirit made an eternal difference in his life and his destiny. He had become a strong Christian and was serving as a faithful deacon in the church.

An Entry Point

I thought I heard two chimpanzees squeal in the distance, followed by the growl of a large cat—maybe a leopard. But nothing fully interrupted my thoughts of the past. I remembered that in my final year of high school I had decided that I wanted to receive the baptism of the Holy Spirit. I went down to the altar in our church, and some adults prayed and laid hands on me. Not long after, I spoke a few words in tongues. "You've got it!" one exclaimed. I didn't feel much different, but accepted what he said. I then thought that speaking in tongues was just an "evidence"—an entry point into the baptism.

By my first year in Bible school, I again wondered if it was valid to be baptized in the Holy Spirit and speak in tongues. So I searched Scripture for myself. I was especially impressed by Jesus' words to His disciples to wait in Jerusalem for the promised Holy Spirit, for "you shall be baptized with the Holy Spirit not many days from now."[28] The disciples already believed in Him, but He wanted them to have something more. Then the Holy Spirit descended, and all were filled and began to speak in tongues.[29] Later the place where they met was shaken, and all were filled again with the Spirit and spoke the Word of God with boldness.[30] Tongues were not mentioned in that Scripture passage, but again the emphasis is on the "filling" of the Holy Spirit.

I noticed that Peter and John prayed for the Samaritan believers to receive the Holy Spirit.[31] Again, the Samaritans already believed in Christ, but there was something more. It was so evident to observers that they had received the Spirit that a manipulating man named Simon offered Peter and John money, saying, "Give me this power also, that anyone on whom I lay hands may receive the Holy Spirit."[32] Perhaps Simon knew that they had received the Holy Spirit because he heard them speak in tongues. Peter's response was clear: "Your money perish with you, because you thought that the gift of God could be purchased with money!"[33]

Peter was later astonished that the Holy Spirit was poured out on the Gentiles who believed, "for they heard them speak with tongues, and magnify God."[34] Paul later placed his hands on twelve male believers in Ephesus, and "the Holy Spirit came upon them; and they spoke with tongues, and prophesied."[35]

I noticed that speaking in tongues was often mentioned when people in the Bible received the baptism of the Holy Spirit. I still considered tongues just an evidence, an entry point, into the baptism. When I prayed, I sometimes spoke a few words in tongues, but not that often. Since I already "had it," I was content with my spiritual walk.

PRAYER LANGUAGE

It sounded like a different chimpanzee squeal this time, melded with other animal sounds from the nearby jungle. My thoughts drifted to Maxine, and I turned on our bed to look at her. My beautiful wife still slept peacefully beneath our broad mosquito net.

After I married Maxine, I noticed that she spoke in tongues almost every time she prayed. Even when Maxine had her vision of heaven and hell, she conversed in tongues. Several times she referred to tongues as her "prayer language."

Maxine had gone to a different Bible school, one connected with a local church in Atlanta, Georgia. She was not just a student, but also taught the children's church that met at the same time as the adult Sunday services. Nearly twenty-five girls and boys, ranging in age from five to fifteen, joined in that children's church. During the time that Maxine taught and ministered there, many received the baptism of the Holy Spirit and spoke in tongues.

One girl in that children's church was six-year-old Jan, daughter of the senior pastor. Maxine prayed for Jan, and she fell backward on the floor. Two hours later Jan stood up, speaking in tongues. Little did Maxine know that Jan would later grow into a beautiful woman, marry Paul Crouch and start Trinity Broadcasting Network. Other notable ministers also came out of that children's church.

It sounded like an owl screeched in the distance, and I glanced again at Maxine. She had such a sweet and consistent dependence on the Holy Spirit. Her example prompted me to once more search Scripture about the believer's use of tongues.

More than an Evidence

Paul's teaching to the Corinthians captivated my thoughts. Paul instructed the Corinthians about the use of spiritual gifts in public services. The "gift of tongues," publicly used, also had to be interpreted so that those present could understand what the Spirit said.[36] Paul wrote boldly about praying "in a tongue" or "praying with the Spirit," and then about singing in the Spirit: "For if I pray in a tongue, my spirit prays, but my understanding is unfruitful...I will pray with the spirit, and I will also pray with the understanding. I will sing with the spirit, and I will also sing with the understanding."[37]

Key Bible Passages on the Baptism in the Holy Spirit

- **Prophesied in the Old Testament:** Joel 2:28; Isaiah 28:9-12 (esp. verse 11)
- **Promised by Jesus:** Acts 1:4-5, 8
- **Experienced by the Early Church:** Acts 2:1-4; 8:14-17; 10:44-48; 19:1-7
- **Further explained in the New Testament:** Luke 11:9-13; 1 Corinthians 14:13-19

Interesting. In those verses, Paul said nothing about interpreting what he prayed or sang in tongues. But what most riveted my attention was the distinction Paul made between the public and the private use of tongues: "I thank my God I speak with tongues more than you all; *yet in the church* I would rather speak five words with my understanding, that I may teach others also, than ten thousand words in a tongue."[38]

So outside the church, in his own private life, Paul spoke in tongues even more than the Corinthians did! He even thanked God for this frequent use of tongues. When I linked what Paul said in these passages, I finally understood. Speaking in tongues was more than an evidence of baptism in the Holy Spirit. As Maxine had often mentioned, tongues was also a private prayer language that the Holy Spirit gave to the receptive believer.

There's Always More

I still wondered why tongues, especially a prayer language, would be important. Paul wrote, "He who speaks in a tongue edifies himself."[39] Jude wrote that we are to build ourselves up "on our most holy faith, praying in the Holy Spirit."[40] Praying in our prayer language builds us spiritually.

Then I remembered what Solomon wrote: "Death and life are in the power of the tongue, and those who love it will eat its fruit."[41] The tongue has great power. Perhaps this is another reason that praying in tongues is so important. It is the one time I can know that I am praying according to God's will, for my tongue is saying only what His Spirit is prompting me to

Seven Benefits I Receive When I Speak in Tongues

1. **I know my spirit is speaking directly to God**—"For he who speaks in a tongue does not speak to men but to God…for if I pray in a tongue, my spirit prays" (1 Corinthians 14:2a, 14a). Praying in tongues can also be like a two-way street. When I pray in tongues, God often gives me wisdom and insight to see better ways of doing what I need to do.
2. **I know I am praying according to the will of God**—The Holy Spirit "makes intercession for the saints according to the will of God" (Romans 8:27b). I am often tempted to pray for what I want, but when I speak in tongues, I know that I am instead praying God's will.
3. **I bring my tongue into subjection to God**—James is clear: "No man can tame the tongue. It is an unruly evil, full of deadly poison" (3:8). But when I speak in tongues, I am finally submitting my tongue to God. Perhaps that is why the tongue is the first thing the Spirit controls when He baptizes us.
4. **I am edified**—"He who speaks in a tongue edifies himself…I thank my God that I speak in tongues more than you all" (1 Corinthians 14:4a, 18). In a world filled with disappointments and unmet expectations, I often need to be edified. Even Paul deeply felt a need to speak frequently in tongues.

say. Maybe that is why Paul concluded his instruction by writing, "Do not forbid to speak with tongues."[42]

As rays of the West African sunrise pierced our bedroom window, I knew that God was stretching me. He was calling me to a new level of bold obedience. It was no longer enough to speak just of salvation in Jesus. I must now also speak of His Holy Spirit and help others to experience Him more fully. There's always more in Jesus. Always.

5. **My faith is stimulated**—Jude explained it best: "But you, beloved, building yourselves up on your most holy faith, praying in the Holy Spirit" (Jude 20). When I find myself struggling with doubt or unbelief, I draw apart and speak in tongues, and my faith is stimulated.
6. **I know I am "giving thanks well" to God**—When I read 1 Corinthians 14:15-17, I realized that I "give thanks well" to God when I speak in tongues, even if no one around me understands what I am saying.
7. **I am spiritually refreshed**—Ever become weary or discouraged? Then speak in tongues. "For with stammering lips and another tongue He will speak to His people, to whom He said, 'This is the rest with which you may cause the weary to rest,' and 'This is the refreshing'" (Isaiah 28:11-12a).

About You

Dr. Cho says that I taught him the importance of the Holy Spirit. But before I could teach anyone about the Holy Spirit, I first had to wash away some of my own wrong attitudes with the water of God's Word.

You and I are in a war. It is not a contest of physical strength; it is a war to conform our thoughts and attitudes to God's Word, to bring "every thought into captivity to the obedience of Christ."[43] Until we do, you and I will never fully be the people God has called us to be.

What about *your* attitudes? Be honest. We are to renew our minds with His Word.[44] As my daughter says, "If you have any attitudes that need cleanin', now is the time to repent and use God's Word to do the washin'." Search His Word for truth as you've never searched it before.

Let the truth of His Word wash away your negative, self-defeating attitudes and replace them with the hope that comes only from Jesus Christ and His sure Word.

GUIDELINES TO RECEIVING THE BAPTISM IN THE HOLY SPIRIT

Scripture is clear: there are a variety of settings and ways in which people receive the baptism of the Holy Spirit. Some receive the Holy Spirit when they are in a powerful service and hands are laid on them; others receive Him quietly when alone in their homes. However, there are some guidelines I followed when I received the baptism myself, and I later found those same guidelines useful in helping others to receive the baptism of the Holy Spirit.

- **Have the assurance of salvation**—Some people receive both salvation and the baptism of the Holy Spirit at the same time (Acts 10:44-48), but most are first born again. Whether you are seeking the baptism, or are helping someone else to receive, start with the assurance of salvation.
- **Understand who the Holy Spirit is**—The Holy Spirit is the third member of the Trinity (1 John 5:7; John 10:30), sent by Jesus after He ascended in order that we would have a Helper, Teacher and Spirit of truth (John 14:16-17, 26). While the Holy Spirit "seals" us in our salvation (2 Corinthians 1:22; Ephesians 1:13-14), He also baptizes the receptive with "power from on high" (Luke 24:49b; Acts 1:8), an experience usually accompanied by speaking in tongues.
- **Ask your heavenly Father for the baptism of the Holy Spirit**—Jesus put it best, "If a son asks for bread from any father among you, will he give him a stone? Or if he asks for a fish, will he give him a serpent instead of a fish?...if you then, being evil, know how to give good gifts to your children, how much more will your heavenly Father give the Holy Spirit to those who ask Him?" (Luke 11:11, 13)

Of all our attitudes, Jesus seemed most concerned about our attitude toward His Holy Spirit.[45] Each believer is sealed with the Holy Spirit when he is born again. But, as one of Karen's friends says, "The Holy Spirit is the only member of the Trinity who chooses to live as a Prisoner until we release Him to speak and flow through us."

If you have never been baptized in the Holy Spirit, if you have never spoken in tongues, now is the time. That might be your best first step in learning to yield more fully to Him. If you already speak in tongues, maybe it's time for you to lead others in the baptism of the Holy Spirit.

I will never forget what happened many years later in Korea. Karen was only ten and wanted to receive the baptism of the Holy Spirit. Dr. Cho and I had already baptized her in water, but she was hungry for more.

However, for many months, nothing happened. One evening service Maxine sat beside her and could hear her begging God to give her the baptism. Maxine leaned over and said, "Honey, the baptism of the Holy Spirit is like a gift. You don't beg someone to give you a gift, you just reach out and receive it. Just relax, praise God and receive."

- **Relax, expect and allow the Holy Spirit to speak through you**—The Holy Spirit is powerful, yet usually works through our choices and decisions. He will not force anyone to be baptized and to speak in tongues, but He will freely give the gift of a prayer language to those who seek Him (Acts 2:1-4; 10:44-48; 19:1-7; 1 Corinthians 14:18-19). If you do not receive the first time you ask, persist until you do.

During a time when everyone in the church was following the custom of praying aloud together, Karen relaxed and softly began thanking God. She suddenly felt the warmth of God's presence and began to speak in a language she didn't understand. "Then," she later related, "I saw a picture in my mind that looked like a demon. His shoulders were bent, his head drooped down and he walked slowly away. In that moment I knew that I'd received the Holy Spirit's baptism. I knew it was a defeat of whatever Satan was trying to do to me."

Maybe you also need a defeat of whatever the enemy is trying to do in your life. Once again, remember Jesus' words: "Ask, and it will be given to you; seek, and you will find; knock, and it will be opened to you. For everyone who asks receives, and he who seeks finds, and to him who knocks it will be opened...If you then, being evil, know how to give good gifts to your children, *how much more will your heavenly Father give the Holy Spirit to those who ask Him?*"[46]

WORD WASH:
DEVOTIONAL AND DISCUSSION QUESTIONS

Sharing Questions

What is one Bible verse or scripture that means a lot to you? Why?

Remember the three guidelines for a sharing question: 1) no one is to take more than one minute in response; 2) go around the circle—if in a small group—and give each person an opportunity to respond; and 3) don't ask other questions at this point, for that stretches out the minute.

Discussion Questions

1. I tell about several times—such as with disappointment, attitude toward authorities and attitude toward the Holy Spirit—when I needed Word wash. With which incident in this chapter did you most relate? Why?
2. Review "Key Facts About God's Word" on page 28. Which one or two things have you often found God's Word doing in your own life?
3. Consider the "Two Attitudes That Need Word Wash" on page 31. Is there another attitude that you would add to the list?
4. Take time to read the verses listed in "Key Bible Passages on the Baptism in the Holy Spirit" on page 35. After each verse or passage is read, respond to this question: What can I learn about the Spirit's baptism from this verse or passage?
5. Review "Seven Benefits I Receive When I Speak in Tongues" on pages 36–37. Which benefit do you notice most often? Which benefit to you feel is needed most in the believer's life?

Application

1. "Three Types of Word Wash," on page 32, describes ways to wash oneself with God's Word. Which type of Word wash have you used most frequently? Share one specific and practical way you plan to wash yourself with God's Word this week.
2. Pair with your spouse or another person of the same gender. Turn to "Guidelines to Receiving the Baptism in the Holy Spirit" on pages 38–39. Let one of you take the role of a person who wants to receive the baptism and the other person lead him or her through the process. Now switch roles and go through the process again.
3. Conclude by praying for each other and for the salvation of one lost person in your area.

Maxine sits on the far left with her children's church, including the six-year-old Jan Bethany Crouch.

Insight Three

PRAY, OBEY AND GET OUT OF HIS WAY

Learn to yield to the Holy Spirit and His promptings

LUSH AVOCADO, PALM and papaya trees encircled us as we set up fifty folding chairs outdoors; it was too hot to meet inside on that Liberian summer day in 1948. When everyone finally sat down, Maxine told the young adult female students how happy we were to be in Liberia, then shared her heartrending vision of heaven and hell. I followed by preaching on the text of Acts 2:38: "Repent, and let every one of you be baptized in the name of Jesus Christ for the remission of sins; and you shall receive the gift of the Holy Spirit."

I ended with an altar call and invited forward those who either wanted salvation or wanted to rededicate their lives to Christ. Nearly all the young women came to the front, and the missionaries who oversaw the women's Bible school in Newake were delighted.

After leading them in a sinner's prayer, I paused and remembered what God had taught me. I gulped, then asked, "Have you received the Holy Spirit yet? Have you spoken in tongues?"

They shook their heads. "No, Pa," our interpreter said, using the local term of respect in interpreting their response. "We have not."

"HELPING" THE HELPER

After I told those gathered that Maxine and I would pray for them to receive the Spirit's baptism, the missionaries over the Bible school stepped to the front. "We know who's more spiritually ready," one informed us. "Let us help you."

So we waited as the missionaries separated the young women in the front into two groups: those who were "ready," and those who were "not as ready." The missionaries told us to first lay hands on those in the "ready" group, for they had shown themselves to be more spiritually stable, and they would therefore be more receptive to the baptism of the Holy Spirit.

We did as the missionaries instructed us. We laid hands on the "ready" group to receive the baptism. Not one responded.

Then I glanced over at the "not as ready" group. Many had started shaking. It looked like God's Spirit was already touching them, so Maxine and I quickly went to pray for them. As we laid hands on the young women in the "not as ready" group, nearly all started speaking in tongues. I particularly noticed one eighteen-year-old; there was a special sweetness when she received her prayer language.

We later turned our attention back to the first group—the "ready" group. What happened to their fellow students had helped them be more open, and several in the "ready" group then received the baptism of the Holy Spirit.

The missionaries were surprised by this turn of events. Those in the "not as ready" group had proven to be the most receptive. The missionaries had tried to help our divine Helper and had misread His intention. Before we could even comment on this, our interpreter motioned to us. "Come quickly," she said. "You must see this woman. Come quickly."

Maxine and I hurried with her over to the "not as ready" group. The eighteen-year-old I had noticed earlier now became the center of our attention. Her eyes were closed and she looked so peaceful. "Her tongue is different," our interpreter told Maxine. "It's like she's talking with someone. Do you think she's having a vision like you did?"

Another Vision, Another Set of Lessons to Learn

As we watched her, our interpreter explained that the girl's father worked in a gold mine. When the young woman stopped speaking in tongues and opened her eyes, the other women joined us—this time to ask her what she had seen.

Our interpreter translated each phrase as the young woman spoke: "I went to heaven. The first thing I saw in heaven was Jesus. He was so beautiful, more beautiful than I have words to say. Heaven was filled with such joy and peace. Then I looked down on streets of gold. It was not like the gold we have, but it was much purer. It was so pure that I could see my reflection."

After her vision, it was not difficult to motivate those women to attend the next two weeks of meetings. Not only did I teach Bible passages about the Holy Spirit, I also pointed to the importance of yielding fully to Him.

By the end of those two weeks, each young woman had made a fresh dedication to serve the Lord. More than twenty of the young women had received the baptism of the Holy Spirit.

I also learned some important lessons. God wanted me to relax and know that His Spirit was already here. He also wanted me to know that no one is to tell Him what to do or when to do it, for only the Holy Spirit knows when a person is ready to receive Him. The Helper doesn't want my help, but does ask me to obey His promptings. The women's Bible school would never be quite the same again, and neither would I.

Our Journey with the Holy Spirit Continues

The next two weeks of our journey with the Holy Spirit continued at our second stop, a leper colony called "New Hope Town," near the same mission station where the women's Bible school was located. New Hope Town had been started by Florence Steidal, a middle-aged missionary nurse with a kind face and a passion to care for lepers. Some called leprosy "living death," for it can have horrifying effects on the human body. In Liberia, leprosy was thought to be a curse from the spirits, a punishment for wrongs committed in the past. Any known leper was forced to be a social outcast, and many were thrown into the jungle to die. So Steidal had started New Hope Town as a place where lepers could find acceptance, medical care and hope.

The missionaries warned us that leprosy caused deformity, but nothing prepared us for what we saw in our first meeting. Because leprosy damages nerves in the hands and feet, victims can have burns, injuries and infections and not even feel them or know that their injuries need to be treated. One man was disfigured beyond anything I'd ever seen. His nose had collapsed, and he had hard nodules instead of cheeks. Several had clawed hands and ulcerated fingers. A few walked on crutches, for their diseased limbs had been amputated. Some had nubs where toes had once been.

Each day we gathered on rows of bamboo benches set up under a thatched roof in a large mud building. Scripture proclaims that "God shows no partiality,"[47] so Maxine and I shared the same messages at the leper colony that we had taught at the women's Bible school. Some warned us to be careful about touching lepers, but we were not afraid. We shook their hands and freely talked and interacted with them before and after every service, with our interpreter by our side.

Most of the lepers at the colony joined us for each meeting. We saw a difference, even after the very first service. Many had filed in, faces reflecting despair. By the time they left that service, they were smiling, glowing with the hope that only Jesus can give.

By the third day, so many came forward to receive the Lord that they could not fit into the front of the building. Maxine pointed out one fifteen-year-old albino woman among the many who had received the Lord that day. She had been flown to New Hope Town by a mission pilot who had lost his way and landed his small plane in the open field of a village deep in the interior. The first day he was in the village, he noticed several people worshiping the girl. Because she was an albino, the villagers felt that the spirits had given her a special status. But the day after his arrival, they discovered that she had leprosy and were about to throw her into the jungle to be eaten by wild animals. The pilot asked them if he could take her. They gave her to him, and he immediately brought her to New Hope Town. Now she stood before us, freshly washed of her sins.

PRAY, OBEY AND GET OUT OF HIS WAY

By the fourth service at New Hope Town, we had developed a pattern. I would first teach, and then Maxine and I would pray as we filtered through those who had gathered, laying our hands on them to receive the Holy Spirit. I remember walking to one section where some male lepers sat. Each one I laid hands on began to speak in tongues. God's Holy Spirit was using us, and we were grateful.

Near the middle of our two weeks, in walked a poorly clad woman in her forties. Her family had just found out that she had leprosy. Instead of leaving her in the jungle, they had allowed her to walk to New Hope Town. As she stood before us, we spoke through our interpreter and told her about Jesus, His cross, His forgiveness and His love. She began weeping uncontrollably and dropped to the floor.

She was an illiterate woman who did not even know the English word "hello." But then, in perfect English, she quoted a passage from Psalm 103: "Bless the LORD, O my soul, and all that is within me, bless His holy name! Bless the LORD, O my soul, and forget not all His benefits: Who forgives all my iniquities, Who heals all my diseases; Who redeems my life from destruction, Who crowns me with lovingkindness and tender mercies, Who satisfies my mouth with good things, so that my youth is renewed like the eagle's."[48]

We stood listening to her, stunned at what we were hearing. This illiterate woman had neither gone forward in an altar call, nor even repeated a sinner's prayer, yet the Holy Spirit marvelously baptized her.

At New Hope Town, God showed us that the Holy Spirit is not interested in our formulas and methods. Instead, He knows each heart, what it needs and when. He is indeed like the wind, blowing where He pleases.[49] We are never to direct Him. We are simply to pray, to obey and to get out of His way.

Before we left that area, a fatal case of malaria struck the eighteen-year-old who had had a vision of heaven in the women's Bible school. We rushed to her side. As she lay dying, our interpreter told us what she was saying: "I can see Jesus now. He's even more beautiful than I remembered. He has His arms out, ready to receive me." She paused, then added, "I'm going to be with Him now." With those words, she stopped breathing.

New Hope Town retested for leprosy at the end of our meetings. They found that twenty-three lepers had been healed and could be released back to their own towns and villages—twice the number they had ever before released at one time.

I didn't understand why the Holy Spirit healed some lepers and let the eighteen-year-old woman die. But I was learning this: He knows best. He doesn't require me to understand His ways, but He does ask me to trust Him. I am to pray, to obey and to get out of His way.

LEARNING TO TAKE AUTHORITY

Our next stop was at the town of Feloke, the place where Henry Garlock had originally assigned us. From the moment we arrived at the young men's Bible school there, we felt that something wasn't right. The students were less committed than any Bible school students I had ever seen; many did not even want to read the Bible. Never once did the missionaries talk about us praying together, nor did they seem eager to discuss spiritual things. It felt as if we had to minister in a fog of oppression. We just couldn't understand what was going on.

KEY BIBLE PASSAGES ON SATAN AND JESUS' AUTHORITY OVER HIM

- **His origin:** Ezekiel 28:13-15
- **His fall from heaven:** Isaiah 14:12-17; Revelation 12:7-9
- **His nature:** John 8:44; 10:10; 1 Peter 5:8
- **Glimpses into his demonic realm:** Luke 11:14-26; Acts 16:16-18; 19:13-16; Ephesians 6:12
- **How Jesus defeated him on the cross:** Colossians 2:13-15
- **All subject to Jesus' authority:** 1 Corinthians 15:27-28; 1 Peter 3:18-22
- **The power in the name of Jesus:** John 14:13-14; Philippians 2:9-11; Acts 3:6-9
- **The power in the blood of Jesus:** John 6: 53-56; Romans 3:25; 5:9; 1 Corinthians 11:25; Hebrews 9:11-22; 10:19; 1 John 1:7, 9

Maxine and I went to our room and started praying. We didn't know what we should pray about, so we prayed in tongues. As we did, one verse exploded in our thoughts: "For we do not wrestle against flesh and blood, but against principalities, against powers, against the rulers of the darkness of this age, against spiritual hosts of wickedness in the heavenly places."[50]

We knew then that we were facing a spiritual battle. But we were novice missionaries, and we were unsure how we should respond. Soon a parade of scriptures became part of our answer: "For God has not given us a spirit of fear, but of power and of love and of a sound mind...because He who is in you is greater than he who is in the world...but you shall receive power when the Holy Spirit has come upon you."[51]

We remembered how Jesus responded in similar situations. Jesus preached "in their synagogues throughout all Galilee, and *casting out demons*."[52] When a man with an unclean spirit cried out, Jesus rebuked the demon saying, "Be quiet, and come out of him."[53] The unclean spirit left.

Jesus then went a step farther. He commanded His disciples to do what He had done: "He gave them power over unclean spirits, to *cast them out*" and He commanded them to "heal the sick, cleanse the lepers, raise the dead, *cast out demons*."[54] Later Jesus told His disciples to wait for the power of the Holy Spirit.[55] After the outpouring of the Holy Spirit, Peter commanded the lame man to walk "in the name of Jesus."[56] Paul cast a demon out of a slave girl, commanding the demon to leave "in the name of Jesus."[57] The name of Jesus has great power, for "at the name of Jesus every knee should bow."[58]

We realized we had the right to take authority over the enemy. I could not pray loudly, for the walls were thin, but I was firm: "In the name of Jesus, we take authority over what the enemy is trying to do at this Bible school. Because of Jesus' power, we command the enemy to stop harassing these missionaries and students. Enemy, we command your plans in this situation to cease. In the name of Jesus, leave. Holy Spirit, have Your way."

After we prayed, even the atmosphere about us seemed to change. When we next saw the missionaries, they seemed more relaxed than before. Each time I preached, the students responded. By the end of two weeks, most of the pastors-in-training had rededicated their lives to the Lord, and several had received the Holy Spirit, speaking in tongues.

GOD AT WORK

I was surprised in one meeting when our new male interpreter asked me a question. "Like you preached," he began, "the Holy Spirit has changed the men students. But they want you to stop for a while. They want two weeks to go back to their villages, in order to preach about salvation and the Holy Spirit to their relatives and friends. Then they'll return for more of your teaching. Pa, could they please do that?"

I looked at the thirty-five eager faces in the rows in front of me, nodded my head, then smiled at Maxine. God was at work.

By the end of those two weeks of recess, the students returned as promised. Nearly all brought us reports about relatives and friends that they had led to the Lord, even in villages formerly hostile to the Gospel. Three of the students even brought back fathers, mothers or

FIVE GUIDELINES FOR YIELDING TO THE HOLY SPIRIT

I want to do things my way. How then can I yield to the Holy Spirit? In my life I have found five crucial guidelines:

1. **Let Him lead**–As Dr. Cho later said, "I learned that the Holy Spirit must be my 'senior partner.'" My greatest problems in life usually come when I try to do the leading, instead of waiting on His direction and timing.
2. **Cling to His Word daily**–God's Word "is a lamp to my feet and a light to my path" (Psalm 119:105). I find that the more I know and value His Word, the more clearly I can hear His Holy Spirit speak. Just as I eat daily for my physical health, I consume His Word daily for my spiritual well-being. This also means I must immediately repent of any sin in my life and be clean before Him (1 John 1:9).
3. **Cherish your times in prayer**–In our busy days with so much distraction and demand, I find it vital to cherish daily times in prayer with Him. I must dwell "in the secret place of the Most High" in order to "abide under the shadow of the Almighty" (Psalm 91:1).
4. **Be in right relationship with authority and others**–Not only am I to be in right relationship to authority figures, but if I have "anything against anyone," I am to forgive him, so that my Father in heaven "may also forgive" me my trespasses (Mark 11:25).
5. **Understand that we are in a spiritual battle**–People are not our enemies, for we are engaged

friends with them. We started meeting in the same small building, but when others from the community joined us, we moved to an open arbor. During the next two weeks, I taught as never before.

in a spiritual battle. We battle not "against flesh and blood, but against principalities, against powers, against the rulers of the darkness of this age" (Ephesians 6:12). Learn to fight the right battle with the power of the Holy Spirit.

Those meetings at the men's Bible school were another turning point for me. I had once thought I would be assigned to that place to teach others. Instead I discovered that I was the main student there, with much more to learn. God's Word was true. Jesus had given us authority over the enemy, and His Holy Spirit had helped us to overcome.

The following month we flew to two other mission stations in the interior. In each place we had a sweet outpouring of the Holy Spirit. During one meeting Maxine sat beside a young tribal man who started to speak in tongues. An older man from a nearby row jumped up and came to Maxine. "This can't be," he excitedly exclaimed in English. "I'm his boss. He works for me in the mines. He's never studied in any school, but he's praising God in fluent French. How can this be?"

Although we had seen God move powerfully, we still had more to learn about our precious Holy Spirit—so much more.

A Change of Plans

I couldn't believe it. We'd had glorious months of teaching in the interior. We returned to Monrovia, expecting to be sent to preach the Gospel to villages and tribes who had not yet heard of Jesus Christ.

But Henry Garlock had other plans for us. His instructions were firm. Garlock now wanted us to oversee the central mission home—a ramshackle three-story house. He also made me the mission's business manager.

The mission home had thirteen rooms and one outside toilet. We never understood why, but our toilet had been built near our only well, making it necessary to boil each gallon of drinking water for a full thirty minutes. There was no indoor plumbing, so we had to carry buckets of water into the kitchen for cooking. For bathing we carried buckets of water into a walled-off segment of an upstairs porch.

Since there were no hotels in Monrovia that missionaries could afford, that sprawling home served as a lodging place for missionaries of all denominations. Some missionaries were dropped off by *Ambassador* flights. A few came in ships, but most came from the interior, both to rest and to restock supplies to take back to their mission stations.

You would have thought it would be a joy to run a home for visiting missionaries. While there were moments of pleasure in serving some, most were only concerned about getting their own immediate needs met. Others felt it their personal duty to tell us novice missionaries what we were doing wrong. We tried to listen, smile and agree as much as we could, but our time in Monrovia was tough on the soul.

Each day Maxine coordinated meals, boiled countless gallons of water and cleaned and rearranged facilities for anywhere from three to eighteen guests. It wasn't easy feeding all those people with a daily budget of only five dollars per person.

The mission also had an endless quantity of details that needed my attention, so I spent most of my time working on my newly acquired duties as the mission's business manager. We became so busy with the mission home and business matters that there was time for little else. It was discouraging to delay our dream of preaching the Gospel in unreached tribes and villages.

THE WILDERNESS PATTERN

In the midst of our difficulty, I noticed a pattern. The Holy Spirit will baptize us afresh, giving us special times of glory; then He leads us into a wilderness: a place or time when life seems bleak, when dreams and hopes—even godly dreams and hopes—die or are put on a shelf.

I remembered that the Israelites had to go through a wilderness to get to their Promised Land. After God's strong arm supernaturally delivered the Israelites from bondage in Egypt, they left loaded with gold and gifts from their Egyptian neighbors. They once again experienced God's glory when they walked across dry land after He parted the Red Sea and then drowned their enemies. But their journey through the wilderness was not short. Because of their ungodly responses, many died before the next generation entered the Promised Land.[59]

Jesus faced a similar experience. When John baptized Jesus in the Jordan River,[60] it was a time of glory. Heaven opened, and the Holy Spirit descended like a dove. The clear voice of the Father rang out, "This is My beloved Son, in whom I am well pleased."[61]

You would have thought that success was imminent for Jesus. But after that time of glory, the Spirit led Jesus into the wilderness[62] where He faced the struggle of weariness and temptation. But Jesus overcame His wilderness struggle and soon began His powerful ministry.

If our Jesus went through His own wilderness experience, we can't expect any less. The way to a Promised Land leads through a wilderness.

Weariness in the Wilderness

To make matters worse in our personal wilderness, ministry in Monrovia was difficult. A few years before, a Methodist church there had hosted a black lady Pentecostal minister from America. While teaching on the Holy Spirit, she had a massive heart attack, slumped over the pulpit and died. "If you receive the Holy Spirit," the common thinking became, "you'll die."

Each Sunday possible, I preached in different inviting churches in towns and villages around Monrovia's countryside. Even when I was able to share about the Holy Spirit, most were not responsive.

It's easy to grow weary in the wilderness. One day Maxine grew so discouraged that she blurted out, "I don't know which way we're supposed to go. This all seems so pointless. We're just a glorified maid and errand boy here. Let's go back to the States. We're not doing any better than missionaries who settle for the status quo. I don't feel like I'm making any impact for God's kingdom here."

I agreed. We went into our empty living room and knelt in prayer. As we prayed in the Spirit, Maxine gave a message in tongues and the interpretation:[63] "You don't need to know the way. Just hear My voice and follow." God's instruction brought us great comfort. From that time on, we spent extended time praying in tongues every day. A fresh discipline and a new resolve were forged in our souls.

I learned that we often fight against being in the wilderness. We rebuke Satan for what we think is his attack, when we should instead thank God for His provision. We try to manipulate a better route, not

Three Signs That You're in a Wilderness Experience

The main characteristic of a wilderness is barrenness. Sometimes my season in a wilderness has been short; at other times, like in Monrovia, it lasted for more than two years. I have observed three signs that let me know I am in a wilderness experience:

- **Financial barrenness**–Your needs are being met, but there is money for little else. When the Israelites were in the wilderness, God gave them manna for only one day at a time (Exodus 16:15-31).
- **Social barrenness**–It is wonderful to have the support and understanding of family and friends. One mark of a wilderness experience is that even the people around us don't understand and accept us. Consider the rejection of Joseph's brothers as he entered his wilderness, sold as a slave to the Midianites (Genesis 37:23-28).
- **Emotional barrenness**–Dreams and hopes grow dim in the wilderness, and that often leads to emotional barrenness. Listen to the distress of the Israelites when the Red Sea was before them and the Egyptian chariots behind them: "Because there were no graves in Egypt, have you taken us away to die in the wilderness? Why have you so dealt with us, to bring us up out of Egypt?" (Exodus 14:11). Sometimes in the wilderness we doubt God's goodness and lose perspective of His purposes and plans for our lives.

realizing that we must journey through the wilderness to arrive at our Promised Land.

Some Fruit in the Wilderness

Soon after, we began to see some fruit in our wilderness. Amin[64] was an alcoholic Muslim who had been born in Lebanon. Amin worked with his brother, trading imported goods such as British cloth for ivory and animal skins brought in by local hunters. They had a store in a small town thirty miles north of Monrovia, in an area accessible only by plane or boat. Amin often came to Monrovia for supplies and stayed at a nearby hotel.

We first met Amin after church one night. Since he was about our age, he spent more and more time with us. We had many spirited talks about Christ and Christianity. During one long, cool walk to the mission home, Amin renounced Islam and received Jesus Christ as his Lord and Savior.

I baptized Amin in the waters of the Atlantic Ocean, and we gave him a Bible. He visited us as often as he could. We soon found that Amin was not only a new believer to disciple, but he also became a close personal friend. In the midst of our wilderness, Amin became like a brother to us—a replacement for my own brother who died young, and the older brother Maxine had never had.

Spirit-Inspired Strategy

After two full and very long years, two single lady missionaries took over our responsibilities at the mission home. Maxine and I moved to a small house in the country. Even though I was still the mission's business manager, we were finally free to visit villages and tribes who had not yet heard the name of Jesus.

But it was not easy. As small as our budget with the mission home was, our budget now was even less, and we often went to bed hungry. Still, we were resolved to do what we felt God had called us to do.

Three Things That the Wilderness Brings

- **Testing and proving**–God led the Israelites in the wilderness and provided times to test and prove them (one example–Psalm 81:7). God can test us in the wilderness, but we are not to test Him (Numbers 14:22-23).
- **Temptation**–While the first generation of Israelites failed the temptations in the wilderness (1 Corinthians 10:1-13), Jesus was victorious over the temptations in His wilderness (Luke 4:1-13).
- **Preparation**–John the Baptist's time in the wilderness prepared him to proclaim the way of the Lord (Matthew 3:1-12). No doubt Paul's three years of wilderness time in Arabia and Damascus helped to prepare him as an apostle to the Gentiles (Galatians 1:15-18).

We first walked to two villages in the interior, neither of which had before heard about Jesus. Several villagers came to our meetings. Amin went with us once and shared his story. I preached about Jesus, but there were only a few conversions. We were not even sure that those conversions were genuine.

Once again Maxine and I became desperate. When we didn't know what to do, we turned to Him. We fasted and prayed, asking God to show us how to better minister to these precious village folk. By now I knew that speaking in tongues allowed God to put things in my heart to do and to say, things I would not have considered on my own.

The Holy Spirit often shows us important things in the wilderness. As we continued praying, the Spirit's directive to us was clear: In each village where we went, we were to ask to speak to the chief; then we were to ask him whether we could pray for some of the sick villagers to be healed. I had never before heard of this Spirit-inspired strategy, but by now I had learned to obey Him and let Him lead.

BREAKTHROUGH

The next village we visited was different. My interpreter and I first found the village chief, regally dressed in a blue and white robe. "I am a missionary," I explained through our interpreter. "I have come to your village because I want to pray for any sick to be healed in the name of Jesus. Jesus is God's only Son. He died for your sins and my sins, and He is also a Healer. Are there any sick in your village?"

The village chief politely nodded. "I have never before heard of this Jesus, but one of my sons is dying, sick with malaria." He pointed, saying, "My dying son is in that hut."

With the interpreter by my side, we walked to that mud hut. The interpreter and I bowed to enter a low opening and then walked slowly around a small fire in the hut's center. Villagers commonly allowed the smoke from such a fire to accumulate under the ceiling, in an effort to keep away mosquitoes that carried malaria. The smoke in this hut was so thick and low that neither the interpreter nor I could stand up. We continued to make our way through the hut, bent over like that, until we were beside the chief's young son—a teenager, who was lying very still on a pallet of rice straw.

I placed my hand on the young man's forehead and felt the heat of his raging fever. I remembered how Jesus gave us authority. "In the name of Jesus," I began, "I take authority over Satan and this sickness, and I command the enemy to take his hands off this young man. In the name of Jesus, be healed."

Immediately, I felt his temperature drop. For the first time, the young man began to move. Within two minutes he raised up on his pallet and declared, "I'm hungry."

My interpreter grew more excited than I had yet seen him. We quickly left the hut to find the chief. When we had found him, we told him that his son was well and was asking for something to eat.

The chief hurried to his son's hut and returned with a large smile on his face, commanding his wife to cook rice for their son. He then told me about three other sick people in the village. We visited and prayed with all three, and each one was instantly healed in the name of Jesus.

"Please come," the chief then instructed us, "to the Palava Arbor and tell my people of this Jesus you speak about."

"Palava" was the accepted term for "talking." While the chief rang the village bell, we walked to the Palava Arbor, a large central area where villagers would gather to settle debates and arguments. The speaker would stand on a small platform, beneath a thatched roof, and talk to those seated on rows of bamboo benches.

It was a great honor to be asked to speak in the Palava Arbor. Soon

Guidelines I Needed in My Wilderness Experience

God allows a wilderness for a season and for a reason. How we respond in the wilderness often determines what He can trust us with in the future.

I found three guidelines important during my wilderness experience in Monrovia:

- **REMEMBER God's past faithfulness**–It is dangerous to allow the difficulties of a current wilderness to block us from remembering God's past faithfulness. One of Israel's chief mistakes in the wilderness was that "they soon forgot His works" (Psalm 106:13a). Instead, remind yourself of the many times in the past when God was faithful.
- **BE GRATEFUL for God's present provisions**–God provides for His children in the wilderness: "Forty years You sustained them in the wilderness, they lacked nothing; their clothes did not wear out, and their feet did not swell" (Nehemiah 9:21). Instead of grumbling and complaining in the wilderness, we need to thank God for His many present provisions.
- **TRUST GOD with your future**–One of the difficult things about the wilderness is that we do not know exactly what the future will hold. Even then we need to understand God's purpose: "For I know the thoughts that I think toward you, says the LORD, thoughts of peace and not of evil, to give you a future and a hope" (Jeremiah 29:11).

young children, grandparents, mothers with crying babies strapped to their backs, and the men of the village were gathered there before us. They were typical villagers—animists who worshiped nature and regularly consulted itinerant witch doctors.

My interpreter and I stood on the small platform and preached salvation. When I told them that there was just one God, and that He was a God who loved them, I was saying something they had never heard before. Ever since their youth, witch doctors had taught them that the spirit world was to be feared and appeased. Their only gods were demanding and angry, bringing trouble and disease if they did not do exactly as they should.

I told them that God had sent His only Son to die for them and to forgive their sins. Never before had they heard of such love, and most wept openly. Nearly the entire village responded to my altar call.

When I taught them that Jesus also wanted to heal them, even more sick people came forward. I prayed for them, and several more were healed.

God gave us our needed breakthrough. In one day, nearly an entire village received Jesus as Lord. After we returned home, we sent back a Bible school graduate to start a church there.

Our wilderness finally came to an end. Over the next several months, we ministered in nine other villages in the same way. Sometimes Amin would go with us and share his testimony as well. Our Spirit-inspired strategy was always to ask the chief whether we could pray for any sick to be healed. When we did that, God did the rest.

Usually the first sick person we prayed for was a family member of the chief. Each one was instantly healed. Each time the chief then invited us to speak about "this Jesus" to his village. We later followed up with other visits to that village and by sending a Bible school graduate who spoke that dialect to plant a church there. Because that church-planter had the chief's favor, he would often be given a prime location to build his thatched-roofed, mud church.

THE SPIRIT'S NOT YET FINISHED

Our first three years in Liberia came to an end, and we finally realized our dream of preaching the Gospel to those who had not yet heard the name of Jesus. Maxine and I packed and got aboard a cargo ship for the ten-day trip to the harbor of New York City. After telling everyone good-bye, we stood at the railing of the ship's deck and watched the Liberian dock grow more distant with each passing minute.

As we stood there watching the sea, I thought back to the time, just a few months before, when we had taken a guide with a team of ten to a village in the interior. Part of our trek led through dense jungle. Often the dirt path was only inches wide, and we could only walk with one foot in front of another.

Once Maxine noticed a poisonous pencil snake dart across our narrow earthen path. If she had placed her foot just two inches farther along the path, she would have stepped on that snake—and she would most likely have died from its venomous bite. Since the walk was long, and Maxine soon grew weary, two men carried her on a hammock draped across their shoulders.

After we walked for seven straight hours, we reached a wide clearing but we were still a long way from our target village. The afternoon sun beat hot, unhindered by forest foliage. I walked in front, our guide now by my side, with sweat dripping down his weathered face. "Sir," I asked, "are you tired?"

The guide looked stunned, as if I'd asked a foolish question. He retorted, "How can I be tired? The day's not finished yet."

The rolling sea brought my attention back to the present. Maxine and I were weary as we stood at the ship's railing. We had made it through the wilderness, but there was still more to learn. He was not yet finished with us.

About You

The Holy Spirit is not finished with you, either. God might be teaching you more about yielding to His Holy Spirit in a Sunday School classroom, as you read His Word, as you drive to work, as you sweep your garage or kitchen, as you are on your knees in prayer or as you go about your busy course of life. Wherever and however He teaches you, learn to obey Him.

Learn first to not limit Him. He is not to be controlled, manipulated or grieved. Let go of your expectations. Allow Him to work outside your personal formulas. Relax. Let God be God.

You might already be filled with the Spirit, but need a fresh touch from God. Maybe you want the Holy Spirit to use you to minister more mightily to others. Relax. The Holy Spirit's here. Just pray, obey and get out of His way!

God might have you in a wilderness experience. Maybe at this moment life seems bleak and even your godly dreams and hopes have died or been put on a shelf. How you respond in the wilderness will help determine your future.

Instead of complaining, thank Him for His provisions. Instead of trying to manipulate your way out of the wilderness, stop. It takes going through a wilderness to get to a Promised Land.

Maybe there's an area of failure in your life. Perhaps it is time for you to once again become desperate before God, to spend time praying and fasting. Seek His face. Let Him give you a Spirit-inspired strategy.

Each one of us grows weary at one time or another. But no matter how hot the heat of your current situation, no matter how distasteful the wilderness might be, remember: your day's not finished yet. Just pray, obey and get out of His way!

Pray, Obey and Get Out of His Way: Devotional and Discussion Questions

Sharing Questions

Has God ever given you a strategy or wise idea in a difficult situation? If so, what was that wise idea, and how did it turn out? (This might concern your work, your family, or another area of your life.)

> *Remember the three guidelines to a sharing question: 1) no one is to take more than one minute in response; 2) go around the circle—if in a small group—and give each person an opportunity to respond; and 3) don't ask other questions at this point, for that stretches out the minute.*

Discussion Questions

1. Which incident in this chapter most caught your attention? Why?
2. What might be some reasons we unintentionally get in the way of the Holy Spirit?
3. Consider "Three Signs That You're in a Wilderness Experience" on page 54. Which "sign" have you seen most in your life or in the lives of those around you?
4. Review "Three Things That the Wilderness Brings" on page 55. Which of these three have you noticed most often? Would you add anything else to this list?

Application

1. Focus on your own relationship with the Holy Spirit. Reread "Five Guidelines for Yielding to the Holy Spirit" on pages 50–51. Which guideline is easiest for most people? Which guideline do many most often overlook?

What do you think God would have you do about this?

2. Pair with your spouse or with another person of the same gender. Be honest: are you (or is someone in your family) now going through a wilderness experience? Review the "Guidelines I Needed in My Wilderness Experience" on page 57. Which guideline do you (or the person in your family) need most to apply?

3. Conclude by praying for each other and for the salvation of one lost person in your area.

Maxine and I perform a skit about missions work in Africa to many in a church who have never before seen a missionary.

Insight Four

PURSUE REVIVAL

Persistent prayer and fasting position us to receive from God

I HAD TASTED REVIVAL in the jungle bush of Liberia, and I was hungry for more. Once you've tasted revival, it increases your appetite for more of God's power and presence, even after you've been in the wilderness. Once you've experienced a move of God, little else satisfies.

But even though I was hungry for revival, in 1952 Maxine and I also needed a year's furlough. Back in the States, we spent time with our parents and siblings and then itinerated in various churches. Dressed in colorful native Liberian costumes, we would perform a skit before I preached.

In the skit I played the role of a missionary sharing the Gospel, and Maxine was a Liberian woman lost in grief. Her only son died while being trained by a witch doctor. I told her of our heavenly Father who gave His only son, Jesus, in order that she might live. After she told me, "I want to hear more about this Jesus," I led her to salvation.

The response to our skit was always positive. We were the first missionaries many had ever met. God helped us not only to raise funds for our own support, but also to help others understand the importance of foreign missions.

WE WANTED A FRESH START

Then, nine months after our return to the States, we made an exciting discovery. Maxine was pregnant. We were excited that God answered our prayer for a child.

Even though we longed for revival in Liberia, we were not happy when the missions department told us we were to return to Monrovia. Revival there was a distant possibility, for the people in Monrovia seemed so closed to the Holy Spirit. Mission business had taken up much of our time in Monrovia, and we knew that same thing might happen again.

We wanted a fresh start. We knew that our denomination desperately needed missionaries in Dakar, the future capital of Senegal and a major coastal city in French-speaking West Africa. The plea for workers in Dakar touched our hearts, and we switched our missionary appointment. The missions department approved us for two years of language study in Paris, France, after which we were to go on to work in Dakar.

We were delighted with our new assignment. A pregnant Maxine and I packed our bags and headed for New York City. We thought we were destined to be God's means of bringing revival to Dakar.

TRUST THE HOLY SPIRIT

As we drove to the dock where we would board the ship to Paris, we stopped by the New York mission office to pick up some supplies. When we arrived at the office, the mission representative was on the phone. Robert McGlasson looked disappointed as he put the phone receiver down. "I know you had your hearts set on language study in Paris," he began, "but that was a call from our mission office in Springfield. They don't want you to go now. Maxine is five months pregnant with one degree of fever, and the doctors said several missionary wives in France have miscarried."

We were shocked. Weeks earlier that same mission office had given us complete medical clearance. Our packed luggage was already in the car, and the ship was soon to leave.

"What are we supposed to do now?" I asked.

McGlasson continued, "They want you to wait eight more months. That way Maxine can have a safe delivery and recuperate here in the States. The missions department will give you an apartment in

Springfield, Missouri. Since you have already raised your own support, you can visit churches and raise funds for other missionaries."

Maxine and I barely nodded our heads and thanked him, then walked to our car. As we drove back to the missionary guest home, we were silent, each pondering what had just happened. Once more the words of Titus rang in my thoughts, reminding us to "be subject to rulers and authorities."[65]

Once again we needed to trust the Holy Spirit to work out His timing. We prayed before going to bed that night, asking God to help us have thankful hearts, even in our disappointment.

People in the Bible Who Experienced Revival

There were several types of revivals in the Bible. While some revivals resulted in religious reform, many involved a renewed focus on God's Word or a show of God's power, and all impacted people to follow the Lord wholeheartedly. Some revivals reached a small circle of people, and other revivals touched an entire nation. People in the Bible who experienced revival include:

- **Asa:** 2 Chronicles 14:2-6; 15:1-5
- **Elijah:** 1 Kings 18:17-40
- **Ezra:** Ezra 10:1-17
- **Haggai and Zerubbabel:** Haggai 1:1-15
- **Hezekiah:** 2 Kings 18:1-7; 2 Chronicles 29-31
- **Joash and Jehoiada:** 2 Kings 11; 2 Chronicles 23-24
- **John the Baptist:** Matthew 3:1-6; 11:7-12
- **Jonah:** Jonah 3:4-10
- **Joshua:** Joshua 5:2-9
- **Josiah:** 2 Kings 22-23; 2 Chronicles 34-35
- **Manasseh:** 2 Chronicles 33:10-19
- **Nehemiah:** Nehemiah 9
- **Paul and Barnabas:** Acts 14:1
- **Peter:** Acts 9:32-35
- **Philip:** Acts 8:5-8
- **Samuel:** 1 Samuel 7:1-6
- **The disciples in Antioch:** Acts 11:19-21
- **The disciples in Jerusalem:** Acts 2:1-41; 4:4; 5:12-14; 6:7

A Vision of Revival

We went to Springfield, and I spoke in churches to raise funds for two other missionaries. One afternoon three months later, I was tired and took an afternoon nap in our apartment. When I woke up, I lay in bed pondering our situation.

Suddenly I had a vision. I saw a massive crowd of thousands of Africans with their hands raised in praise to God, many speaking in tongues. I had a clear sense that those Africans were Liberians in the midst of revival.

The very next day the missions department called. They needed a pastor for the only Assembly of God church in Monrovia. If we would not take the position, they were going to close the church.

I turned to Maxine and told her about my brief vision and the phone call. As we prayed, we both knew God's will: even though we had thought it impossible, He wanted to use us to bring revival to Liberia. Our disappointment over Dakar became instead God's divine appointment to Monrovia.

I called the next day and accepted the appointment as pastor of the church in Monrovia. I had learned an important lesson about revival: God is God. We cannot mandate where or when revival will come.

SHOWERS ARE NOT ENOUGH

By February of 1954, we were back in Monrovia with our new baby daughter, Karen. There were only twelve people left in the church I was to pastor, for the congregation had become a religious social club for the faithful few. We had to change if we were to grow.

To sharpen our focus, I first changed our name to "Monrovia Evangelistic Center." We held several revival meetings and saw many come to the Lord. We also had frequent baptismal services, and we organized follow-up for the new believers.

I read several articles about the "indigenous church," and I was committed to growing our church to be self-supporting and self-governing, eventually with a Liberian pastor. I taught on tithing and developed a structure of Liberian leaders within the growing membership.

I made mistakes, but God turned each one to my benefit. Once I wrote the secretary of state, who also owned Liberia's only national newspaper. I did not know how to use proper wording and government protocol in my letter, and he responded by writing that I had offended him. I then wrote a lengthy letter of apology. He wrote back, expressing surprise that anyone would write such an apology and said that he would cooperate with me in any way he could.

By June of 1955, while Liberia was in the midst of its rainy season, our church experienced its own shower of spiritual refreshing. Despite my mistakes, our members grew in faith and in ministry to others. For example, the friends of Deborah Lymas, one of our recent converts, urged her to go to a doctor about her heart trouble. With her newly found faith, she instead declared, "I want to trust God." During a church service one Sunday night, God instantly healed Deborah; she never had heart trouble again.

Victor Ford, like others in our church, received the baptism of the Holy Spirit and immediately wanted to minister to others. So Victor started visiting hospitals and jails, praying for the sick there. Josiah Johnson, the head of our youth group, heard a woman screaming one night. He ran to where he had heard the sound and found the woman. He discovered that she was demon possessed, so he laid hands on her in the name of Jesus and rebuked the demons. That very hour she was free from demonic influence.

Our home also became a refuge for many. Amin, the Lebanese trader and our close friend, started visiting us again. He often played with Karen, then a young toddler, and we would talk about the Bible and what God was doing in his life. The illegitimate son of a Spanish ambassador repeatedly shared meals with us, pouring out his heartfelt rejection. A Liberian woman, beaten by her husband, came to spend the night and pray with us. Visiting missionaries, ministers and friends stayed in our two guest rooms, calling our rented house a home of peace.

Our church met together once a month for a day of prayer for various ministries and for revival in Liberia, but somehow that never seemed enough. We experienced showers of refreshing, but we needed a deluge of spiritual rain. There was still so much darkness throughout Liberia.

Persistent Corporate Prayer and Fasting

As I considered what God would have us do, I remembered that the disciples had wanted the promised Holy Spirit. But before He baptized them with power, they first "all continued with one accord in prayer and supplication."[66] When persecution began, they again joined together in prayer, and the place where they met was shaken.[67]

Unity brought amazing results. "All who believed were together," and the Lord "*added to the church daily* those who were being saved."[68] Later, Acts records that when "those who believed were of one heart and one soul...*with great power* the apostles gave witness to the resurrection of the Lord Jesus, and great grace was upon them all."[69]

I remembered different Old Testament examples when God had honored corporate fasting by changing a country's or a city's destiny. When a multitude of enemies came against Judah, King Jehoshaphat gathered the people to pray and fast, and God divinely defeated their enemies.[70] When King Ahasuerus decreed the death of all the Jews in his kingdom, they and Esther fasted, and God delivered them and gave them victory.[71] When Jonah pronounced God's impending overthrow of Nineveh, the entire city fasted and repented, and God stopped the promised destruction.[72] Scripture shows clearly how God responds when people come together to pray and fast.

I learned that it was not enough to want revival; we had to actively pursue it. As I studied and prayed, I knew revival would not come until we first came together for a weekly time of corporate prayer and fasting. Since Saturday was the most convenient day of the week for the majority of people, we held a day of "Prayer and Fasting for Revival in Liberia" each Saturday at our church.

By now I had learned proper government protocol. I put an announcement for our Saturday time of "Prayer and Fasting for Revival in Liberia" in the secretary of state's national newspaper and invited everyone to come. I sent personal invitations to all the government officials, from the president to the lowest ranking bureaucrat, as well as to each of the pastors in Monrovia.

Each Saturday we started at six in the morning and continued until six in the evening. Our objective was clear: to pray for God to bring revival throughout Liberia. The president's own pastor joined us, as did the secretary of state and several other government officials. Different people led in prayer for matters of national concern. Others led sessions of spirited song, and we often had unison prayer. The twelve hours flowed easily, with a growing number coming for a portion or all of the day of prayer and fasting.

Several came because other dignitaries were there, but God touched them nevertheless. One government official came to salvation, and the Holy Spirit convicted him about the woman he had been living with for many years. We married them in our church; the government official dressed in a black suit and his six-months-pregnant bride in a white wedding gown. The little ring bearer and flower girl were their own children. God was already at work in response to our prayer and fasting.

Increasing Faith and Expectancy

I gave brief words of exhortation each Saturday, in order to increase faith to believe God for greater things. On two consecutive Saturdays I read reports about the salvations and healings that took place in the Philippine campaigns held by Ralph Byrd, a friend and pastor of a church in Atlanta.

Revival Defined

In our day, revival means different things to different people. To some it means full church altars, a strong sense of God's presence, or repentance and confession. To others revival means experiencing joy, long church services, rededication or exuberant praise and worship. To still others revival means a greater hunger for God and His Word, miracles, large crowds or walking in holiness.

One thing is certain. No matter what one's personal definition, revival restores Jesus' ministry to the church. His ministry includes repentance, salvation, healing, deliverance and a greater understanding of the Father. Because Jesus has sent us the Comforter, revival also means a fresh outpouring of His Holy Spirit. Some revivals focus on one or two of these elements, but the most powerful revivals have all of these components.

Although we should always operate in the Holy Spirit's ministry, we often turn to our own ideas and approaches. As soon as we realize that we are relying on our own strength and wisdom, we need to repent and let the Holy Spirit's ministry be revived—within us and through us.

The reports told how Byrd had conducted his campaigns in ten towns in the Philippines over a period of three months. Thousands of people came to salvation. Part of that report read: "God used Byrd in a mighty way in praying for the sick and in leading hundreds of believers into the baptism of the Holy Spirit…On one occasion several crippled people waiting directly in front of the platform were healed…Without anyone saying a word, some of the lame would rise and throw aside their crutches.

"Quite a number of deaf and dumb were healed instantly without a human hand being laid upon them. Several blind who had been led to the meetings walked to the platform without any assistance to testify of their healing...An old woman who was 102 years of age walked to the platform and joyfully testified that she had been healed of her blindness. Another woman, who the night before had stood on the platform to be prayed for, was completely healed of a huge goiter..."[73] Another report told that a "man, who had been deaf for forty years, was instantly healed and heard clearly."[74]

On the second Saturday I read reports, we were in our third month of weekly prayer and fasting days. As those gathered heard about the healings and miracles, I could sense an almost electric expectancy. Several months earlier, while I was in the States, I had informally asked Byrd if he would come to Liberia to hold a revival campaign. When I saw the response of that Saturday gathering, I got serious. We prayed as a

GUIDELINES FOR PRAYER AND FASTING

- **Understand the biblical basis**–Throughout Scripture, people have fasted and prayed to God, serving as examples so that we would do the same: Exodus 34:28; Judges 20:26; 1 Samuel 1:1-20; 2 Samuel 3:35; 12:16; I Kings 21:27-29; 2 Chronicles 20:3-30; Esther 4:1-3; 4:16-17; Psalm 35:13; 109:22-26; Isaiah 58:6-14; Jeremiah 14:7, 11-12; Daniel 1:11-17; 6:18-23; 10:2-21; Joel 1:13-20; 2:12-19; Jonah 3:4-10; Zechariah 7:5; 8:19; Matthew 4:2; 6:17-18; 17:19-21; Mark 1:13; 2:18-20; 9:28-29; Luke 4:2; Acts 9:9; 10:30; 13:2-3; 14:23; 1 Corinthians 7:5.
- **Use practical wisdom**–If you have a busy and demanding schedule, or if you have a limiting medical condition, you might not be able to fast entirely from food and just drink water. Rather, you might need to go on a juice fast, or a partial fast. If you have never fasted before, you might start by simply praying and fasting one meal. Be sure to schedule your time wisely.
- **Be clear about your target**–Hannah wanted a son (1 Samuel 1:1-18) and Daniel wanted to understand a revelation (Daniel 10:12). There are times when God might prompt you to fast without a specific reason, but those times are rare.
- **Join with others of like mind as much as possible**–There is power in the prayer of agreement (Matthew 18:19), and this is especially true when we fast for the same purpose.

group that God would send Byrd to Liberia.

God at Work Behind the Scenes

Mrs. Ida Parker led us in song and prayer that Saturday morning. A Spirit-filled Methodist woman and the wife of Monrovia's mayor, Mrs. Parker was a close friend of Liberia's president and his wife. By that point in the service, people packed into our 400-seat sanctuary, some even standing against the walls. Mrs. Parker was enthusiastic in song and fervent in prayer, and we had a great time that morning.

- **Plan your time of prayer and fasting**—We carefully planned our Saturdays of prayer and fasting. Years later Jashil Choi, Dr. Cho's mother-in-law, taught me one of the best personal plans I've yet seen:

1. **Decide** how many meals or days you will pray and fast.
2. **Repent** of your sins during the first portion of your fast. Allow the cleansing power of the blood of Jesus through the Holy Spirit to become a reality.
3. **Petition** God with specific requests during the second portion of your fast. Be sure to align your desires with God's will.
4. **Resolve and worship**—Resolve to do God's will during the final portion of your fast. Thank God for His answer(s). Then transfer faith into action and return to your regular schedule with new resolve and faith, continuing to worship God.

At about noon, Mrs. Parker turned aside to speak to me on the platform. "I need to go for a while, Rev. Hurston. Could someone else please lead the meeting?"

I nodded and went to the pulpit to direct a time of unison prayer. Mrs. Parker walked out hurriedly, holding a written report of Byrd's last campaign in her hand. One hour later, an almost breathless Mrs. Parker returned, walked quickly to the platform and whispered in my ear: "The president wants to see you. Please turn the prayer meeting over to someone else. You must come with me right now."

I was stunned by her invitation, but promptly turned the meeting over to someone else and went with her. Monrovia was small as capital cities go, with major buildings only a short distance apart. As we walked to the president's executive mansion, called the "Blue House," Mrs. Parker explained that she had shown the Byrd report to the president.

The president had then told Mrs. Parker that he wanted Byrd to come to Liberia to hold a revival for the inauguration. The idea of a presidential invitation surprised me; I needed to hear this for myself.

The President in His Pajamas

As we walked to see the president, I remembered what little I knew about him. Before entering public service, President Tubman had studied to be a lay Methodist preacher. Because he was a politician, I had wondered about the genuineness of his commitment to God, but I also knew that people considered Tubman a generous and God-fearing man. In Liberian tradition, his first term as president was eight years. Tubman had just been elected for a third four-year term with 90 percent of the vote. Even one of his greatest critics admitted that Tubman had done more for Liberia in ten years than had been achieved in the previous century. But all was not calm. There had recently been an assassination attempt on his life.

We walked to the back of the Blue House where a guard greeted us. After Mrs. Parker spoke to the guard, he called the president's room and took us to an elevator. I was surprised that we were going to visit the president just then; it was the custom in Liberia to take a siesta and to nap from noon until two o'clock.

As we got off the elevator, the president met us in his pajamas. "Rev. Hurston," he began, "my country needs revival. You might not know this, but my mother is a Spirit-filled, Pentecostal Christian and a great woman of prayer. We need more of God in this nation.

"My third inauguration is coming in just a few weeks. I have seen the report of this Ralph Byrd. Please invite Byrd to come to Liberia soon to hold an 'Inaugural Salvation and Healing Revival Campaign.' I will arrange for the revival to take place not only in Monrovia, but also in one or two major cities or towns around Liberia. We would have the campaign as the concluding event of my official inaugural celebration."

I could hardly believe what I was hearing! Visitors from all over Liberia and from other countries in Africa and beyond would be in Monrovia for the inauguration. It would be an incredible time to share the Gospel!

As Mrs. Parker and I walked back to the meeting, she surprised me again. "Rev. Hurston, when the president asks for something like this, it also means that he will pay for all the arrangements—including Rev. Byrd's fare, lodging, meals and expenses—with government monies."

Imagine. We had prayed and fasted, and God had worked behind the scenes. I had never thought revival would come to Monrovia, and now the president planned to pay from his inaugural fund to have a salvation and healing campaign! I was so elated I could hardly type the letter of invitation to Byrd. When he later accepted, even the president was excited. I knew the coming days would be extraordinary, but I never dreamed what a phenomenal work God would do.

About You

Please understand. God's will for you doesn't depend on your talents or your gifts. God instead looks for ordinary people who persistently cry out to Him, people through whom He can display His extraordinary presence and power.

This means that you and I need to be sensitive to His Holy Spirit. This means we should focus on having the right, Word-washed attitudes and actions, so God can easily put us in the right place at the right time.

What do you want God to do for you? Hannah wanted a son. She pursued her desire with prayer and fasting, and God gave her Samuel and five more children.[75] When Daniel wanted to understand a revelation, he fasted three weeks, and God gave him a vision of an angel who explained what was to come.[76] Jesus Himself fasted forty days in the wilderness.[77] The New Testament even gives guidelines to married people for the times they pray and fast.[78] Whatever you want God to do, first check how willing you are to pursue God; then deny yourself and focus on Him.

What bondage or obstacles do you want God to break in your life? Jesus once faced an "unbelieving generation"[79] and a boy with a demon. He responded, "This kind does not go out except by prayer and fasting."[80]

What do you want God to do in your work? In your family? In your church? In your country? Rally as many people as possible to fast and pray. When God's people pursue Him passionately, pray persistently and fast diligently for specific breakthroughs, He specializes in doing the impossible.

Maybe you also want revival. I learned that you can't just wait for revival to happen; it must be pursued. As you persist in prayer and fasting, you and all those who stand with you position yourselves for revival. Know that God is God. We cannot manipulate Him, but we can position ourselves to receive. No matter how much the cost, never forget this: nothing on earth tastes as sweet as God's presence in revival.

Pursue Revival: Devotional and Discussion Questions

Sharing Questions

What is an answer to prayer that you or your family has experienced? How did that impact you?

Remember the three guidelines to a sharing question: 1) no one is to take more than one minute in response; 2) go around the circle—if in a small group—and give each person an opportunity to respond; and 3) don't ask other questions at this point, for that stretches out the minute.

Discussion Questions

1. Have you ever wanted a fresh start in life? If so, did you do anything about that, and what happened?
2. What is your personal definition of *revival?* How does that compare with "Revival Defined" on page 69?
3. Choose one of the people who experienced revival in the list on page 65. Read the scripture(s) listed. In one or two sentences, verbally report about the revival that person experienced.
4. Have you ever joined with others in a time of corporate prayer and fasting? If so, briefly share what impact that had on you and the situation.
5. God worked "behind the scenes" through Mrs. Parker. Consider something similar God might have done in your or your family's life. What is one way God has worked "behind the scenes" for you or your family?

Application

1. Consider the "Guidelines for Prayer and Fasting" on pages 70–71. Which guideline do you think is most important for a Christian to apply? Which guideline would you like to consider using this upcoming week?
2. Pair with your spouse or with another person of the same gender. Be honest: what do you want God to do for you? Share your answers to these questions:
   - How can I better join with others at my church for prayer?
   - Do I sense that God would have me plan a time of prayer and fasting concerning my desired breakthrough? When and how?
3. Conclude by praying for each other and for the salvation of one lost person in your area.

Maxine and I with Karen before leaving for Liberia the second time.

Insight Five

The Violent Take It by Force

Follow the Spirit's flow of faith and watch Him do wonders

THERE'S SOMETHING YOU should know about me. Long before the Lord would use me to mentor Dr. Cho, he used someone to mentor me. Ralph Byrd was the most positive man I've ever known, and he taught me more than anyone else about faith in God and praying for the sick.

I first met Ralph Byrd when I was twelve years old. He had just become a traveling evangelist and had held a revival in the church my family attended. Byrd and his wife stayed in our home because our family was noted for hospitality. His focus in those days was solely on evangelism, and my father encouraged him to take the pastorate of a church in Atlanta, Georgia.

Byrd later became a pastor in Atlanta. God even used him to rescue the Bible school Maxine attended.[81] His church provided facilities for the school, and he served as president during Maxine's first year there. The following two years, Edgar Bethany (Jan Crouch's father), pastored there and served as president of the school.

Byrd purchased a larger building in a more central area of Atlanta, and a portion of the congregation moved there with him. About the time that Maxine and I married, Byrd had heard about several healing evangelists and invited them to minister to the members of his growing congregation. Those evangelists not only brought a better understanding of God's healing power to the church, they also transformed Ralph Byrd. He already loved and studied the Bible, but then he clearly saw the extent of Jesus' healing power in Scripture. At that point Byrd seized hold of a bold faith that would ultimately bring healing to thousands of people.

He believed strongly that God used our *positive words* to build faith, but the enemy used our *negative words* to bring problems. Byrd had only a fifth-grade education, but he never let that limit him. He talked and preached about Jesus' roles as Savior, Healer and Deliverer. He also preached about specific incidents in Jesus' ministry when He healed the sick and cast out demons.

Byrd explained that Jesus sometimes simply prayed for the sick to be healed. At other times—such as with the epileptic boy,[82] Peter's mother-in-law[83] and the woman bent double for eighteen years[84]—Jesus would cast out demons. So Byrd did exactly the same thing. Sometimes he sensed that he just needed to pray for the sick. At other times he would pray with authority and cast out demons of sickness.

"Unbelief," Byrd would often say, "is the greatest hindrance to healing." He talked about the time Jesus was in His own hometown and marveled at the unbelief of his fellow townspeople because He couldn't do anything but lay His hands on a few sick people and heal them.[85] God gave Byrd a gift of discerning the level of faith in a person and in a crowd. He could sense when God's Spirit was present to heal and when people were receptive. "Faith," he said, "opens one to receive."

Not only did Byrd believe in the Word, he also believed in bathing everything in prayer and fasting. To Byrd, fasting was denial of the flesh to focus on prayer and God's Word, the only way to get into the Spirit's flow of faith. He would spend hours praying before each service, both in English and in tongues. Since Jesus did only what He saw His Father doing,[86] Byrd also believed in and practiced a moment-by-moment dependence on God's Holy Spirit.

A great hindrance to one's destiny is to be passive, waiting lazily for God to force one to make every move. Byrd was certainly not passive. He instead was a God-pleasing risk-taker, one of those people who boldly obey God no matter what the cost. One scripture calls them the "violent," expressing this important truth in this way: "The kingdom of heaven suffers violence [the NIV translation says 'forcefully advances'], and the violent take it by force."[87]

The "violent" are not people of physical force. Rather they are those who have learned to persist in obedience and prayer until the kingdom, God's rule and reign, is established in the immediate situation. Though more timid souls may be content with the status quo, God-pleasing risk-takers like Byrd follow His Spirit and do great exploits for Him. These godly risk-takers do not hold back, but leave a mark on our world and in the realm of the Spirit that benefits all concerned.[88]

Byrd became one of God's "violent," and dedicated his life to the pursuit of healing the way I pursued revival. He boldly obeyed God and the promptings of His Spirit, no matter what others thought. It was Byrd's dependence on the Holy Spirit that would make Liberia's 1956 "Inaugural Salvation and Healing Campaigns" so phenomenal.

A Nation Prepared and Expectant

After several letters and radiograms, Byrd and his wife finally arrived in Liberia, accompanied by Rev. Glenn Horst, the denomination's secretary of overseas evangelism. They stepped off the plane at eleven o'clock Friday night, on December 30 of 1955.

The Liberian government literally rolled out a red carpet that stretched from the airplane to the limousine. Not only did the president's personal aide greet them, but one of the president's cabinet members also declared, "All Liberia is waiting for you, from the president down to the least of us." A senator then said that the inaugural ceremony was incidental, because the "big thing" would be the revival.

Three days later, on January 2, 1956, William V. S. Tubman was officially inaugurated into his third term as Liberia's president in Monrovia's Centennial Pavilion. Byrd, his wife, Horst, Maxine and I were seated near the front.

The senate chaplain prayed with the fervency of a fiery preacher, and

President Tubman delivered a moving inaugural address. Then, quite unexpectedly, he moved from behind the podium, knelt on the floor and prayed. Tubman's prayer was simple, asking God for guidance and grace, and asking the Holy Spirit to always dwell within him. By the end of his prayer, most were in tears.

We joyfully participated in a colorful parade to celebrate the inauguration. That evening we joined the presidential banquet and sat at a table with several prominent missionaries. Some near the front started to talk about the upcoming revival.

I was shocked when the president's staid Methodist pastor publicly declared to the banquet guests: "Prepare your hearts, for God's Spirit is about to be outpoured. The Lord has smiled on Liberia and will visit us with signs that 'shall follow them that believe,' because 'they shall lay hands on the sick, and they shall recover.'[89] This message is for today, and we shall keep these gifts and this revival after Rev. Byrd has returned to America."

Four days later, Byrd, Horst and I went to the inaugural ball. According to government protocol, we wore white clergy collars with black suits and shirts.

At first we sat at a round table not too far from the president's table. Then the president called us to join him at his personal table. As we talked, the president told us that he wanted the fullness of the Holy Spirit. I was speechless. If we had any doubt before that God was at work, there was only expectancy now. God had answered our prayer—He had prepared an entire nation for revival.

THE FIRST NIGHT OF REVIVAL

The president arranged for the revival to begin in the largest facility in the nation, one week after his inauguration. On the first night of the revival, at least 3,000 people crowded into Centennial Pavilion, with several people even hanging over the balcony. More were standing outside than were sitting inside.

After the choir sang, President Tubman introduced Byrd and Horst. The president reminded those gathered, "Healing is not new. In the Old Testament God used prophets to bring healing. Jesus ministered healing when He was on earth. God always wants to heal the sick, if He can only find men who will believe...Get into this revival and you will see something you have not seen in a century of Liberian history."

God was giving us an unprecedented opportunity for evangelism with the potential to sweep an entire nation. In the words of the president, this could well be Liberia's "revival of the century."

Dignitaries and leading pastors filled the platform. Byrd preached a short, faith-filled sermon on Jesus as both our Savior and our Healer, and ended by asking those with severe pain to raise their hands. Dozens of hands shot up, and he selected several to come to the platform for prayer.

Though Byrd didn't know it, the first man he prayed for was Senator J. L. Gibson. The senator had endured six major stomach operations, the last two in the States. The doctors finally admitted that there was nothing more they could do for him.

God instantly healed Gibson when Byrd prayed for him, and Gibson's pain lifted for the first time in fifteen years.[90] I don't know when I've ever seen a happier man. Overwhelmed, Gibson exclaimed, "I'm healed! I'm free of pain!" Tears of joy streamed down his face as he shook hands with the president and thanked him for bringing Byrd to Liberia.

Many others were healed in that first service. After one crippled man was healed, he put his cane over his shoulder and sauntered down the platform. When a crippled woman walked freely with straight steps, the undersecretary of the treasury remarked loudly, "Why, she doesn't even limp!"

Near the end of that first service, we established a pattern that carried throughout the revival meetings. We held an altar call for salvation and invited to the front those who wanted to repent of their sins and receive Jesus. Hundreds came to the Lord each night.

After the first service was over, Byrd, his wife and Horst left the pavilion to go to the lodgings the government had provided for them, and I went home. The next day a man came to our house because he had heard about the meeting and wanted to know if Jesus had come again. Even the president commented, "When I saw people healed, I felt as though I were living in the days of Christ."

The Second Night

On the second night of revival, we moved to the Army's soccer stadium, where at least 10,000 attended—an incredible number for a city of 41,000. There was space for only about 500 on the benches in the stadium risers, so most had to sit on quickly prepared bamboo benches, stand in the field, or sit on chairs and benches they brought from their homes.

As I stood on the platform and led the song service, I noticed that many raised their hands. It looked exactly like my vision years before, where I saw thousands of Africans with their hands raised in praise to God. If we obey, God keeps His promises.

Byrd then stepped to the microphone. He was a man of bold faith who knew how to encourage others' trust in God. Before Byrd started preaching that second night, he asked those healed the first night to come and share what God had done. I could hardly believe the number of people who responded. We allowed about thirty to share publicly how God had healed them.

Byrd again preached a pointed sermon on Jesus' saving and healing power. Just as he was about to ask for those who needed prayer, BoBo ran quickly to the platform. BoBo was one of the most well-known figures in Monrovia. He was in his early thirties and had been a deaf mute since birth. BoBo had worked for years as a courier, especially with government and military officials. They would write or gesture to explain where a document was to be delivered, and BoBo would faithfully take it to the right person or office.

BoBo pointed to his ears as the people around Byrd told him about the deaf mute. Byrd prayed for BoBo, and he instantly started hearing. Byrd spoke in BoBo's ear, one word at a time, "Jesus healed me! Thank you, Jesus!" BoBo correctly repeated each word.

The entire crowd erupted, and our first problem developed. The president's office had arranged for soldiers and policemen to help with crowd control. But when those soldiers and policemen saw Byrd pray for their acquaintance BoBo, and heard BoBo talk, many left their posts to better see and hear the deaf mute who had never before spoken a single word. Others left their positions because they wanted to receive prayer themselves.

Soon after that, Byrd prayed for a middle-aged blind woman who instantly started to see. Once again, the crowd erupted. Since many of the soldiers and policemen had already stopped helping with crowd control, the crush of the crowd became dangerous. We closed the meeting early that night to avoid any accidents...and even found it difficult to leave the stadium ourselves.

I was responsible to officiate and make comments at the inaugural revival meetings, and to coordinate arrangements behind the scenes. The following afternoon I called a meeting of the soldiers and policemen who oversaw crowd control. I thanked them for their involvement and reminded them how important it was that each stay in his position. I also promised that one night we would pray especially for them. We didn't have any problems with them after that.

> ### Jesus' Recorded Healings
>
> In His earthly ministry, there were times when Jesus healed large numbers of people (Matthew 12:15; 14:14; 15:30-31; 19:2; 21:14; Luke 5:17; 9:11). Scripture also records Jesus' specific healings:
>
> - **Cleansed a man of leprosy:** Matthew 8:2-4; Mark 1:40-42; Luke 5:12-13
> - **Healed the centurion's paralyzed servant:** Matthew 8:5-13; Luke 7:1-10
> - **Healed a paralytic man:** Matthew 9:2-7; Mark 2:3-12; Luke 5:18-25
> - **Healed a woman who'd had a flow of blood for twelve years:** Matthew 9:20-22; Mark 5:25-29; Luke 8:43-48
> - **Restored sight to two blind men:** Matthew 9:27-31
> - **Healed a man's withered hand:** Matthew 12:10-13; Mark 3:1-5; Luke 6:6-10
> - **Healed the nobleman's dying son at Capernaum:** John 4:46-54
> - **Healed a man sick for 38 years at the Pool of Bethesda:** John 5:1-9
> - **Restored sight to two other blind men:** Matthew 20:29-34; Mark 10:46-52; Luke 18:35-43
> - **Opened the ears of a deaf mute:** Mark 7:31-37
> - **Restored the sight of a blind man at Bethsaida:** Mark 8:22-26
> - **Healed a man of dropsy:** Luke 14:1-4
> - **Cleansed ten men of leprosy:** Luke 17:11-19
> - **Healed the cut ear of the high priest's servant:** Luke 22:50-51

So Many Healings

We held morning services each day in our church. Some mornings the building was so packed that Byrd, Horst and I could hardly get through the crowd to walk to the pulpit.

It was difficult to individually interview the large number of people to find names and facts before Byrd, Horst or I prayed for them. To simplify the process, we gave out cards for people who wanted individual prayer. On a card each wrote his name, where he was from and what his sickness was. When a person was healed and wanted to publicly testify what God had done, we read the basic facts on his card before he briefly shared. We gave out more than 4,000 of those prayer cards during that first campaign.

Healings continued throughout the nearly five weeks of revival in Monrovia. A friend brought an old preacher to an evening meeting. This elderly man was blind and paralyzed, and his memory was gone. He had spent ten years in the hospital, and nurses had nicknamed him "hospital baby." After the old preacher received prayer, he instantly moved around and talked freely. When he publicly shared about his healing with the crowd, the old preacher spoke with such eloquence that he amazed us all.

Horst and I prayed for an elderly woman with a visible cataract. The cataract disappeared as we watched, and she could see clearly again. When several blind people were healed, one shouted, "I see the lights… Now I see the people!"

Even Maxine was healed. For a year she had suffered from chronic back pain. While she was sitting on the front row, Byrd and I merely walked by and God instantly healed her.

Mrs. Parker, who had introduced Byrd's ministry to the president, was healed of diabetes. She then went to the hospital to pray for one of her friends, Miss Thomas. After Mrs. Parker prayed for her, Thomas walked for the first time in four years.

There were so many healings and so many cases of personal salvation that we stopped trying to keep an exact count. We estimate that for each person healed, at least one was born again.

DOUBTS DISAPPEAR

There were dozens of healings each night, but some had more impact than others. The second Tuesday of the meetings, three young deaf people were instantly healed. One girl with a paralyzed arm was healed while she just sat in the crowd. The following Wednesday, a paralytic was instantly and completely healed, while several deaf mutes heard noise for the first time in their lives. Several blind saw light and could count their fingers. A number of women with female disorders reported instant healing.

On Thursday we prayed for Amanda, who had been a servant of the president's wife for many years. She was hard of hearing and could barely walk. She was instantly healed. Once again Amanda could hear clearly, and told the crowd, "I want to do something before all of you that I have not been able to do for twenty-five years." Amanda then ran off the platform and through the crowd, leaving most of us laughing with delight. During mass prayer for the sick, another woman was healed of blindness; she was so happy that she shouted praises to God until she was hoarse.

JESUS' MINISTRY OF DELIVERANCE

Scripture shows how Jesus not only healed many sick persons, but also cast demons out of large numbers of people (Matthew 4:23-24; Mark 1:32-34; 3:10-11; Luke 4:40-41; 6:17-19; 8:2). In addition, Scripture records specific cases when Jesus delivered an individual person and cast a demon/s from him or her:

- **Rebuked the fever from Peter's mother-in-law:** Matthew 8:14-15; Mark 1:30-31; Luke 4:38-39
- **Cast the demons from two demon-possessed men:** Matthew 8:28-34; Mark 5:1-15; Luke 8:27-35
- **Cast a demon from a mute man:** Matthew 9:32-33
- **Cast a demon from the Canaanite woman's daughter:** Matthew 15:21-28; Mark 7:24-30
- **Cast a demon from a boy:** Matthew 17:14-18; Mark 9:17-29; Luke 9:38-43
- **Cast an unclean spirit from a man in the synagogue:** Mark 1:23-26; Luke 4:33-35
- **Loosed a woman from a spirit of infirmity that bent her double:** Luke 13:11-13

On Friday, a crippled woman was healed and started dancing on the platform. A deaf boy was instantly healed that same night. On Saturday, Chief Justice Russell was healed of rheumatism. On Sunday, we spent two hours praying for the sick. We saw even more healings of deaf mutes and of those with abdominal diseases. When we asked for those who had been healed to give their testimonies, the line never seemed to end.

The president asked Byrd to pray for all of Liberia's Supreme Court justices. God instantly healed Justice Davis of a longstanding sickness. Justice Davis sent a wire to his doctor, "You've lost a good patient. I have been perfectly healed." When Davis was next at a social function, he refused offers of liquor and cigarettes. The revival brought not just healing, but also a greater sense of God's holiness. "Not drinking or smoking,"

Davis proclaimed, "is the price God wants me to pay for my healing. And it is a small price indeed."

In the weeks that followed, the healings only seemed to intensify. The sheriff of the Supreme Court was instantly healed of painful crippling arthritis; deaf mutes heard perfectly, lame persons were healed, then leaped and jumped throughout the crowd.

A number of government officials attended revival meetings from the beginning. Some missed scarcely a single service, while others were skeptical. The undersecretary of the treasury, the Honorable Mr. Dennis, told how he and many of his friends had doubted that there were miracles in today's world. However, after they attended the meetings and saw what God was doing, their doubts disappeared.

Not only were thousands saved and many healed, but scores also received the baptism of the Holy Spirit. The first one to receive was Senator Gibson, who had been healed earlier. The president's own pastor, who oversaw a Methodist church, was filled with the Holy Spirit, as was Dr. Delaney, the chaplain of the House of Representatives. Ministers of other denominations grew hungry to receive the baptism, and many did.

At one point we decided to pray for the sick only in the morning services, and to focus the night services on the baptism of the Holy Spirit. However, the demands of the sick were just too great. As word of the healings spread, the sick came from all over Liberia, Nigeria, the Gold Coast and the surrounding French territories. Tribal chiefs from the remote interior even paid the way for some of their sick people to fly to Monrovia to be in the revival; the airlines had to add additional flights to bring the sick and the curious. We had to focus on salvation and prayer for the sick in both the morning and evening services.

There were many touching moments. One young man, born deaf, heard music for the first time as Byrd played the piano for him. He clapped his hands, swayed back and forth, and shook his head with the music's rhythm. His father then ran to the platform, embraced his son and wept as he shouted, "My boy can hear! My boy can hear!"

Favor with the Press

God gave us great favor with the secular press. One front-page newspaper article boldly proclaimed, "Miracles of Faith Healing Sweep

Monrovia," and reported how the crippled walked and chronic diseases vanished.[91] The next day another front-page article referred to "vast crowds" that came to the inaugural revival from its opening meeting, and that "so far many cures have been claimed by persons who were once blind, lame, or afflicted for years with incurable maladies."[92]

One columnist wrote: "Faith in God has won more battles than any atomic invention...Rev. Ralph Byrd repeatedly says that he has no power of his own...he is but a mere man. But here is the secret: Ralph Byrd believes in God; he has completely surrendered his life to God, and God is using him to manifest His power in a wonderful way...[only] living faith in a living God who keeps and fulfills His Word can give the kind of security humanity so much desires."[93]

That same columnist later wrote about the miraculous healings and told how some healings even occurred miles away from the seat of the meetings. She ended that column with a warning: "The Great Physician heals both body and soul. He warns us, however, to turn away from the old life of sin. He says, 'Sin no more, lest a worse evil befall you.'"[94]

There were a total of twelve articles about the inaugural revival in the secular newspaper,[95] with only one negative article. In that article, written nearly ten days after the inaugural revival began in Monrovia, the Catholic bishop in Liberia warned that all Catholics who attended the meetings would be excommunicated.

Yet even that article ended on a positive note, "The Inaugural Salvation and Healing Campaign has had a tremendous effect...many who were either lame or dumb have been given relief only by prayer and faith. The American pastor, Ralph Byrd of Atlanta, has healed a good number of persons who had little or no hope of recovery from their various disabilities. He had the largest crowd ever in Liberia's history."[96]

Not Disappointed

The president was so delighted with what God had done in Monrovia that he scheduled the "Inaugural Salvation and Healing Campaign" in six more cites. As was his custom, Byrd prayed and fasted...and then we went by plane to our next location.

Our plane first landed at the dirt airfield in Lower Buchanan, the largest city in Liberia's Grand Bassa County. God had so blessed the meetings in

Monrovia that we wondered what revival would be like in this smaller city.

We were not disappointed. During that first service nearly everyone we prayed for was healed. By the next service a government official stood beside us to keep count of all the people we prayed for, as well as those who were healed. We prayed for sixty people that night, many of whom were deaf. According to the official's records, over 90 percent of the people we prayed for were instantly healed. The next morning 600 people came for prayer, and we prayed for 1,600 sick that night.

I best remember a man dressed in rags who had traveled on foot for three days to get to the revival. The people who brought him told us that he had been deaf and mute since birth; he had never heard a sound in his life, nor had he ever spoken a word. The poor man stood before Byrd

THREE BIBLICAL ELEMENTS IN JESUS' PRAYERS FOR THE SICK

Jesus used a wide variety of ways in which He prayed for the sick. He spoke over the centurion's servant (Matthew 8:13), touched the eyes of two blind men (9:29-30) and put clay with saliva in the eyes of another blind man (John 9:6). While there are many differences in approach and method in biblical prayers for the sick, I find three common elements in many:

1. **Point of Contact**–Jesus and New Testament believers usually used some point of contact in their prayers for the sick, whether that involved the laying on of hands (Mark 16:18; Hebrews 6:2), the symbolic use of oil (James 5:14), a simple touch (Matthew 9:29) or even cloths or handkerchiefs (Acts 19:11-12).
2. **Action of Faith**–"Faith without works is dead" (James 2:26b), and Jesus often asked the sick to perform some action that expressed faith. He told the man with a withered hand to "stretch out your hand" (Matthew 12:13), He told the blind man to go wash in the pool of Siloam (John 9:7), and He told the leper to go show himself to a priest (Mark 1:44).
3. **Prayer of Command**–When demons were present, Jesus did not cast them out with a gentle word. He commanded and "rebuked the demon" out of the boy (Matthew 17:18a), rebuked the unclean spirit out of the man in the synagogue (Mark 1:25-26), and encountered the possessed man of the Gadarenes by saying, "Come out of the man, unclean spirit" (Mark 5:8). When I sense demonic oppression or bondage, I must also pray a prayer of command.

and pointed to his ears. Byrd prayed for him, and God healed him. When he heard the singing, tears welled in his eyes. He embraced Byrd and wept for joy. When God's power is present, He does not show favoritism.[97] He will heal a wealthy senator from the capital city, or a poor, ragged man from a remote interior village.

One last note: While Jesus prayed for people who were in His presence, there were times when Jesus spoke the word from a distance, and the sick were healed (Matthew 8:5-13; 15:22-28). This is also the essence of intercessory prayer—praying in faith in the name of Jesus for another's healing or breakthrough.

The power of God intensified. The morning of the fourth and last day of the Lower Buchanan meetings, the three of us prayed for the sick for nearly four hours, with only brief pauses. It made no difference who prayed, nor what the sickness was; nearly all the sick we prayed for were immediately healed. God does not show partiality in who is ministering any more than in whom He chooses to heal. He will use anyone who prays in faith for the sick to be healed.

God Had Still More

The next four nights and three days in Greenville there were fewer sick than in any other place we visited, but God was still present with power. Again we met in an open area to allow as many as possible to come, and 2,000 attended our first meeting. The day after we arrived, a deaf and dumb man was healed. Friends carried a lame woman into the service; she was instantly healed, and left to run down the city's central street shouting and praising God for her restoration. Dozens were born again at each meeting.

The next week we were in Cape Palmas and Harper City, in the southernmost coastal area in Liberia. Senator James Anderson telegrammed the president: "In both the mornings and evenings the entire parade square is packed to the fullest attendance in its history…thousands of sick flood in from the nearby French Territories, as well as a leper camp."[98]

With the large number of sick, Byrd wisely changed his strategy. When he sensed what he termed a "spirit of faith" in the crowd, he called other missionaries and local pastors to help him pray for the sick. We no

FIVE REASONS WE SHOULD PRAY FOR THE SICK

1. **Because Jesus modeled praying for the sick**—If we want to be like Jesus, we must follow His example. Jesus was "moved with compassion for them, and healed their sick" (Matthew 14:14b). We also need His perspective and compassion as we pray for the sick.
2. **Because Jesus commanded us to pray for the sick**—When Jesus sent out both the twelve and the seventy, He gave them power over the enemy (Luke 9:1, 10:19), and told them to heal the sick (Luke 9:1, 10:9). Jesus' closing words in Mark were that we should "go into all the world and preach the Gospel to every creature…lay hands on the sick, and they will recover" (Mark 16:15, 18b).
3. **Because Jesus' work on the cross provides healing**—Isaiah prophesied that Jesus "was wounded for our transgressions, He was bruised for our iniquities, the chastisement of our peace was upon Him, and *by His stripes we are healed"* (53:5 [emphasis added]). This thought is repeated at the end of 1 Peter 2:24, *"by whose stripes you were healed."*
4. **Because the early church prayed for the sick**—They prayed for the lame man at the temple gate (Acts 3:1-10, 4:22); prayed for the multitude of sick people (Acts 5:16); delivered the demonized (Acts 8:6-8); prayed for the cripple in Lystra (Acts 14:8-10); witnessed special miracles by the hand of Paul (Acts 19:11-12); prayed for Publius's father (Acts 28:8).
5. **Because the New Testament gives guidelines for praying for the sick**—"Is anyone among you sick?

longer waited for the sick to complete prayer cards and come individually to the platform to receive prayer. Byrd, Horst, I and local missionaries and pastors fanned out in the crowd and laid our hands on the sick.

By our third day, the crowd was electrified when a young deaf man was healed. We then prayed for a woman with internal problems so severe that the hospital had sent her home to die. She could not eat, she could not walk, and she was so weak she could barely speak above a whisper. After we prayed the prayer of faith, she immediately got up from her homemade cot and began to dance. Many in the crowd knew her. Her healing caused such a commotion that we had to close the service because we could no longer keep order.

Roosevelt Tubman, the president's well-known cousin, had been paralyzed and mute for fourteen years. When Byrd gave a blanket prayer of deliverance and healing over those gathered, God's Holy Spirit touched him, and Roosevelt freely walked to the platform. The formerly helpless cripple, who had not spoken a word for fourteen years, stepped to the microphone as he began to tell about his healing and said, "You all know me." The crowd went wild with joy, and he was never able to finish his testimony.

> Let him call for the elders of the church, and let them pray over him, anointing him with oil in the name of the Lord. And the prayer of faith will save the sick and the Lord will raise him up. And if he has committed sins, he will be forgiven. Confess your trespasses to one another, and pray for one another, that you may be healed. The effective, fervent prayer of a righteous man avails much" (James 5:14-16).

That week we prayed for 6,000 sick people, and we again saw God's awesome power displayed. Senator Anderson wrote a summary report on revival in Cape Palmas, declaring, "Thousands felt their pains and diseases healed and gave testimony to glorify God…At the close of the last service, nearly all the people marched with Rev. Byrd and his party through the city, joyously singing parting hymns and sacred songs…(it was) thrilling and stirring."[99]

Our next stop was New Hope Town, the leper colony in the interior. While nearly 600 lepers now lived in this village, eight tribal chiefs from other villages also came, bringing nearly all their people with them. We never understood where they found enough room to sleep at night, but they came to each meeting of the revival campaign.

From the very first night, nearly 5,000 jammed into the church and the extensive arbor built on three sides of the building. We prayed for more than 11,000 people during those four days and three nights, including all of the tribal chiefs. One had been blind, another had been lame for more than ten years, and the other six had a wide assortment of sicknesses. Each chief testified of his healing to the crowd in his own dialect. Fifty blind people and several deaf people were also healed, as were some lepers. In one service we stressed the importance of the baptism of the Holy Spirit, and more than 200 people received the baptism and spoke in tongues.

SEVEN GUIDELINES IN PRAYING FOR THE SICK

The most important guideline in praying for the sick is to quickly obey the promptings of the Holy Spirit. If I don't do that, none of these other guidelines will be effective.

1. **I first prepare myself**–Before Jesus began His ministry of power, He fasted forty days (Luke 4:2). I found that I also must prepare myself with prayer and fasting, repent of any sins, reject doubt and unbelief, and read God's Word to fill my heart and mind with Jesus' example.
2. **I stir and challenge faith in the hearts and minds of the sick**–I use three basic ways to build faith in the sick. I share:
   - **Biblical examples of healing,** such as the many times Jesus healed the sick;
   - **Biblical promises of healing,** such as 2 Chronicles 7:14; Psalm 30:2; 107:19–20; Isaiah 53:5; 57:16–19; Hebrews 13:8; James 5:14-16; 1 Peter 2:24;
   - **Testimonies of people recently healed** to remind people that Jesus still heals today.
3. **I use and lift up Jesus' name**–Believers in the New Testament church used the name of Jesus when they prayed for the sick (Acts 3:6), delivered the possessed of demons (Acts 16:18), and knew that "at the name of Jesus every knee should bow...and that every tongue should confess that Jesus Christ is Lord" (Philippians 2:10a, 11a). I pray for the sick in the mighty name of Jesus, for He is the Healer.
4. **I am sensitive to the Holy Spirit in choosing which way He wants me to pray**–Sometimes the Holy Spirit might lead me to lay hands on the sick.

The morning we left, more than a thousand people came to sing good-bye to us. I will never forget the scene of those lepers, some without hands, waving farewell as they sang in their own dialects. But God had still more for us to do. Much more.

MAN OF THE YEAR, REVIVAL OF THE CENTURY

Nearly three months earlier, when we attended the president's inaugural ball, there had been a time when others got up to dance. We instead drifted to different tables to personally invite seated officials to the first inaugural revival. While Byrd and Horst went in one direction, I noticed an empty seat at a diplomats' table. As I sat there, I introduced myself to each one. Through an interpreter, I discovered that I was inviting Russian diplomats to our upcoming revival in Monrovia, so I took the opportunity to share the Gospel as well.

One Russian diplomat I met was the stubby and bald Nikita Khrushchev, then secretary of the Communists' Central Committee. We never knew whether Khrushchev attended any of the revival meetings, but the following month in Moscow he gave a landmark speech that denounced the intolerant excesses of Stalin's former rule. *Time* magazine honored Khrushchev as "man of the year" in 1957, and by 1958 Khrushchev had become Russia's undisputed premiere.

Neither Byrd, Horst nor I would ever be made "man of the year," but God gave us an even greater honor: He was using us to bring what many later called Liberia's "revival of the century." While Khrushchev built an earthly kingdom of military might, God used us—His spiritually "violent"—to establish His rule and reign in the hearts and bodies of the broken and receptive.

At other times He might direct me to anoint the sick person with oil. There are occasions when I sense a demonic problem, and pray a prayer of command. Only He knows the key to bringing healing to that person; I must follow His leading.

5. **I persist**–Bartimaeus persisted in crying out before Jesus turned in his direction and healed him (Mark 10:46-52). If there was one occasion when our perfect Jesus had to pray twice for the same man to be healed (Mark 8:22-25), then we might also need to pray more than once for a specific sick person to be healed. God values persistent prayer (Luke 18:1-8).
6. **If needed, I give proper follow-up instructions**–Jesus told a man He'd healed to "sin no more" (John 5:14). He told the demon possessed man He'd delivered to "go home to your friends, and tell them what great things the Lord has done for you" (Mark 5:19). Sometimes the Spirit also prompts me to give a sick person who's been healed a specific post-prayer directive.
7. **Throughout all, I let love prevail**–"Now abide faith, hope, love, these three; but the greatest of these is love...a more excellent way" (1 Corinthians 13:13; 12:31b). Even if that sick person is not healed at that time, I want him to leave knowing that God and I love him.

About You

There were many healings in the inaugural revival, but I had a favorite.

A father and mother carried their lame eight-year-old girl on a stretcher to one of our services. Byrd first said to her, "If you believe that Jesus can heal you, I will pray for you."

"Yes, Pa, I believe," she responded in her Liberian slang. "Please pray God for me."

After Byrd prayed for her, the little girl immediately jumped up and started to walk. I was deeply touched when she testified, "I'm just a little girl, but God was sorry for me and made my foot straight. Now I can walk and run like other children, and can play with them. I thank God plenty. Even though I'm just a little girl, Jesus didn't pass me by."[100]

Jesus doesn't want to pass you by, either. Maybe you personally need a demonstration of God's healing power. Persist in prayer, feed your faith with His Word, be sensitive to the Spirit's promptings and find someone with strong faith who will agree with you for healing.

I don't know all the reasons why God's healing power flows so powerfully in some situations and not in others. Maybe healing is more frequent when people are convinced of the reality of a spirit realm, instead of being skeptical. Maybe God is so desirous of reaching the lost that He freely heals in an atmosphere with even a little faith in His Word.

I do know this: Jesus is not just our *Savior,* He is also our *Example.* Jesus did not just pray[101] and teach.[102] He spent much of His ministry healing the sick,[103] casting out demons[104] and doing miracles.[105] When Jesus sent out the Twelve and the Seventy, He commanded them to do the same.[106] Jesus later declared, "these signs will follow those who believe,"[107] and said that those who believed in Him would do even "greater works."[108]

Understand *who* Jesus is. Understand *what* He has called you to do. The work of God is to believe.[109]

Does this mean that it's wrong to go to medical doctors and take medicine? Absolutely not! God often uses doctors and medicines to accomplish His purposes. But it is wrong to depend on doctors and medicine instead of depending on the God who works through them.

You might have many questions. "Is it really true," you might wonder, "that praying for the sick is part of what God wants me to do?" Before you answer your own question, go back to Scripture. Let the record of Jesus' ministry and teaching wash away your worries. Then "pray the cost" as you bathe your concerns in prayer and fasting. Cry out for Him to anoint you with the Holy Spirit and with faith-filled boldness.

Years later a young Dr. Cho would ask me many questions about healing. "John," he once questioned, "do you really believe that God still heals the sick today?" Another time, after reading a book by Oral Roberts, he commented, "Some say that healing is part of God's plan to evangelize the world. What do you think?" I could understand Cho's personal struggle when he asked, "John, what if I pray for a sick person and he is not healed? What should I do then?"

My answer would be the same to you today as was my answer to him. Whether you and I work in a factory, an office, run a home business or are on a construction crew, Jesus is our example, and we are also to pray for the sick. God's healing power causes many lost persons to believe in Him. We are not to focus on those who are not healed. Instead, we are to obey and thank Him for those He does heal and deliver.

If you want to demonstrate God's power in healing, the degree of your "violent" desperation will create the level of your determination. Pray and fast like you've never prayed and fasted before. Get around people whom God is already using to pray for the sick. Ask them to teach you, to pray with you and to help you learn to be more sensitive to His Spirit.

Jesus wants to use *you* to establish His rule and reign in broken hearts and bodies, and bring healing to others. The sick are all around us—whether coworkers on the job, next-door neighbors or fellow Christians at church. Jesus' ministry shows that your heavenly Father still loves you, still cares for you and still performs wonders. Jesus is still serious about healing when we pray with faith for the sick, but only those "violent" in faith obey.

He wants you to step out of your comfort zone into His flow of faith, and watch Him do wonders through you. Jesus doesn't want to pass you by, either. He just needs to know how serious you are.

Ralph Byrd prays for a blind woman who was healed.

Ralph Byrd and I pose with our wives during a free day of the Liberian Revival

This picture was taken the second night of the revival in Monrovia when we moved to the Army's soccer field. I am the figure in the white suit standing on the platform, microphone in hand, making announcements and later leading the song portion of the meeting; the crowd extended the full length of the field.

The Violent Take It by Force: Devotional and Discussion Questions

Sharing Question

Who is one person you greatly respected while you were growing up, and why did you respect that person so much?

Remember the three guidelines to a sharing question: 1) no one is to take more than one minute in response; 2) go around the circle—if in a small group—and give each person an opportunity to respond; and 3) don't ask other questions at this point, for that stretches out the minute.

Discussion Questions

1. What is one area of life where many believers are passive? How do you think God would have them be "violent" to change that?
2. Which healing in the inaugural revival touched you the most? Why?
3. As you look over the list of "Jesus' Recorded Healings" on page 83 which of those healings stands out to you? Why? Which item on the list in "Jesus' Ministry of Deliverance" on page 85 most strikes you?
4. Of the "Three Biblical Elements in Jesus' Prayers for the Sick" on pages 88–89, which have you seen most often? Why do you think that's important?
5. What reason(s) might believers give today for not praying for the sick?

Application

1. Review "Five Reasons We Should Pray for the Sick" on

pages 90–91. What reason means the most to you? Why?

2. Consider the "Seven Guidelines in Praying for the Sick" on page 92–93. Which guideline do you think many often overlook? Which guideline do you personally think is most important to apply?
3. Ask if anyone in your group is sick or struggles with a physical problem. Follow the seven guidelines as much as possible, and pray for that person(s) to be healed.
4. Conclude by praying for each other and for the salvation of one lost person in your area.

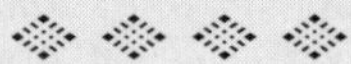

Maxine and I pose in front of a mission plane that took us into the jungle bush for ministry.

The revival meeting in Tchien, Liberia

Insight Six

The Ministry of the Plowman

Good follow-up conserves and increases the harvest

THE INAUGURAL REVIVAL continued. The government chartered a plane to fly us, our groceries and our equipment to Tchien, a remote town in the interior. As in several other places, the officials in that area declared the days of the revival to be public holidays. All businesses and shops closed so that people could go to hear the Gospel preached.

When we arrived, it seemed that the entire city of Tchien had turned out to greet us. The district commissioner said he wanted to give us a Bible welcome: "When Jerusalem welcomed Jesus, they welcomed him with palm branches." It was quite a sight. School children waved palm branches as we marched from the airstrip to the city, walking with the district commissioner, an army general and his officers, hundreds of townspeople and dozens of soldiers.

The people in Tchien opened their hearts to us and to revival. So many gathered for each service that most had to stand in the open field. Some sat on simple seats or chairs that they brought with them.

In one service, a Muslim tribal chief was healed. In another, a blind witch doctor—called a "country doctor" by some and a "shaman" by others—was healed. He had lived by selling occult medicine and occult fetishes, called *jujus,* in Liberia. Each *juju* was supposed to ward off evil spirits and bring its owner good luck. Many of the witch doctor's teeth had been filed to sharp points. He stood at the microphone and instructed the crowd, "Throw away all your *jujus* and all your devil medicine. It will do you no good. I have thrown mine away, for only Jesus, the Son of the living God, is able to save and to open the eyes of the blind. I was blind, but now I see."

Each meeting seemed more filled with God's presence and power than the service before. On the morning of our final meeting, God's power instantly healed an eight-year-old lame boy. When Byrd told him to stand up and walk, he took hold of Byrd's hand and began walking through the crowd with steady steps. Immediately the district commissioner shouted, "That boy has never walked in his life!"

Within two hours we had prayed for more than one hundred blind or vision-impaired people, and they regained their full sight. I remember one row of blind girls who instantly started seeing as they were sitting in the service. Others were led to the platform. After we prayed for each one, he would walk back to his seat without the aid of a person or a cane. Many ran home to tell their good news.

When the time came to leave, we held a farewell service in Tchien. In appreciation for the revival, the district commissioner presented each of us with a tribal chief's robe, the highest honor one could pay a guest in the interior. The Muslim tribal chief, who had been healed earlier in a revival meeting, stayed up the night before to make sure the tailor made the robes properly and on time.

During our ten days there, hundreds were wonderfully saved and healings abounded. Tchien was in lion and elephant country, but the only lion we heard roar was the Lion of the tribe of Judah.

CONTINUED FAVOR WITH THE PRESS

Byrd clearly explained to the press that he could not bring any healing unless the people themselves had faith in God.[110] One article later pointed out, "One of the reasons Byrd is so successful is his keen love for humanity. He didn't just say it, his every act showed it. I would shrink from some of those who came to him for healing, but he never found them too dirty or too offensive."[111]

The secular press continued to give us favor, with nine more articles outlining what God had done in other towns and cities.[112] One columnist wrote, "Our country has experienced a wonderful spiritual period... [that gives] strength and fervor to towns and cities."[113]

One of the final news articles on the inaugural revival reported that Byrd and his party "prayed for over 40,000 sick persons" and that "ninety percent of this number include the blind, lame, deaf and dumb who were healed." They described it as "the most successful revival in the world." That same article quoted Byrd as saying that "no [other] president has manifested such a great faith" in inviting him to come for this inaugural event.[114]

Knights Official

We held our last inaugural revival in the even more remote interior towns of Kolahun and Foya Kamara, where missionaries of a Swedish Pentecostal denomination had done a great work. There were fewer people in those towns than had been at Tchien, but their level of faith was high. I remember one day when we prayed for 200 sick people in the morning and several hundred sick that night. Not only were many born again during our meetings, but we also witnessed dozens of healings and saw scores of believers baptized with the Holy Spirit.

As we were leaving, I saw my friend Manne Paulson, a Swedish missionary, under a tree, surrounded by hundreds of tribal Liberians. He was praying for the sick and several were being healed. Horst served as the revival's historian; his last journal entry read: "We did not come to merely bring revival, but rather to leave revival. This has been our prayer and our prayer is being realized."[115] The inaugural salvation and healing campaigns came to an end, but God's healing power did not stop.

We went back to Monrovia, and the Byrds and Horst packed to return to the States. The next day the president held a special ceremony for us.[116] The president first outlined what God had done through Byrd, Horst and myself through the inaugural revival. "As a public testimony of my gratitude," the president continued, "I decorate each of you a

'Knight Official in the Liberian Humane Order of African Redemption.'"

The Liberian government was a blend of American structure and British protocol. Knighthood was the highest honor the president could give us. We were delighted, but we were even more grateful for what God had done through us during the past three months.

That evening the president gave us a reception in the Executive Pavilion and presented Byrd, Byrd's wife and Horst with parting gifts. We were sad when the Byrds and Horst left for America the next day, but the inaugural revival fires continued to grow. One pastor remarked, "This revival brought Liberia back into the times of Christ. It gave us faith to pray for the sick and believe God to heal."

Many arrived late for the inaugural revival in several places, including New Hope Town. Our missionaries there prayed for them, and God healed several. We also received reports of the revival spreading in the western county of Kolahun. In one town a new believer led more than fifty people to the Lord. Similar reports came in from the young women's Bible school in Newake, Tchien and Putuken, an interior town near some of Liberia's tallest mountain ranges. At least three local churches were started as a result of that revival.

WHAT WAS HAPPENING?

Yet, in the midst of all the wonderful things that happened, something continued to bother me. I kept wondering what churches were doing to follow up the thousands of new converts who had come to the Lord through the revival. An altar call represents a beginning, not an end. I was bothered by the thought that our Lord wants us to "make disciples,"[117] not just converts, and to bear fruit that "should remain."[118] What was happening to all the people who had made decisions for the Lord?

One night, after I talked with Maxine and played with Karen, I went to my office to think and pray. For a long time I didn't understand Jesus' parable about the four kinds of soil.[119] Why would any sower place seed on a pathway, or on stony or thorny ground? In the West we first plow, then we sow the seed; we would never knowingly place seed in such inhospitable places.

As a warm African breeze blew through an open window in my small study, I remembered learning a common Mideastern practice: two people are usually involved in planting a crop—a sower and a plowman. Even now in some Mideastern areas, the sower first sows seed and the plowman comes behind to loosen ground under the seeds. The sower does not decide where the pathway or the thorny or stony ground is; the plowman does.

Just before the revival began, the missionaries had elected me general superintendent of Liberia's Assemblies of God. I had been able to do more in the inaugural revival because of that position, but now I needed to seek God for the future.

As I prayed, I sensed God's sweet presence and direction. In the revival in Liberia we had sown the seed of the Gospel. But now we needed the ministry of the plowman; we needed to follow up on the seeds God had helped us to plant. I knew we were to return to places where revival meetings had been held, with special focus on those areas where only a few people were baptized in the Holy Spirit. We were to further teach and train local pastors and workers. We were also to hold revival meetings in places where the inaugural revival had not been able to go. The inaugural revival was officially over, but the work of this "Knight Official" had just begun.

The Ministry of the Plowman in Monrovia

I first had to care for our church in Monrovia. We grew to capacity crowds after the inaugural revival. In May we had a "first ever" event. On Pentecost Sunday there were thirteen different Pentecostal churches from various denominations in Monrovia that held a "United Pentecostal Service" at our church. In July we held a two-week revival in a church to begin the "200 Souls Campaign," with a focus on salvation, praying for the sick and helping people receive the baptism of the Holy Spirit. We didn't want to lose our evangelistic thrust.

Also, the primary chaplain of Liberia's Frontier Force, equivalent to our Army, was baptized in the Holy Spirit during the Monrovia revival. He asked our church to conduct a week of revival services in August for the soldiers.

It was the first time in forty-seven years that such a revival had been held for Liberia's military. During that week, nearly 100 soldiers and soldiers' wives were born again. The national newspaper reported that many were then baptized in water in an indoor stadium; the following week the military's Sunday morning chapel attendance reached a record high.[120] In a later issue the same reporter wrote, "The Army Chief of Staff, Major General A. R. Hooper, stated that the religious revival resulted in a great change in the soldiers' discipline...there is no doubt that the revival created new impetus in the men, both in body and in spirit."[121]

THE MINISTRY OF THE PLOWMAN IN TCHIEN AND BEYOND

In November I went back to Tchien. It again seemed like the entire town came, this time for the follow-up revival. Over the next two weeks, I taught on evangelism to more than sixty local pastors and workers from eight different tribes, showing them how to promote revival campaigns in their own churches.

Each evening in Tchien I held revival meetings in a vacant lot next to a church. I spoke on Jesus as our Savior, Healer and Baptizer, then gave an altar call and prayed for the sick. I told those who wanted to receive the baptism of the Holy Spirit to go into the church building, where missionaries and local pastors waited to minister to them. I was determined that this follow-up revival was going to be tied directly to the local church.

One night while I was praying for the sick, I noticed a man who had several teeth filed to sharp points. He looked like the blind witch doctor who had been healed, but I wasn't sure. When people outside began to be filled with the Spirit and speak in tongues, he sat near them, stared and listened. Once he came close to me as I prayed for the sick and just stood there, watching. When I gave instructions for those who wanted the baptism of the Holy Spirit to go into the church, he joined the rest filing inside.

Early the next morning Maxine and I were sleeping when two missionaries woke us. The witch doctor had come to them with a bag filled with broken *jujus* and the mortar he used to make occult medicine and told them he had a story he wanted us to hear. Since he spoke English, he didn't need an interpreter. "I have sold my medicine and *jujus* from here to the Ivory Coast," he began. "God forgave my sins and saved me in the inaugural revival. But I went back on God and sold *jujus* again.

When I heard about this follow-up revival, I came.

"Last night I again gave my heart to God. I also went into the church and received the baptism of the Holy Spirit. During the night I took all my *jujus* and the things I use to make medicine, and I broke them to pieces. This time I will not go back on God. I will preach the Gospel." I never doubted the importance of follow-up after that former witch doctor's story. Months later we heard that he was indeed preaching the Gospel.

Three Benefits of Good, Caring Follow-Up

1. **Bonding**–When a person experiences caring follow-up from leadership, he more easily bonds to that church or group; lack of caring follow-up causes a group or church to "scatter" (Matthew 9:35-38; Ezekiel 34:2-6).
2. **Two-dimensional growth**–First, caring and appropriate follow-up gently call a person into accountability and personal growth. Second, when a person receives the godly follow-up he needs, he tells others about it. A group or church with caring follow-up is a growing group or church (John 4:5-29, 39).
3. **It pleases Jesus**–You follow the example of Jesus and please the Father's heart (Matthew 14:14; 20:34; 22:36-39; Mark 8:2-3).

In Tchien, I realized we needed to stay an extra year for follow-up, even though we were scheduled to leave for furlough in the States. It was also in Tchien that God revealed to me His plan for the next year: we were to have daytime conferences to teach and train local pastors and workers, and we were to hold revival meetings at night.

I then visited the interior town of Plebo, where several of our Bible school teachers and students had attended the nearby Cape Palmas revival in late February. They caught a spark of revival, and by April God had fanned it into continuous nightly revival meetings. By the time I arrived, hundreds of people were coming from miles around to the meetings on the "Plebo Hill" grounds, and the school there was forced to build a new, larger chapel to contain them. People looked on Plebo Hill as a place to find salvation for their souls and healing for their bodies.

Before 1956 ended, we held a two-week revival in Feloke, home to one of our mission stations and the young men's Bible school, and several of

An Overview of Nine Gifts of the Holy Spirit

Several Bible passages mention the gifts of the Holy Spirit—also called giftings, offices and manifestations—including such passages as Romans 12:6-8; 1 Corinthians 12:7-10; Ephesians 4:11-12; and 1 Peter 4:10-11. During our follow-up teaching sessions, I focused on the Spirit's gifts in 1 Corinthians 12:7-10:

REVELATION GIFTS are similar to the eyes of God, helping us see from His perspective:

- **Wisdom**—This gift reveals a part of the total wisdom of God. While knowledge is information, wisdom is the right use of information for proper ends. Examples: Genesis 41:33-36 and 47:13-36; 1 Kings 3:16-28; Matthew 22:15-22.
- **Word of knowledge**—Inspired by God, this gift reveals the truth of facts which the Spirit wishes to declare. Examples: 2 Samuel 2:1-14; John 4:17-18; Acts 5:1-6.
- **Discernment of spirits**—This gift allows us to discern the human spirit (John 1:43), God's working (1 Samuel 3:8; Matthew 16:15-20) and the presence of the demonic (Matthew 12:22-24).

POWER GIFTS represent the hand of God touching us with His accomplishment:

- **Faith**—This gift involves a supernatural anointing for a specific act or pronouncement of faith. Examples: 1 Kings 18:1-40; John 11:41-42.
- **Healing**—This is correctly called "gifts of healing," and delivers the sick and destroys the works of Satan in the human body. Examples: 2 Kings 5:1-14; Matthew 8:2-4; Mark 10:46-52.
- **Working of miracles**—This gift results in a

the students helped us pray for the sick. Nearly one hundred were born again, more than ninety received the baptism of the Holy Spirit and scores were healed. It was the greatest revival that mission station had experienced in its twenty-five-year history.

One More Year

Our extra year in Liberia was strategic. There were thousands of tribal people in Monrovia who did not speak English well, so our church established prayer groups in different languages and dialects. The first Sunday of each month these groups joined together at our church for worship, communion and baptism of new converts. Dozens were born again and received the baptism of the Holy Spirit.

We prepared training courses for pastors, evangelists and workers, as well as Bible studies for pastors to use in teaching converts. We then held ten-day conferences and revivals in nine different locations, including four cities where the inaugural revival had not been. I had learned from Byrd, and I always prayed and fasted for two days before each conference and revival; I wanted to be in the Spirit's flow of faith.

Our pattern was the same in each town or city. From nine o'clock in the morning until three-thirty in the afternoon, we held a conference for local pastors, evangelists and workers. We taught about various types of evangelism and about the spiritual gifts in 1 Corinthians 12; we gave Bible studies on how to teach new converts, and we had one session on evangelistic preaching. At seven in the evening, we held revival meetings in one of the local churches.

supernatural intervention in the ordinary course of nature. Examples: Joshua 10:12-14; Matthew 8:23-27; Mark 8:1-9; Luke 7:11-15; John 2:1-11.

VOCAL GIFTS represent the mouth of God speaking to us:

- **Prophecy**—This gift is a supernatural utterance in a known language, usually given in a public setting. Examples: 1 Samuel 10:6-11 and 19:20-24; Acts 11:27-30; 21:10-14.
- **Tongues and interpretation**—These twin gifts involve the Spirit-inspired speaking of a language unknown to the speaker, then interpreted through God-given inspiration into the language of the listeners. They are used in a public setting, and they are distinct from the prayer language of tongues. Some guidelines: 1 Corinthians 14:13, 22, 27-28.

There was keen interest in the daytime conferences, especially when I explained the spiritual gifts. I was concerned, for in most places missionaries were the only people who had publicly operated in the spiritual gifts. During the conferences, I often held one special afternoon service to pray for God to give these gifts to the local pastors, workers and churches.

The church that was our host in the interior town of Vionjama had never before seen spiritual gifts expressed in public worship, so I even taught about the gifts during a revival service. After we prayed, one of the church leaders burst forth in a message in tongues, and a young man who could not talk without stuttering gave the interpretation. In flawless English he declared, "Jesus is coming soon! Jesus is coming soon!"

An African teacher at the Bible school in Plebo was delighted when

God used several students to prophesy and give messages in tongues. "I am so glad," she kept saying, "that God has granted these gifts to the Liberian church." Often when a message was given in tongues, and interpretation was granted, people exclaimed, "God is talking to us!"

When a missionary at another Bible school heard God use students to prophesy, she cried, explaining, "We have been praying for more than seven years for this to happen!" When three lepers in New Hope Town gave messages in tongues followed by interpretations, an older African worker declared, "God has brought heaven down to us. It seems like God is right here."

Our focus in the evening services continued to be on salvation, praying for the sick and leading people in the baptism of the Holy Spirit. Not only did scores repent of their sins and respond to the nightly altar calls, but many also were healed. In one city a woman was not able to eat without vomiting, and she had been told that she was going to die. God healed her during an evening service, and she ate that night. By the end of our ten-day stay, she was once again strong and back at her usual work.

In the town of Plebo, a man had gone blind one month earlier. When we prayed for him, God instantly restored his vision. The next night a husband brought his wife for prayer. She had a visible infection on her arm and hand, and she looked terrible. Her husband told me he had taken her to witch doctors, as well as to medical doctors, but no one was able to help. The day after we prayed for her, the infection dried up and she returned to normal.

Those evening meetings allowed pastors and workers in the conferences to see revival in action; we wanted to stir their hearts. At the end of each conference, we encouraged local pastors and evangelists to put into practice what they had seen and to hold revival meetings after they returned to their churches and towns.

While we had busy months, Liberia's president went on a tour of several European countries, including Italy, France, Holland and Germany. Each place gave him a warm dignitary's greeting, and that same year Liberia was elected to the vice presidency of UNESCO. After President Tubman returned home to a hero's welcome, Swiss and Israeli firms invested large amounts of money in businesses in Liberia. President

Tubman had honored God by having the inaugural revival; God was now honoring him and the country he served.

By the end of 1957, we knew that God had used our follow-up. Churches throughout Liberia had held revival meetings, and they had taught new converts basic Bible studies. Several churches reported prophesy, messages in tongues and interpretations in many worship services. Local pastors prayed for the sick, and many were instantly healed. Several government officials were now serving God and living righteous lives. God was still at work.

About You

Consider Paul. Gamaliel, the most honored rabbi in that century, trained Paul in the best Jewish education of his day. Yet Paul believed that the kingdom of God "is not in word but in power."[122] Paul wanted to demonstrate God's power instead of using human logic to persuade people to believe in Christ.[123]

Paul knew people. Most people are more convinced of God's reality from seeing one miracle than through hours of clever speech and logic. God worked unusual miracles through Paul, "so that even handkerchiefs or aprons were brought from his body to the sick, and the diseases left them and the evil spirits went out of them."[124]

But Paul wasn't just a man who demonstrated God's power through miracles; he also provided follow-up for those he had led to the Lord. The Bible says that Paul and Barnabas made many disciples in Lystra, Iconium and Antioch, and then returned to each city to encourage them.[125] Paul wrote his letters to believers in Galatia, Ephesus, Philippi, Colosse and Thessalonica in order to follow up with churches he had started or established further. With his follow-up, Paul also helped to train and encourage young ministers such as Timothy.

Consider yourself from the time of your salvation until now. Did you mature in a vacuum, without anyone to help or encourage you? If so, you'd be an exception. There were probably one or more persons along the way who prayed for and with you, who answered your questions about God and the Bible, who invested time and energy to help you be where you are now.

SEVEN WAYS
I APPLY THE MINISTRY OF THE PLOWMAN

How does one rightly follow up on a new believer? I have found seven ways:

1. **I pray**—The pull of the world can be strong on the new believer, but there is much power in prayer. I pray daily for God to strengthen, guide and guard the new believer.
2. **I resource**—The new believer might need a Bible, or a better Bible version. There are also excellent teaching books, Bible studies, classes and other resources that can help to increase his knowledge or further stimulate his faith and relationship with the Lord.
3. **I connect**—Scripture is clear: we need each other, and we are to "not forsake the assembling of ourselves together" (Hebrews 10:25a). As soon as possible, I introduce the new believer to other Christians, especially to those strong in the Lord with whom the new believer can relate. I also connect the new believer to a Bible-believing local church led by a caring pastor who provides opportunities for greater spiritual growth.
4. **I model**—Paul told the Corinthians to "imitate me" (1 Corinthians 4:16). One doesn't learn to drive a car by reading a textbook, nor does one learn the Christian walk by just reading the Bible. I learned to pray by being with a believer who knew how to pray and touch God. I better learned how to yield to the Holy Spirit by observing my wife, Maxine.
5. **I teach**—We are to "teach and admonish" one another in God's Word (Colossians 3:16). All

Maybe God has used you to lead someone to salvation. Consider what you have done since. It's not enough to be a sower; that new believer might also need the ministry of the plowman.

Maybe you have prayed for him. That's great, but we often need to put feet on our prayers. Offer to do Bible study with him and to answer his questions. Tell him about the Holy Spirit and about how much God wants to give him a prayer language. Make sure he is firmly planted in a Bible-believing, Spirit-filled church.

Maybe you oversee several leaders or workers in your church. Like Paul, wisely teach and train them on an ongoing basis. Pray for them and for their families, and care for them as people, not just as workers.

When you have visitors in your church, or people who respond to altar calls, beware of simply rejoicing in the number of responses. Instead, realize that your work has just begun. Enter the ministry of the plowman and do loving and appropriate follow-up with each individual. If you don't, neither that person nor your church will ever grow as God intended.

believers, especially new believers, need to be informed, corrected and challenged.

6. **I encourage**—We are to "edify" or encourage one another (Romans 14:19; 1 Thessalonians 5:11). The new believer can easily grow discouraged and often needs an encouraging word through a telephone call or personal visit.
7. **I hold accountable**—One management principle states that people do not do what they're told to do, but what they're held accountable for. As Jesus held His disciples accountable, I found I also need to lovingly hold the new believer accountable.

Maybe you have prayed for a sick person, but he wasn't healed. Pray again. If that still doesn't bring a breakthrough, pray and fast. Let the Holy Spirit lead and show you any obstacles; then pray again.

Years after this, in Korea, I would find that healthy home groups can help a church provide good follow-up. Whichever avenue you choose, apply the ministry of the plowman: follow through with follow-up. In a culture that idolizes the instant, God calls us to follow through and persist. In a world that values large numbers, God asks us to care for and minister to the individual.

Be like Paul. Don't rely on logic and clever words, but pray and demonstrate His power. Then follow up and follow through with those who respond. We did after Liberia's inaugural revival, and God helped us both to conserve and to increase that harvest. He'll help you to do the same.

THE MINISTRY OF THE PLOWMAN: DEVOTIONAL AND DISCUSSION QUESTIONS

Sharing Questions

Think of a time when someone expressed care to you at a point of need in your life? What did that mean to you?

Remember the three guidelines to a sharing question: 1) no one is to take more than one minute in response; 2) go around the circle—if in a small group—and give each person an opportunity to respond; and 3) don't ask other questions at this point, for that stretches out the minute.

Discussion Questions

1. Consider the impact of the inaugural revival on the country of Liberia. How do you think the year of follow-up helped?
2. Compare the two meetings in Tchien—the one during and the other after the revival. What did the story of the witch doctor teach about follow-up?
3. Why do you think the apostle Paul thought it was important to demonstrate God's power? Why then did he also think follow-up was important?
4. Consider the "Three Benefits of Good, Caring Follow-Up" on page 105. Which benefit do you think is most important? Why?
5. Review "An Overview of Nine Gifts of the Holy Spirit" on pages 106–107. Which gift have you seen used most often? Which one do you feel is most important in ministry to others? Why?

Application

1. Read "Seven Ways I Apply the Ministry of the Plowman" on pages 110–111. Which of these ways have you observed to be most important? Why? Which of these ways have you used most often, and what was the result?
2. Think of one person in your area who needs some form of follow-up. What one way do you need to apply the ministry of the plowman to that person this week? Share with your spouse, or another small group member, what you sense God is leading you to do.
3. Conclude by praying for each other and for the salvation of one lost person in your area.

Insight Seven

LET GO AND GO ON

Forgiveness clears the road to destiny

IT STARTED LIKE a typical September Sunday. I preached in the morning service at the Monrovia church, and people responded well; some were born again, others were filled with the Spirit. But that evening Maxine felt ill and stayed behind to recuperate in our bedroom on the second floor of our rented house. I returned home from my evening preaching as early as I could to see how my gentle wife was faring.

When I walked into our bedroom, Maxine sat up, but she remained quiet as if weighing her words. "John," Maxine finally spoke, her lovely brown eyes brimming with tears. "There is something I've wanted to tell you for several days now, but I couldn't. I was afraid, very afraid. But something terrible happened, and now I must tell you…"

Maxine trembled with fear and paused for a moment. Then she looked up at me. Tears flowed as she asked, "Do you remember the last time you went to New Hope Town?"

"Yes, Maxine." I had been gone for only three days. A missionary had sent me a frantic message warning that the government might take possession of our mission's leper colony. I quickly arranged to fly into the jungle bush on a small, private mission plane, leaving my precious Maxine alone with Karen. To make matters worse, as I sat on the bed and looked into Maxine's tear-filled eyes, I couldn't shake the regret and disappointment that the entire trip with its endless meetings had been unnecessary. The missionary's fears had been entirely unfounded. Later the government had even given us a citation commending our work among outcast lepers.

Maxine began to tremble again, drawing my thoughts back to the present. "John, I do not want to tell you this. It means you will lose one of your best friends."

My thoughts began to race. Which friend could she be talking about? What had happened that could cause the loss of a friend?

Maxine carefully searched my face with her tearful brown eyes. I knew she could sense my alarm and concern. "John," she said again, breaking the silence, "It's about Amin."

BETRAYED

Amin?! What had he done? Busy in the revival and in the follow-up meetings, we had not been able to spend time with Amin as before, but we still considered him part of our family. When not with us or in a hotel in Monrovia, he was with his brother at the trading store.

Maxine's voice drew me back to the present: "John, we considered Amin a man of honor whom we could trust. But while you were at the leper colony…" Maxine's lip trembled and she paused again. Finally she took a deep breath and said, "Amin raped me."

I could hardly believe what I was hearing! Was this the same Amin who was our trusted friend? The same Amin with whom we had prayed, laughed and spent countless hours talking?

"You left for the leper colony in the afternoon," Maxine continued, "and that night I brought Karen to our room to sleep with me. We were already asleep when I heard a loud knock on the bedroom door. It startled me because I knew I had locked the downstairs doors. I didn't know how anyone had gotten in so easily, or why that person would knock on my bedroom door. I was hesitant to open the door, but the knocking continued.

"I glanced at Karen; she was sleeping so soundly. Then I heard Amin's voice, 'Maxine, I just want to talk with you.' I knew that Karen would wake up if Amin continued knocking and talking, so I quickly put on my robe, opened the door and stepped into the hallway."

Maxine shook her head as if to dislodge an unpleasant memory. My stunned emotions began to come to life, and rage began to build inside me. Then Maxine looked me in the eye and said, "John, he was different from the Amin you and I know. It seemed as if a demon from hell had invaded his personality. He grabbed me by the shoulders and shoved me into the guest bedroom across the hall. Then he threw me onto the bed and ripped off the robe and blue gown you gave me.

"At that point," Maxine said, "my fear was so strong I could hardly think, much less pray. I wanted to yell and scream for help, but I knew no one would hear me. Even if someone did hear my cry for help, no one would have believed me. It would have meant the end of our ministry in Liberia."

No Word for Rape

Maxine was right. Liberians had a casual attitude about sex. There wasn't even a word for "rape" in any of the Liberian dialects. Most believed that if a man and woman were alone together, sex would naturally occur, even if they were married to other spouses. I'd lost track of the number of times I had counseled Liberian pastors about the sin of adultery. To make matters worse, our house was too far from surrounding homes for anyone to hear her cries.

Two young Liberian men from jungle villages stayed in our basement so they could attend our mission school. They received free room, board and some money in exchange for work around our house. If Maxine had been able to get from the guest room to our bedroom and scream for help, those two young men might have heard her and come to her aid.

They might have stopped Amin from going farther, but they would never have believed that he was forcing Maxine. They would have assumed that Maxine was having an affair with Amin and that she called out because she was tired of him and wanted him to go.

Such an innuendo would have compromised the integrity of our ministry. Never again could we be effective in missionary work in Liberia. The shadow of an alleged affair would have cast its pale on everything we tried to do for God.

It was all so unfair to Maxine. My gratitude for her sensitivity to our situation softened my growing rage, but part of me still found it hard to believe that Amin would do such a treacherous thing.

FRANTIC FEAR

"After Amin raped me the first time," Maxine said as she lowered her gaze, "he grew even more frantic. He grabbed me by the throat and started to choke me, saying, 'John will never sleep with you again.' I feared for my life as his fingers wrapped tighter and tighter around my throat, but somehow I sensed that the more fear he saw in me, the more abusive he would become.

"John, I started praying silently at that point. Even as Amin continued to choke me, God's peace surrounded me like a blanket. Then Amin let go of my throat. I gasped for air, grateful to God for His help."

The more Maxine talked, the more I wanted to get my own hands around Amin's throat. He had violated my wife and betrayed our trust. Amin deserved death.

"All night long," Maxine's words drew me back to her story, "Amin had his arm around me, forcing me to lie next to him on the bed in the guest room. He turned and violated me whenever he wanted. I knew he would kill me if I kept resisting, so I had no choice but to yield to him. I was thankful that at least Karen remained asleep and didn't know what was happening."

In that moment everything within me wanted to find Amin and kill him. But I knew that my main focus now must be Maxine. She breathed deeply, grateful for a moment's pause. "Early the next day Amin took all my keys and left me in the house with Karen. He told me he would burn the house to the ground if I ever tried to leave, and then he drove away in our car. I don't know where he went. At that point I did not care."

THE NIGHTMARE CONTINUES

"John, I so wanted to call you at the leper colony, but I knew there was no phone there. I thought about taking Karen, sleepy as she was, and walking to the nearest house for refuge, but it was too far away. That was when I remembered that Amin had purchased a gun. John, I was afraid of what he would do if I left, so I decided to wait it out. By late morning I began to realize that Karen's unusual drowsiness was a signal that she was deathly sick. I didn't know what was wrong, but I'd been on the African mission field long enough to know she needed immediate medical help."

I pulled my gaze away from Maxine long enough to consider my little

Karen, sleeping in the next room. I knew that she and Amin had a special relationship. She even called him "Uncle Amin," and often rode on his back while they played "horsie." I remembered how the two of them frolicked together around our downstairs living room with their laughter ringing through the house. I felt betrayal greater than I'd ever known before. A pain seared inside me like the jabs of a sharp knife. How could Amin have done this to Maxine?

Maxine again breathed deeply and then plunged back into her nightmare. "When Amin finally returned that afternoon, Karen's temperature was high, and he rushed us to the hospital. The doctor in the emergency room examined Karen and told us she had a bad case of malaria. You know how malaria is, John. You're fine one day and on the point of death the next. The doctor gave us some medications and told us to take Karen home and put her to bed. He assured us that the medicine would soon have Karen well again.

"John, I thought Amin would leave that second night, but he didn't." Maxine shook her head in stunned disbelief and went on. "After Karen went to sleep on the bed in our bedroom, Amin once more grabbed me and threw me onto the bed in the guest room; I endured another night just like the first. This happened again the third night! John, it was a nightmare that just wouldn't go away. Each day, Amin would leave with my keys after threatening to burn down our house if I tried to leave."

By this point I was struggling to keep calm. Amin deserved death, but Maxine needed assurance and comfort. I took her in my arms and held her as gently as I could, and we wept freely. Only our deep sobs and uncontrollable tears broke the pained silence.

Fear and Betrayal Deepen

Maxine swallowed hard and then continued. "The morning after that third night, I could hear the sound of the mission plane buzzing our house—the signal that you were coming home. When Amin heard the buzz of the mission plane, he started begging me, 'Please, Maxine, don't tell John what I have done.'

"At first I told him that I would tell you. But he kept begging, and I kept remembering the gun he had bought. I felt it would be safer if you did not know, so I promised Amin that if he would never touch me again, I would not tell you. Amin agreed. I know now that I was wrong not to tell you when you returned. Amin would not let me go to the airport to meet you, but went and met you himself.

"By the time he brought you home, Karen's fever had broken and she was better. You looked tired from your three-day trip, and I acted as if nothing out of the ordinary had happened while you were away." As Maxine paused, I remembered seeing bruises on her arms and legs. Since she bruised easily and was a hard worker, I had thought nothing of the bruises. Now I knew better.

"The first chance I could," Maxine continued, "I went to our family doctor and asked him if I was pregnant. He examined me and told me he couldn't be sure. At that point I broke and told him that I had been raped, careful not to mention Amin's name.

"John, do you remember how our doctor's wife left him? Well, our doctor urged me never to tell you about Amin raping me. I think he was afraid you wouldn't believe me, and our marriage would end. John, he was wrong. I should not have listened to him, but I didn't know what else to do."

A Flurry of Emotions

A flurry of conflicting emotions swirled inside me. I felt both an unbelievable sorrow for Maxine and a growing rage toward Amin. For a moment Maxine buried her tearful face in her hands. Then she looked up and continued, "So many times I have asked God to forgive me for yielding to Amin. But I felt I didn't have a choice. I thought he would kill me if I kept resisting, and I wanted to live. I wanted to continue to be your wife and mother to our daughter. But I have been so ashamed, John ...so ashamed."

I took her in my arms once more. Maxine was an upright woman who lived by godly principles. I knew she had done nothing to trigger Amin's treachery. As I listened to the pain in her voice and saw the hurt in her eyes, I could hardly comprehend such a tragic betrayal. How I wished that our embrace would take away her pain. How I grieved that I had let my busyness with mission work blind me to Maxine's plight.

Maxine rested her head on my shoulder and continued, "You know how I stayed home tonight, sick in bed, while you went to preach in the evening service? Not long after you left, Amin suddenly came into our bedroom. I didn't even hear him until he was standing by the side of the bed. He began by saying, 'Maxine, I made plans to kidnap you. Then I decided that you'd only be a slave, and I don't want a slave.'

"John, I thought that he would leave after he said that. Instead, he started unbuckling his belt. I realized that he was going to rape me again, even with our bedroom door open and me sick on our bed. I mustered all the strength I could and stood up, clutching the sheet around me. A rush of emotion came over me that I never before felt: I hated Amin with a hatred I never knew I was capable of having.

"Amin could see the hatred in my eyes. He stopped unbuckling his belt, saying, 'Maxine, if you had a gun in your hand now, you would kill me, wouldn't you?'

"I told him I would. Then he said, 'You're going to tell John what happened, aren't you?'

"When I told him I would, Amin retorted, 'Then you might as well kill me now.'

"I was grateful to God that Karen was downstairs, playing with one of the students. Slowly I walked to the door, calling loudly for Karen to be brought to the bedroom to see me.

"Amin lost no time. He ran out of the bedroom and down the stairs before Karen came. You know how easily we hear the sound of cars in our driveway? By then I could hear the laughter of his friends waiting in a car outside. He started the motor and screeched out of the driveway to a nearby road. Weak from trembling, I crawled into bed again, soon joined by our playful Karen.

"Oh, John," her voice broke, "it was awful. Just awful." Maxine began to cry uncontrollably.

I would confront Amin, but this was not the time. I embraced Maxine as closely as I could. Throughout the hours of the night we talked and shared our questions and our pain, gently holding each other when words were no longer enough.

An Unheeded Warning

As our embrace grew closer, we thought back to the past. For years we had opened the doors of our home, especially to the downtrodden. In that spirit we had also ministered to Amin, answering his questions about God, developing a close friendship of trust.

Older missionaries had warned us not to keep our home open to others. "People will hurt you," they said. "Eventually someone will do you wrong. Mark our words, John and Maxine."

We had not listened to their warning. Jesus trusted, even when He knew Judas would betray Him. How could we do anything less?

As dawn appeared in the West African sky, we wondered: had those missionaries been right? Should we have guarded ourselves and our hearts more? The friend we had once loved and trusted had betrayed us both, shattering Maxine's innocent trust for his own carnal pleasure. As we held each other in dawn's early light, the searing pain of betrayal gnawed at our souls.

We realized that Amin had drifted far from God. Worse than betraying us, he had betrayed his Lord and Savior.

CONFRONTING AMIN

By mid-morning my anger could no longer be contained, so I called the hotel where Amin stayed when he was doing business in Monrovia.

"Hello, this is Amin," he finally answered.

"Amin, this is John." There was no pleasant ring to my words. "Last night Maxine told me what you did to her." I needed to talk face-to-face with Amin, but there was no place for discussion at that hotel. Besides, I wanted to confront him on our turf. "Amin," I demanded, "come to my house so we can talk."

After a moment of uncomfortable silence, Amin responded by banging the receiver down. I wasn't sure whether he would ever come. While Maxine waited with me, my thoughts drifted.

Our personal tragedy stood in stark contrast to our greatest triumph in ministry. But on this September day, with a somber Maxine by my side, I did not feel like a knight in shining armor bringing salvation, healing and revival to an entire nation. Instead, I was a tired warrior, weary from the battle without and the battle within.

Three hours after I called, Amin finally came. A carload of four Lebanese men pulled into our driveway, and a drunken Amin stumbled out and staggered toward our house.

Amin was no fool. He was fluent in five languages and a graduate of the American University of Beirut. But now he was so drunk that he was walking on the edges of his shoes, and I had to help him up the stairs to my private study, where no prying ears would overhear our conversation.

Seeing Amin drunk like that quieted the rage within me. My desire for revenge changed to disgust. Amin sank onto the couch in my study. Maxine sat in the chair beside me as I repeated what I had said on the telephone, "Last night Maxine told me what you did to her."

Amin's eyes glazed over with drunken stupor. "Old man," he used the Liberian title of respect as his slurred words rolled out, "you told me to take care of Maxine while you were gone."

How to Stay Strong in God

Because Amin grew weak in his faith and walk with God, he returned to his worldly ways. Consider these four guidelines to staying strong in the Lord:

- **Stay connected**–I find and stay connected to godly friends who give wise counsel, for ungodly friends draw me away from the Lord. I also am connected to a good Bible-believing church, and I am consistent in my attendance at faith-building worship services (Hebrews 10:25).
- **Eat a good daily spiritual diet**–As I daily eat food for my physical body, I daily read and study God's Word for my spiritual nourishment. I also daily spend time praying and praising Him, including praying in my prayer language.
- **Be active in ministry to others**–Jesus said that His food was "to do the will of Him who sent Me" (John 4:34). For full health, I must move beyond daily spiritual devotions and apply His Word as I minister to others; it is then that "the joy of the LORD is [my] strength" (Nehemiah 8:10). This will often include faithful service in an area of ministry in a local church.
- **Guard your attitudes**–There are many attitudes we must guard, but the most important is our attitude toward God. The writer of Proverbs put it this way: "The foolishness of a man twists his way, and his heart frets against the LORD" (19:3). When I make a mistake or even when life grows difficult, I am tempted to blame God. I instead must know that "God is not a man, that He should lie…[for] every good gift and perfect gift is from above, and comes down from the Father of lights, with whom there is no variation or shadow of turning…for God is love" (Numbers 23:19; James 1:17; 1 John 4:8b).

Again anger welled up inside me. I looked him in the eye and retorted, "Amin, I never asked you such a thing. You know better than that."

Amin turned his head and rambled incoherently. For the next few minutes we could only understand a few words he spoke: "I just can't believe you haven't killed me...I used to think I was a good man, better than anyone else. But John, you're a better man than me...I just can't believe you haven't killed me..."

As I sat listening to Amin, I realized that God alone was responsible for vengeance. Amin was pathetic. There was no way to reason with our drunken betrayer. The best I could do now was to protect Maxine in the present and the future. "Amin," I insisted, "I don't want you to ever come back to our house again. Leave us alone."

Amin never apologized to Maxine. As I helped the drunken man back to his carload of waiting friends, I knew his main concern was to justify himself. His focus was on consequences, not repentance.

Struggles

When Amin left our house that day, he did not walk out of our lives. During the days that followed, Maxine and I struggled with a confusing mixture of anger and guilt. How could our trusted friend have done such a heinous thing? How could he? Then again, why hadn't we clearly seen the signs of someone turning from God? Had we failed Amin?

Though he had seen us often, he lived in a small town, far from the city and any church fellowship. Although he often read the Bible we gave him, he was surrounded by his Muslim brother and friends, drinking buddies from former days.

During the inaugural revival, his business hit hard times. Instead of growing closer to the Lord, Amin turned to the world. I encouraged him not to go to the local theater for entertainment, but to grow closer to God. Then he announced that he was smuggling diamonds, a profitable practice common among traders wanting to escape government taxes. I warned him, "Amin, you could lose your soul for just a few dollars." I had thought he would take my warning seriously, but I was wrong.

The Journey to Forgiveness

In the days that followed, Maxine and I learned more about forgiveness.

Jesus clearly taught about our need to forgive: "For if you forgive men their trespasses, your heavenly Father will also forgive you. But if you do not forgive men their trespasses, neither will your Father forgive your trespasses... Whenever you stand praying, if you have anything against anyone, forgive him, that your Father in heaven may also forgive you your trespasses."[126]

Jesus modeled a life of forgiveness. Even while He hung on the cross, deserted by His disciples, His accusers railing and mocking Him, Jesus asked His Father, "Forgive them, for they do not know what they do."[127]

Five Reasons We Must Forgive

1. **Jesus modeled forgiveness**–Even while being treated unfairly by people who did not repent, Jesus forgave (Luke 23:34).
2. **Jesus taught us to forgive**–Jesus repeatedly taught His disciples to forgive (Matthew 6:12; 18:21-35; Luke 17:3-4).
3. **Forgiveness opens the flow of God's forgiveness to us**–When we refuse to forgive others, God refuses to forgive us (Matthew 6:14-15; Mark 11:25-26; Luke 6:37).
4. **Forgiveness releases our faith**–Mark 11:25-26 connects our faith with our forgiveness. When we refuse to forgive, we block our faith. When we forgive, we release our faith.
5. **Not forgiving allows the enemy a place in our lives**–Paul forgave "lest Satan should take advantage of us; for we are not ignorant of his devices" (2 Corinthians 2:11). Unforgiveness is a sin that the enemy uses as a "device" against us.

As terrible as Amin was for such a treacherous betrayal, we knew we had to forgive him. As insensitive as we had been to Amin's downward spiral, we knew we had to forgive ourselves.

In the months that followed, Amin visited us often when we were at home. We quickly learned that forgiveness is not an emotion, but a choice—an act of our wills. We soon grew accustomed to the sound of a taxi dropping an inebriated Amin at our door, leaving the befuddled drunk to stumble into our house.

We dropped whatever we were doing to listen to Amin's intoxicated ramblings, justifying himself and blaming God for unfairness. Whenever possible, we said, "Amin, what you did was wrong, but we forgive you. Now you must repent and turn back to God."

There was no reasoning with our drunken betrayer. I ended each visit by helping the pathetic Amin to our car, and Maxine and I would then drive him to his hotel. Before he walked inside, I would exchange my watch for his more expensive timepiece—an exchange that reflected our forgiveness and desire that he return. The next morning when he woke and saw my watch, he knew that he had paid another drunken visit to the Hurstons. When he returned to our house, I would give him back his timepiece and encourage him to turn back to God.

Through the weeks we discovered that, though the path of forgiveness begins with a decision, it is also a journey in which we continue to walk in forgiving kindness. Soon we were able to help Amin out of his alcoholism, and a measure of friendship was restored among the three of us.

We often grew weary of the journey, yet no longer thought of Amin as our betrayer. God still loved Amin, a sinner desperately in need of our Savior. Yet as much as we tried, Amin's spiritual state continued to deteriorate. One of the other men involved in diamond smuggling betrayed Amin for his own selfish purposes. When we urged Amin to give his heart back to God, he would reply, "Later. I will later. First I must get revenge." Our forgiven betrayer chose not to forgive his own betrayer.

As the days progressed, we saw Amin less and less. Finally, at the end of 1957, we left Liberia for furlough in the States.

WE SOMETIMES QUESTION

We did not know it then, but the enemy was trying to use unforgiveness as a roadblock to our destiny in God. Our greatest days of ministry were still ahead. If we had refused to forgive or had not gone on in ministry, we would have allowed the enemy to steal our destiny.

We sometimes question why God allows certain things to happen. Years later, we finally told the full story to an adult Karen. She was badly shaken, asking why God would allow such tragedy when we had been so committed to Him and to His ministry. Our answer came to her through a gentle question: "Karen, your mother's still alive, isn't she?"

We are, to a great extent, the beneficiaries and victims of the actions of others. The rich man's son inherits wealth, the poor man's child his father's poverty. But God, in His infinite goodness and mercy, sets boundaries, ever listening to our cries for deliverance. Paul worded it this way: "God is faithful, who will not allow you to be tempted beyond what you are able, but with the temptation will also make the way of escape, that you may be able to bear it."[128]

You and I are not responsible for the actions and reactions of others. We are, however, responsible for our own actions and reactions. No matter how another treats you, you are to "let all bitterness, wrath, anger, clamor and evil speaking be put away from you, with all malice. And be kind to one another, tenderhearted, forgiving one another, even as God in Christ forgave you."[129]

Three Types of Forgiveness

1. **Forgive those** who have sinned against you (Matthew 6:14-15; Ephesians 4:32).
2. **Ask forgiveness** of those you have sinned against and offended (Matthew 5:23-24).
3. **Forgive yourself** for past mistakes. When you block your conscious sense of God's forgiveness, you enter into condemnation (Romans 8:1). If you repent and ask God to forgive you, He does. When—for whatever reason—you block a sense of that forgiveness, you have entered into a subtle form of idolatry by putting your standards above God's.

Even now Maxine and I sometimes talk about Amin. When one is disappointed and begins to doubt God's goodness and care, he often turns to worldly sources of fleeting satisfaction. Amin accelerated his downward spiral by watching the movies in the theater he frequently visited. Not long after, we discovered that the theater had been showing pornographic films—movies banned even in America. Their explicit content had planted the seeds of violent sex that grew to full bloom when Amin raped Maxine.

We later learned that Amin had become a government agent, hoping to use his power and influence to wreak vengeance on the man who had taken advantage of him in diamond smuggling. Later we were told that someone shot and killed Amin when he was in the middle of a "diamond war" in the jungle. We only hope that, in those few minutes before dying, Amin turned fully back to God.

About You

I've noticed another pattern. When God grants you a great victory, the enemy tries to attack you with something to bring future defeat—often something that involves offense, pain and hurt.

NINE POSSIBLE STEPS IN FORGIVING SOMEONE

Karen struggled several years trying to forgive Amin, then realized that there were often steps in the process of forgiving someone:

1. **Remember**–Ask God to remind you of areas of unforgiveness in your life (John 14:26; 16:13). When unforgiveness is dismissed and not dealt with, it can sometimes develop into a root of bitterness (Hebrews 12:15).
2. **Be honest**–Tell God openly how you feel about the person who hurt you (Psalm 62:8).
3. **Choose to forgive**–Forgiveness is not an emotion; it is a choice. Choose to forgive and even verbally tell God you forgive that person for that specific hurt (John 20:23).
4. **Intercede**–Be like Jesus and ask God to forgive the person who hurt you (Luke 23:34).
5. **Admit your sin**–Ask God to forgive you for having held the sin of unforgiveness (1 John 1:9).
6. **Release God from any blame**–Release God from any false blame for allowing that person to hurt you (Proverb 19:3), and thank God even in the middle of that hurt (1 Thessalonians 5:18).
7. **Ask God to replace**–Ask God, by His Holy Spirit, to put His fruit of love, joy and peace into your heart and mind in the place where the fruit of unforgiveness once was (Galatians 5:22-23).
8. **Renew your mind**–Not only are we to renew our minds with God's Word (Romans 12:2), but also with God's perspective. Renew your mind about that person, and choose to remember him not as "that person who did such and such to me," but rather as one God loves and for whom Jesus died.

A man once told me that the hardest thing in the world was to help people. I didn't believe him at the time, but I've since discovered that he was right. It's ironic that the more you help and minister to people, the more likely you are to face hurt, offense and betrayal.

Later there would be times in Korea when a fellow missionary could have offended me. There were even rare occasions when Dr. Cho could have hurt me by what he said or did. Talking and even preaching about forgiveness is easy—until you have to apply it.

In the midst of our follow-up revivals, the last major truth I learned in Africa prepared me to quickly let go of hurt and offense, and go on. It was probably the most important truth I learned in Africa. I know it was the most costly.

Maybe you, too, suffer the pain of betrayal. Perhaps you are also the victim of someone else's wrong actions. Maybe you face personal tragedy in the midst of public triumph. Or worse yet, even though you look fine on the outside, inside you have grown cool to the Lord. Maybe you have felt that God is somehow unfair.

> **9. Bless**—Ask God to bless the person who hurt you (Matthew 5:44), sometimes also doing an unexplained act of kindness and blessing to that person.

If you are now in any form of a downward spiral away from God, stop! Stop and consider what you are doing. Stop focusing on what God has not yet done, and instead turn your attention to what He has already accomplished.

If something has happened to discourage you, don't give up. Learn not just to let go, but also to go on. After a tragedy or disappointment, if you will respond with love and forgiveness, God can use you even more mightily than before.

If we had given up ministry after Amin's betrayal, if we had focused on the question "Why, God?" we would have abandoned God's plan and purposes for us. We would never have gone to Korea nor met Dr. Cho, and we would never have had an impact on the lives of thousands of people on two other continents.

When you and I let go and go on, we clear the road to our divine destinies. The words of the psalmist are true: "Those who sow in tears will reap with songs of joy. He who goes out weeping, carrying seed to sow, will return with songs of joy, carrying sheaves with him."[130]

LET GO AND GO ON: DEVOTIONAL AND DISCUSSION QUESTIONS

Sharing Question

Name a time when you extended forgiveness to someone. What did that mean to that person?

Remember the three guidelines to a sharing question: 1) no one is to take more than one minute in response; 2) go around the circle—if in a small group—and give each person an opportunity to respond; and 3) don't ask other questions at this point, for that stretches out the minute.

Discussion Questions

1. Amin had grown weak in his faith and in his walk with God, and was therefore open to be used by the enemy. Review "How to Stay Strong in God" on page 123. Which way have you personally found to be important? Why?
2. Jesus told an important parable on forgiveness in Matthew 18:21–35. Let each person read a different verse until your group (or you and your spouse) has read this entire passage. What one or two specific things do you notice about forgiveness in this passage?
3. Have a different person read each of these passages: Matthew 6:14–15; 2 Corinthians 2:10–11; and Ephesians 4:30–32. After you read each passage, answer this question: What can I learn about forgiveness from these verses? How can a lack of forgiveness be a roadblock to one's destiny?
4. Which of the "Three Types of Forgiveness" on page 127 do you feel most believers most often neglect to do? Why do you think that is so?

5. Of the "Five Reasons We Must Forgive" on page 125, which reason do you personally find most important? Why? Would you add any reasons to this list?

Application

1. Pair with your spouse (if you are having devotions together), or with someone of the same gender (if you are in a small group). Together review "Nine Possible Steps in Forgiving Someone" on pages 128–129. Which of these steps do you think many people overlook? Which of these steps have you found it important to do?
2. Be honest. Is there someone—past or present—that you need to forgive? Tell your partner and allow him or her to help you walk through the steps in forgiving. Allow your partner to tell you if there is someone he or she needs to forgive, and help that person walk through the steps.
3. Conclude by praying for each other and for the salvation of one lost person in your area.

Insight Eight

THE RIGHTEOUS TAKE RISKS

God-directed risks lead to Spirit-empowered results

WE SEARCHED FOR a map. Ralph Byrd had invited me to go with him to South Korea to preach on the Holy Spirit and to pray for the sick in week-long campaigns in that nation's six major cities. We didn't even know where Korea was, so Maxine, Karen and I finally located it on an encyclopedia map. The mountainous peninsula in northeastern Asia had a population of about twenty million people at that time. Although many were Buddhists, many others believed in shamanism, an animistic form of ancestor worship.

We had finally returned from Liberia. We were supposed to rest, travel to sponsoring churches to thank them for their support and raise more money. We had much to do during this furlough in the States, and we needed to stay away from overseas ministry involvement. In Liberia I already had great favor with the president and was highly regarded. I had never before ministered in Asia. Common sense and logic argued that I should guard what God had already done through me. There was no logical reason why I should go to Korea during the summer of 1958.

We had purchased an older, wooden house that used to serve as Sunday School classrooms for the Brownsville Assembly of God (a church in Maxine's hometown of Pensacola, Florida) and had made it into a duplex. Since the house was on a lot next door to the church, we worshiped at Brownsville whenever possible.

One of the times I was asked to preach at Brownsville, Karen was so stirred by the sermon, and so convicted of her sins, that she nearly ran forward when the altar call was given. Some say a five-year-old is not mature enough to become born again, but Karen was as repentant of her sins as any adult I have ever seen. Now I even wondered whether I should stay at home to nurture the new convert in our own household.

A Deeper Reason

But there was a deeper reason for staying home in the States. Ever since Maxine's rape, I longed as never before to protect her. While that was a good thing, I also found myself wanting to guard everything else that I held dear. Then I would think about Jesus' parable of the talents in Matthew 25.[131]

You remember the story. A man was about to leave for a trip, and he called three of his servants. He entrusted five talents to one servant, two talents to another and one talent to a third. A talent was a large measure of silver or gold, and some say that one talent was worth 6,000 days of labor on a farm. Even at today's minimum wage, those were not small amounts.

Both the servant with five talents and the one with two talents invested their money. When the man returned, each of them had doubled the amount entrusted to him. That pleased the master. But the third servant didn't even leave his money with bankers to earn interest, and that angered the master.

One truth in this parable stirs my soul. When the good servants invested their money, they took a risk. The servant who displeased his master was the one who had been too afraid to take any risk.

While I wanted to hold on and protect what I had, I remembered that faith in God requires taking risks—not risks that we think might be beneficial, nor risks that seem good, but risks that we know God is directing. Taking a God-directed risk is not always easy, but it is the only way that we, like the first two servants, can please Him.

As a family we prayed and decided that I should obey God and take the risk in this new ministry venture. When I left for South Korea, Maxine and Karen stayed behind in our apartment in the wooden frame duplex, praying for successful revival campaigns and for my safe return.

Desperate Postwar South Korea

When Byrd and I got off the plane in Seoul, South Korea's capital, we were shaken by what we saw. The economic situation in postwar South Korea was desperate. As crying children pulled on their skirts, war widows fanned flies off the few vegetables they were selling as sidewalk vendors. While mutilated war veterans pulled themselves around on homemade carts, healthier men struggled to transport large loads on primitive, ox-drawn wagons. War orphans roamed nearby streets as beggars and pickpockets. The mountains we passed through were filled with shantytowns, houses made of pasteboard walls covered by roofs created out of flattened beer cans—cans that had been discarded by the American military. South Korea was filled with people in need of the saving love of Jesus Christ.

Thirty-five years of occupation by the Japanese and three long years of the Korean War had left the nation in shambles. During the early 1950s, thousands of refugees from the north had fled to South Korea, putting an even greater strain on the devastated country. Bombs and mortar fire had demolished one out of three homes and, in some areas, four out of five factories. Even the trees were gone, confiscated by the Japanese for their earlier war effort, or burned as fuel in desperate times. Jobs were scarce, and every day the Korean people struggled to survive until the next meal. Poverty and disease were widespread, and an estimated half of the population had tuberculosis.

The old ways of the formerly strong Buddhist and animist Korea also lay in desolation. Most felt that Buddha had deserted them during their nation's darkest hours. Others felt that it was now useless to tend the graves of ancestors and pray for their assistance. Many were not even turning to the local shamans for help.

NINE RISK-TAKERS IN THE BIBLE

There were dozens of risk-takers in the Bible, but I have my favorites:

- **Abram** risked leaving the comfort of his own country when God instructed him; as a result he became the father of a great nation (Genesis 12:1-3) and a blessing to all believers (Galatians 3:14).
- **Joshua and Caleb** risked appearing like fools when they encouraged the Israelites to enter the Promised Land after the other ten spies had said it was impossible. Because of their stance of faith, they were the only ones of their generation to enter the Promised Land (Numbers 13:16-14:30).
- **Rahab** risked her life by hiding the two Jewish spies; because of her obedience, her entire family was spared (Joshua 2:1-21; 6:22-25), and she later became an ancestor of Jesus Christ.
- **The sinful woman** risked rejection when she wiped Jesus' feet with her tears and hair, then kissed and anointed His feet with fragrant oil. She instead received Jesus' forgiveness (Luke 7:36-50).
- **Stephen** risked death when he spoke the truth to the religious leaders. The persecution that spread after he died resulted in Christians scattering beyond Jerusalem to share God's Word (Acts 6:8-8:4).
- **Peter and John** risked punishment by the religious authorities when they continued to preach God's Word, and the church in Jerusalem grew stronger as a result (Acts 4:4-33).

The stage was set for an incredible move of God. And why not? Already the small number of Christians then in Korea were praying, crying out to God. I obeyed God by risking a new ministry venture, and God responded by putting me in the right place at the right time.

GOD BLESSES

God blessed our revival meetings. It was the first time in Korea's history that campaigns of that magnitude had been conducted in strategic areas. From the first night of the first revival meeting, attendance was surprisingly high for Korea at that time, with crowds of 3,000. Three of the six campaigns were under our large tent.

During the Sunchon campaign, the tent was so packed that people had to stand on the outskirts. Crowded inside were unbelievers, curious onlookers, Methodists, Presbyterians and other churchgoers, some of whom had never been saved. I gave the opening message, and then Byrd preached a simple Gospel message. Hundreds responded to the invitation to receive Christ, and one could sense God's precious presence.

- **Paul** risked an uncertain future when he appealed to Caesar. As a result of his imprisonment, he shared the Gospel with many (Acts 25:10–28:31) and wrote several epistles, now part of our New Testament.

Byrd then asked for people who were totally or partially deaf to raise their hands, and he picked three of those who responded to come to the platform. The first was a woman deaf in one ear. After Byrd prayed for her, and she could hear clearly out of that ear, the crowd started clapping. The next was a woman hard of hearing. When she could hear even low whispers, you could sense the faith growing in those gathered.

The third was a deaf mute. When he repeated the words Byrd spoke into his ear, the crowd erupted. By the next night there were so many sick that Byrd prayed for half of them on one side, and I prayed for the other half on the other side.

At one meeting there was an old Korean man who had been tortured by the Japanese for some minor act of disobedience. The Japanese had thrust a chopstick into each of the man's ears, bursting his eardrums. He had not been able to hear in thirty years. During that service the surprised elderly man suddenly started hearing again. The next day the old gentleman brought his entire family, including his grandchildren, to the meeting. That entire extended family became born-again Christians.

Risk Obeying God by Investing in Another Person

That was the summer when I first met Yonggi Cho. The thin, young Bible school student was in the last year of his studies. In spite of all the difficulty that he and his own country were facing, Cho had a pleasant and kind personality, and he was eager to talk about the things of God. I had worked with dozens of interpreters in Liberia, some of whom had also been Bible school students. But none had been quite like Yonggi Cho.

Byrd assigned Cho to be my Korean interpreter in four of the crusades, three of which were held in churches in strategic cities. During the morning sessions, our focus was to encourage people to be filled with the Holy Spirit; the evening services focused on salvation and healing. The pace was fairly rapid, with four daily services, but Cho and I often talked between meetings.

I discovered even more about Cho when we shared the same room in two Korean homes. He was the oldest son of seven children. His father and mother were Buddhists who had ostracized him because he had become a Christian. He had learned English, studied some law and some medicine in the midst of that war-torn situation, but he hadn't received a diploma for either course of study. Later a missionary named Lou Richards had helped him go to Bible school. Cho had become an ardent student, and he read every Christian book he could find.

I've rarely seen anyone with a hunger for God like Cho had. He and I talked and prayed together more than any other interpreter I had ever worked with. He also asked a parade of questions about the work of God.

Above all, most of the young student-preacher's questions were about divine healing. Because there were few Pentecostal and Charismatic missionaries in Korea at that time, guest lecturers at his Bible school had often been strong in their knowledge of the Word but weak in the things of the Spirit. They had explained that the age of miracles had passed with the death of the last of the twelve apostles. Divine healing and miracles, they contended, were no longer needed. Even though Cho himself had been healed of tuberculosis, he thought that his healing might have been a theologically unacceptable exception to the rule. One of his many questions was, "Do you really think that healing is part of God's plan for today?"

I quickly learned another principle: sometimes God asks us to take a risk by investing time and energy in another person. To do that, we must listen well, pray fervently and plant the best seeds of truth possible.

When Cho asked about divine healing, I responded by showing him some scriptures about healing. I reminded him of Jesus' example and then told of healings I had seen in Liberia and in Korea. "Healing," I emphasized, "is vital to God's present-day plan."

CHO'S PERSONAL BREAKTHROUGH

We held one revival campaign in a local church in Pusan, near Cho's hometown area. After one evening service, Cho came to me laughing. He told me how a local pastor in our meeting had prayed unsuccessfully for a possessed man, "Please, Mr. Devil, come out of this man."

We both went to the local pastor, and Cho interpreted as I told him that we must do what Jesus did. "Christians are not to beg demons to leave," I said. "Like Jesus, we are to command them to go."

Cho and I prayed for that same demon-possessed man, this time commanding the demon to leave. The man was instantly healed and delivered, and the pastor was joyful in what he'd learned.

Cho's personal breakthrough finally came when I prayed for a man who had been deaf in both ears for many years. Cho stood next to me, and when that man said he could now hear, Cho wanted to test him. Cho whispered Korean words in both his ears, asking him to repeat the words. When he did, an excited and marveling Cho exclaimed, "He can hear! He can hear!"

Before the six campaigns were over, Cho himself was praying for the sick.

The Plane Ride Home

On the plane ride back to America, we rejoiced at the many who had been healed, the hundreds who were saved and the many others who were filled with the Spirit. After we talked for a while, Byrd grew weary and settled back to sleep. But my mind was too full to allow my body to rest, and I began to think again about my childhood.

During the Great Depression, my family lived in a rented house on two acres of land. My father had grown up on a farm and wanted to teach me responsibility, so he allowed me to plant a few rows of peas and beans. I tended both crops, and, when it was time to harvest them, I went with Dad to get pint- and quart-sized woven baskets.

I took my red wagon and packed it with pints and quarts of peas and beans. I sold a pint for a nickel and a quart for a dime. I went door to door in my neighborhood and in surrounding areas and found that many were happy to purchase fresh, home-delivered vegetables.

I returned home as rich as a nine-year-old could be and put my nickels and dimes on a table to count them. Just then Dad came into the room. "Son," he said with a warm smile as he walked toward the table,

SIX REASONS I TITHE

1. **Tithing is biblical**–Abraham and Jacob tithed before God gave the Mosaic Law (Genesis 14:18-20; 28:20-22). God later commanded tithing (Leviticus 27:30, 34).
2. **Tithing pleases God**–I tithe as an act of faith in God's ability to provide for me and my family. The release of my faith when I tithe pleases God (Hebrews 11:6).
3. **Jesus endorsed tithing**–Jesus said that my righteousness is to exceed that of the scribes and Pharisees (Matthew 5:20; 23:23). Tithing is therefore a minimum for me.
4. **Tithing shows that I put God first**–Tithing is one way to give God my "first fruits" (Exodus 23:19a; 2 Chronicles 31:5; Proverb 3:9), a practical way to show that I make God the priority in my life.
5. **Tithing brings spiritual protection**–When I tithe, God responds by "rebuking the devourer" for my sake (Malachi 3:10-11).
6. **Tithing brings blessing**–God also responds by pouring out blessing when I tithe (Malachi 3:8-10), and tithing can even bring prosperity to a nation (2 Chronicles 31:4-8; 32:27-29).

"I want to teach you a lesson."

Dad carefully took ten dimes and stacked them on top of each other. "Son," he continued, "one of these dimes belongs to God. Which one is it?"

"The top one, sir," I responded as best I could. I reasoned that it belonged to God because the top one was closest to heaven.

Dad held one coin up and said, "That's right. I know you want to spend this dime on yourself. But God wants you to take a risk, for God has a better idea. When you give this dime, this tithe, to God through the church, you release your faith in Him. God blesses you for that release of faith."

No matter what my desires or my own thoughts, I knew my father was right. God *does have* a better idea. From that point on I faithfully tithed, and God always provided enough money for me to pay my bills and to bless others.

Once, several years back in Liberia, we were struggling greatly with finances, so I decided to review our books. I found that I had not been tithing consistently, and I made an immediate adjustment. Not long after, our finances had started flowing again.

As our plane continued hurtling through the air, I realized that God's risks and "better ideas" were not limited to tithing. Most would think that we should stay in Liberia and enjoy the president's favor, but God had a better idea.

As our plane back to America rode high above the clouds, I knew two things about the future. As wonderful as our ministry in Liberia had been, God was now calling us to be missionaries in Korea. As great as it had been to be on our own, God had destined us to work with Yonggi Cho. I only hoped that Maxine would see our change in that same light.

The Importance of Humility in Risk-Taking

Maxine and Karen were glad to see me back home. They were happy when I shared what God had done in the revivals in Korea and when I told about the wonderful young interpreter named Yonggi Cho.

Then, when I announced that God was calling us to Korea, Maxine's usual bright expression faded. "Honey," she cried, "I want to go back to Africa. Africa's my home. I want to live and die in Africa."

Taking a risk is not always easy, and sometimes opposition comes from those closest to us. God had given us great favor in Liberia, but there were several missionaries and trained pastors who could carry on the work there. Yet little had been done in Korea. I held Maxine in my arms and shared my heart: "Darling, we must obey God. The need in Korea is so great. People there are ready for revival. This Cho has the commitment it takes to build a great church. I want us all to go to Korea and start a church with him."

After a few days Maxine finally seemed somewhat open to the idea of going to Korea, so we went to the national missions headquarters in Missouri. When I told the mission board that I knew God was leading us to Korea, the board chairman was firm: "We can't let you leave Liberia. Why would you ever want to switch to Korea? You already have Liberia in the palms of your hands. Besides, most missionaries don't change fields; most remain in the same country their entire lives. Stay in Liberia."

Maxine was relieved. I knew I had to stay humble, submit to authority and pray. God's Word was clear: "Humble yourselves in the sight of the Lord, and He will lift you up."[132]

RISK BY SPENDING TIME IN PRAYER

HOW TO RESPOND WHEN PEOPLE AROUND YOU DON'T UNDERSTAND

When Joseph told his dreams of greatness, his brothers became so angry that they sold him into slavery (Genesis 37:1-28). When young David talked of killing Goliath, his oldest brother was angry, and Saul thought David was presumptuous (1 Samuel 17:22-33). I use four basic guidelines to respond in similar situations:

- **Maintain a godly attitude toward others**–In the midst of his difficulty, Joseph forgave his brothers (Genesis 50:15-21). Young David properly questioned his skeptical older brother and tried to do all that Saul asked him to do (1 Samuel 17:28-29, 38-39).
- **Keep your focus on God's faithfulness**–Throughout his dilemma, Joseph trusted God's faithfulness (Genesis 50:20). Even with the giant Goliath looming near, David focused on the fact that God had helped him earlier to kill a lion and a bear (1 Samuel 17:34-37).
- **Do what you know to do**–Joseph tried to be the best slave and prisoner he could be (Genesis 39:2-5, 20-23) and even made the right decision when he resisted Potiphar's wife (Genesis 39:6b-20). David could not wear Saul's armor and instead went to a brook to choose five smooth stones to use in his own slingshot (1 Samuel 17:38-40).
- **Expect God's supernatural favor and ability as you persist in obedience**–God gave Joseph supernatural favor and an ability to interpret dreams that later resulted in Joseph becoming a ruler in all of

I stayed near our headquarters for a few days to spend time in prayer. One day as I went for a walk, a tall, white-haired man called out to me as I rounded a corner. "Are you John Hurston? I've been looking for you. My name is Maynard Ketchum, and I'm the mission secretary for Asia.

"We need good missionaries in Korea," he continued. "I talked with the mission board after I heard about your new burden. I got them to allow you to go to Korea for two years before returning to Liberia.

"There's more, John," he added. "Global Conquest is one of our foreign missions programs. Its aim is to plant evangelistic centers in major cities around the world. Seoul, Korea, is our first target city. Several men—including Gordon Lindsay, the man who founded Christ for the Nations—have raised thousands of dollars to build a center in Seoul. We would like to put that project under you."

> Egypt (Genesis 39:3-5, 22-23; 41:1-57). God gave David the supernatural ability to sling one stone in just the right place on Goliath's forehead, bringing defeat to the Philistines (1 Samuel 17:41-54).

I smiled, nodded my head and thanked him. God had used what He did through me in Liberia to give me credibility. I couldn't help but wonder what God had planned for the future.

When I went back and told Maxine what Ketchum had said, she cried again. A few months later, the doctors discovered that Maxine had colon cancer. When I was finally able to see Maxine after her surgery, she told me, "As I lay flat on my back in the hospital, I promised God that if the surgeon got all the cancer, I would gladly go to Korea for two years. You won't have to beg me anymore to go to Korea with you."

Because of Maxine's surgery, the mission department said we needed to wait one more year before leaving for Korea. During that year, Karen went to first grade in Brownsville Elementary School, and I raised even more money for the projected church building in Seoul, for our fares to Korea and for our monthly budget. By the end of that year, we had all the finances we needed. I had risked obeying God amid opposition, and God worked on our behalf.

Risk Obeying God in Humble Beginnings

We finally arrived in Korea on a cold winter day in December of 1960. We went directly to the Assemblies of God mission compound in Seoul and met the missionaries there. We told them about our plans to join them and to live in a 32- by 8-foot silver Spartan trailer we were bringing to the compound. The missionaries showed us the spot where the trailer could rest, not far from where Cho lived.

I was anxious for Maxine to meet Cho. The next day we left Karen with some of the missionaries and walked through the snow as the chilling cold of the Korean winter winds pierced our clothes. We knocked on the door of the modest Korean home where we had been told that Cho lived. A pleasant, middle-aged woman opened the door, smiled and greeted us warmly. She called out in Korean. After a few minutes, Yonggi

Cho looked over her shoulder, asking, "John Hurston, is that you?"

It was good to see Cho again. After I introduced Maxine to Cho, he introduced the middle-aged woman to us: "This is Jashil Choi. She and I started a tent church together."

As we four sat on the floor, Korean style, Maxine shivered. Most Korean homes of that era were heated with a system of coals underneath the floor. When Jashil felt Maxine's cold hands, she immediately placed them on the heated floor and covered them with her own hands until they were warm.

We prayed together, thanking God for our safe trip, and then I learned more of their story. They had attended the same Bible school. During the winter of 1957, Cho had grown ill with a severe case of the flu. For 15 days, Jashil Choi, a former midwife, had nursed him and prayed for him. From that time on, a strong bond formed between the two.

Because of the wide difference in their ages, and the fact that Cho's Buddhist parents lived so far away, Cho called Jashil "Mom," and she called him "Son." Little did they know then that Jashil would years later become Cho's mother-in-law when he married her daughter Grace.

Cho and Jashil had often gone together with a group of students to nearby Pagoda Park, singing and preaching the Gospel in busy streets. Jashil respected Cho's intellect and dedication to the Gospel; Cho admired her unwavering persistence in prayer.

A few years earlier, Jashil and her husband had helped a man during lean times. He had later become a public official, and he gratefully gave Jashil 10,000 square feet of land next to a cemetery. The property was in a poor, outlying area of Seoul known as Taechodong, adjacent to the mission compound. After she graduated from Bible school, Jashil applied to work in a nearby orphanage, but she was rejected in favor of another worker. So Jashil built a simple cement-block house on the property and decided to start a church.

But Jashil did not want to be a senior pastor. She wanted Cho to become the pastor, and she wanted only to be his supportive coworker. She asked Cho to come and preach in the opening service in 1958, shortly before Cho served as my interpreter in the summer campaigns. Only five people heard Cho's first sermon in the living room of the small home in Taejodong: Jashil, her three children and a farmer's aging widow who had come in out of the rain. Cho's pulpit was a stack of wooden apple crates covered by a thin cloth. While Cho spoke, the tired old woman went to sleep and started snoring. Cho almost walked out.

Cho tried to quit several times over the next few months, heading to the central train station to buy a ticket home. But his faithful ministry partner, Jashil, followed after him, begging him to obey God's "better idea" no matter how hard it was. He never boarded the train.

After Cho returned from interpreting for me during the summer revival campaign, he focused on praying for the sick as never before. He and Jashil struggled to get the new church on its feet, daily throwing themselves on God in desperate prayer.

Jashil even bought a tattered military tent, set it up on that property and got ready for growth. Every morning at 4:30 they used an empty gas container as a bell to summon the growing number of believers to pray. The rest of the day they visited the homes of their poor community, ministering and praying with any who would allow them. Meanwhile, at most any hour of the day, people were praying under the tent. Many joined in teams, some with Yonggi Cho and others with Jashil, to go to homes and pray for the sick.

Cho told his growing congregation that God had healed him of tuberculosis and that God could do the same for them. Then the Holy Spirit brought a breakthrough. A paralyzed woman started to walk. A man who had suffered for seven years with palsy was healed. A local shaman renounced her witchcraft, received Jesus Christ as Lord and burned her idols. A well-known alcoholic was converted. News of all this spread in the small community, and church attendance started to climb.

They soon joined another tent to their existing one, built wooden extension sides and "papered" the wooden portions with newspapers. They installed small pot-bellied stoves down the middle to give warmth in the cold weather and put straw rice mats on the ground for flooring.

Cho and Jashil risked obeying God in humble beginnings, and He answered their persistent prayers. As we four sat and talked, more than our hands grew warm; our hearts also warmed in friendship to each other. Cho proudly told us that they now had 250 members in their tent church, and we encouraged him to continue on.

But all was not well. The missionaries had told us how disappointed

TEN RISKS GOD ASKS ME TO TAKE

The primary risk God asks each of us to take is to make our unseen Jesus the Lord of our lives, then to "walk by faith, not by sight" (2 Corinthians 5:7). In order to do this I need to:

1. **Risk my priorities** by adopting God's priority on the lost, for He is "not willing that any should perish but that all should come to repentance" (2 Peter 3:9b). This means I gladly share the Gospel in an appropriate and relevant way whenever I have the opportunity.
2. **Risk my frequent self-centered focus** by choosing to love the Lord [my] God with all [my] heart, with all [my] soul, with all [my] mind, and with all [my] strength...and to love my neighbor as [myself] (see Mark 12:30-31).
3. **Risk my control** on my life by instead obeying God's Word and His Spirit's promptings.
4. **Risk my daily time** by spending a portion of it reading, studying and/or meditating on God's Word and praying to Him.
5. **Risk my money** by tithing to the church and giving to others (Malachi 3:8-12; James 2:14-18).
6. **Risk my preferred activities** for faithful participation and service in my local Bible-believing church (Hebrews 10:25).
7. **Risk my relationships** by choosing to always put God first and "to speak the truth in love" (Ephesians 4:15).
8. **Risk doing what I want or think best** by rightly submitting to authority and trusting God in the midst of unfairness and disappointment.
9. **Risk my pride and self-sufficiency** by humbling myself in the sight of God (James 4:10;

they had been when Cho pulled out of the denomination. There had been political infighting among some of the Korean pastors, and a Korean pastor with a small congregation was illegally occupying the downtown property where I was to build a church.

When I mentioned this to Cho, he hesitated. "I didn't want to be a part of that faction," he explained. "I learned much about healing through interpreting for you in those summer revivals. My belief in divine healing is stronger than that of those men, and I did not want to get caught up in anything. So I left the denomination. We are an independent work."

We soon finished talking and walked back outside into the snow, this time to look at the adjacent, tattered tent church. Their beginnings were humble, but the touch of God's blessing was there.

It was only a short walk back to the mission compound. There was still much to be done on that winter day in 1960.

1 Peter 5:6). This may include repentance, making restitution, admitting mistakes and asking forgiveness.

10. **Risk my pain and desire for human justice** by instead choosing to forgive others and trust God.

About You

We often want security and protection, but God's way is different. God took a risk when He created man and gave him choice.[133] God took the greatest risk of all time when He "so loved the world that He gave His only begotten son."[134] God knew that if He did not take that risk, we could never be restored to Him.

Noah took a risk when he built an enormous ark as neighbors scoffed, at a time when there had never been any rain on earth.[135] Elijah took a risk on Mount Carmel when he openly challenged 450 prophets of Baal.[136] Mary took a risk when, as a virgin, she allowed God to divinely impregnate her.[137]

Noah, Elijah and Mary took risks and obeyed God in spite of opposition. Because he obeyed God, Noah saved his family when the flood destroyed everyone else on earth. Elijah clearly showed God's superiority to the Israelites. Mary gave birth to our Lord.

I know you want to fulfill God's destiny for your life. Like Noah, Elijah and Mary, you must step outside your comfort zone, take God-directed risks and humbly obey God, even when opposition comes from those closest to you. Be sure your direction is from God, and be as kind and loving in the process as possible. Know that God-directed risks lead to Spirit-empowered results. If you have understood God correctly, in time God will prove that you were right.

Proverbs words it this way: "The wicked flee when no one pursues, but the righteous are bold as a lion."[138] Some of those bold risks God wants you to take might be small, such as sharing the Gospel with someone when you're not sure how he or she will respond. Other risks might be greater, such as taking a new venture.

What are the risks you know God is asking you to take now? Those risks might be personal, or might relate to family, to work or even to your spiritual life. Don't hesitate to obey.

Like Peter, when Jesus directs, you must step out of the boat of your comfort zone, and keep your eyes on Him as the waves of circumstance swell around you.[139]

I found that risk-taking obedience is not always easy. But I knew I had to persist, for the benefits of obedience are eternal.

The Righteous Take Risks: Devotional and Discussion Questions

Sharing Question

What is one risk you have taken, and how did it turn out?

Remember the three guidelines to a sharing question: 1) no one is to take more than one minute in response; 2) go around the circle—if in a small group—and give each person an opportunity to respond; and 3) don't ask other questions at this point, for that stretches out the minute.

Discussion Questions

1. What impressed you most about Yonggi Cho in these earlier days? What were some struggles he had? What kind of risks did he take?
2. Turn to Matthew 25:14–30. Take turns reading verses until your group (or you and your spouse) has read this entire passage. What do you learn about risk-taking from this parable?
3. Consider the nine risk-takers listed on pages 136–137. Which one would you most want to be? Why?
4. You might have thought it strange that I wrote about tithing in this chapter, but tithing is one of the most important "risks" a believer can make. Review "Six Reasons I Tithe" on page 140. Which reason is most significant to you? Why?
5. Of the "Ten Risks God Asks Me to Take" on pages 146–147, which risk have you personally found most challenging? Why? Would you add any other risks to this list?

Application

1. Pair with your spouse (if you are having devotions together),

or with someone of the same gender (if you are in a small group). Be honest: share one specific risk you sense that God is asking you to take. Then ask that person to pray for you, that God would give you wisdom, boldness and all that you need to take that risk.

2. Maybe you are already taking a risk and find that people around you don't understand. Whether that is the case or not, review the four guidelines in "How to Respond when People Around You Don't Understand" on pages 142–143. Consider one way you might practically apply each of these guidelines.
3. Conclude by praying for each other and for the salvation of one lost person in your area.

Ralph Byrd and his interpreter pose with Cho and me during the 1958 Korean revival tour.

A 1960 picture of the tent church after expansion

Insight Nine

THE BARNABAS FACTOR

It takes a Barnabas to make a Paul

THE NEXT TIME I saw Cho, it was early spring. We had spent a few months in a southern coastal city, holding revival meetings and waiting for materials that had been sent into that port.

Cho was grim. The Korean army had sent him a draft notice, and he was soon to enter the military for two years. Cho talked of his concern for his growing congregation; Jashil could not carry the load by herself. By the end of our talk, Cho decided that I was to pastor the tent church with Jashil while he was in the army. I left a smiling and relieved Cho.

After we returned to Seoul with our new furnishings, Jashil gathered several of the men from the tent congregation. They poured a concrete slab for our trailer on the part of the mission compound nearest the tent church.

Maxine and I went regularly to early morning prayer meetings under the tent, and we stayed half an hour afterward to spend more time praying and talking with Jashil. During the rest of the day, we went with Jashil to visit people in their homes—sometimes to cement-block houses, but mostly to dwellings made of pasteboard. Wherever we went our message was the same: Jesus came to save, to heal, to bless and to meet needs.

ENCOURAGE THROUGH PRACTICAL ACTS OF CARE

I soon learned that one of the best ways to encourage others was through practical acts of care. When we finally got the trailer in place, I paid to have electricity extended to that lot. My payment also gave me the right to extend electricity to Jashil's nearby modest home and to the tent church.

Jashil and others in the church were praying that Cho would somehow be released early from his military duty. God gave me a clear word during an early morning prayer meeting: "Cho is going to be out of the military in seven months." When I shared that word with Jashil, she smiled, but she remained doubtful and returned to her praying.

I visited Cho in the army whenever I could. Each time my message was the same: "God will soon bring you back to us. We need you."

Once I found Cho hospitalized in the army hospital in Seoul, sleeping on a pad on the floor. On my next visit I took him a cot with a mattress. If God was going to arrange a quick release for Cho, we wanted him as comfortable as possible in the meantime.

While Cho was in the army, I knew we must go forward with God's work. We had brought a new, large tent with us from the States; we pitched it near the marketplace in our area and held a locally advertised revival meeting. Though I preached with a strong focus on the Holy Spirit, I really missed Cho. The Korean man who interpreted for me did as poor a job in translation as anyone with whom I have ever worked.

It was there I discovered that God is not limited by an interpreter. Though I had never before had such an inadequate interpreter, I never before had such a great outpouring of the Holy Spirit. During one morning meeting I felt such a strong presence of the Holy Spirit that I wondered if I were in a Korean Pentecost. As I walked among the nearly 800 gathered for prayer, I heard each person speaking in tongues. It was a touch of heaven.

After the revival meetings in the marketplace, we put the new tent on top of a nearby hill and took down the tattered tent. Within a short time, the tent congregation grew to 600.

At that time the dispute over the downtown mission property had already been in the courts for several months. After the court ruled in the mission's favor, the missionaries asked me to deal with the pastor who had illegally taken possession of that property. Since that pastor was fluent in English, I went alone to talk with him. I first showed him the papers with the court ruling. Then I told him, "If you find a place to move, we will give you enough rent money for six months." I was surprised when he quickly agreed.

While in the States, we had raised the total amount of money needed to purchase the components for a prefabricated building that would seat 1,500 people. Now I was finally able to start construction on that Global Conquest church building on our property in downtown Seoul. I knew God would do great things through this church; even in Liberia I had learned that Paul's New Testament pattern still works today. If we could establish a strong church in a primary city, God would use that church to spread its godly influence in the nation.

Seven months after Cho went into the military, he was honorably discharged for medical reasons. God honored His word, and later healed Cho. It was good to have him back; there was much work to be done.

Encourage by Showing Honor and Respect

My respect for Cho increased with each passing day. While I was visiting one of our members, he told me that he had seen Cho one cold winter morning. Cho had wrapped himself in a straw rice mat to keep warm, and he was loudly crying out to God in Korean, after which he prayed in tongues. Cho had given his all for that tent church, and I knew that God had great things in store for him. I wanted to honor him to the best of my ability.

One day, not long after Cho returned from the army, we started talking. "Cho," I began, "I want you to consider coming back into the Assemblies of God."

Cho had been disillusioned by the political infighting in the denomination, and he was hesitant to get involved again. He gently shook his head, as if to shake off a negative thought. "John," he responded, "I don't know about that."

FOUR BENEFITS IN ENCOURAGING OTHERS

1. **I receive the blessings of obedience,** for God's Word instructs us to encourage—that is, to comfort, to exhort and to edify—others: 1 Thessalonians 4:18; 5:11, 14; 2 Timothy 4:2; Hebrews 3:13; 10:25.
2. **I become more like God's Spirit,** for Jesus asked the Father to send Him as our "Paraclete," our Comforter and Encourager to help us: John 14:16, 26; 15:26; 16:7.
3. **I improve my relationships with others,** especially those I consistently and appropriately encourage. "Death and life," even the health of relationships, "are in the power of the tongue" (Proverb 18:21a; see also 12:18b; 15:4a).
4. **I find myself encouraged.** Jesus taught, "Give, and it will be given to you...for with the same measure that you use, it will be measured back to you" (Luke 6:38). It is a kingdom dynamic that the more I rightly encourage others, the more I myself am encouraged.

"Cho, there's more I need to ask," I continued. "While we have been putting up this prefabricated building in the downtown West Gate area, I have been praying. I know God wants you and Jashil to come and work with me at the new location. I also feel that God wants you to be senior pastor of the West Gate church some day. That's why I am talking to you about coming back into the denomination."

I could sense Cho's growing hesitancy, so I said, "Let me share my viewpoint. I think of a missionary as the scaffolding used to construct a building. Once the building and all the finished touches are done, they take the scaffolding down and move it on to another location. Once a church is established, the missionary is to move on. Leadership in the Korean church is to come from Koreans."

Cho agreed, but he still shook his head and said, "I cannot come with you to West Gate." Cho was genuinely concerned for his congregation in Taechodong. Less than a handful could afford the long and expensive bus ride to West Gate. It would be like starting over.

We said good-bye that afternoon. I knew of nothing else to do but to pray and to release the situation to God.

A few days later there was a knock at my trailer door. Cho stood smiling. "I've been praying, and I've changed my mind. I'm ready to go with you to West Gate. Jashil will come as well."

I was thrilled, but I soon discovered that not everyone was excited about Cho's decision. Within the denomination some felt that Cho was too young, too arrogant or too strong in his beliefs about healing. Even godly people can be wrong in their judgments. But Cho remained resolved in his decision to move to West Gate with me.

Encourage by Believing in Another's Vision and Dream

Cho soon applied for his license to preach, and he was accepted back into the denomination. During the new building's construction, Cho's vision grew. He often talked about how he sensed God's leading to build the largest church in Korea.

One day, at my prompting, we visited what was then the largest church in Korea; they held multiple worship services and had a membership of about 10,000. Cho stepped off the size of their empty sanctuary in meters, while I stepped it off in yards. Much to our surprise, our new sanctuary was even wider. That simple act excited us because we wanted to work in cooperation with the vision we knew that God had planted in Cho's heart.

Construction on the new building continued, and we rented the vacant lot next to the construction site. We took down the tent in Taechodong and moved it to the vacant lot to start a series of revival meetings. The few who could come from Taechodong made the move with us. The others stayed with John Stetz, a missionary who built and pastored a church for them on the mission compound.

We had three weeks of daily morning and evening revival meetings under the tent on that vacant lot. During the morning meetings, Cho or I would speak. During the evening meetings, Sam Todd, an invited American evangelist, spoke while Cho interpreted.

Even on the first day of the revival meetings, we had nearly a thousand people crowded under that tent. Each day there were dozens of conversions and healings, and many people were filled with the Holy Spirit. Before we officially dedicated the church, Jashil and eighteen women visited a thousand surrounding homes, inviting people to attend the upcoming dedication meetings.

On October 15 of 1961, we held the afternoon dedication service in the newly built 1,500-seat auditorium. Three thousand streamed from all directions toward the busy West Gate downtown intersection, packed the building and overflowed into the adjacent tent that we had used for the earlier revival. Speakers included Dr. M. S. Kim, who represented the office of the minister of education; Dr. Yoon Ce Yung, vice-speaker of Korea's National Congress; and Chung Dall Bin, retiring chairman of the joint chiefs of chaplains of the ROK (Republic of Korea) Armed Forces.[140] Each seemed to share our dream that the West Gate church should be a place where people could see the power of God in action.

The crowd grew even larger by the time of our night service. One woman, unable to walk, crawled on hands and knees from the street into the new auditorium. She lay in the aisle and listened to the message. As Cho and I preached the Word, she felt her paralyzed muscles come to life. At the close of the healing prayer she

SEVEN SOURCES OF ENCOURAGEMENT IN DAVID'S LIFE

David was frequently discouraged; a few examples are in Psalm 10:1-12; 12:1-2; 13:1-4; 22:1-2, 12-18; 31:10-13; 35:19-26; 38:21-22. As I studied David's life, I found that he had seven sources of encouragement–ones that I often need as well:

1. **God's Word and works**–David often turned to God's Word for encouragement and hope, and I need to do the same (Psalm 119:25, 28, 41-42, 49-50, 92-93, 146-147). David also allowed God's works in creation to build his faith (Psalm 19:1-11; 97:1-6).
2. **Prayer**–David cried out to the Lord, praying for His divine encouragement and help (Psalm 5:2; 32:6-7; 119:76). One of the most important things I do when discouraged is to pray.
3. **Praise and song**–David often chose to praise and sing to God, even when he felt discouraged (Psalm 7:1-2, 17; 61:1-2, 8; 138:1, 3; 147:2-3, 7). Paul and Silas chose to do the same in prison, and God delivered them (Acts 16:25-26).
4. **Friends**–The friend who most encouraged David was Jonathan; perhaps this is who Solomon had in mind when he later described "a friend who sticks closer than a brother" (Proverbs 18:24b). Read more about David and Jonathan in 1 Samuel 18:1-4; 19:1-7; 20:1-42. I also need godly friends who speak encouraging words to me.
5. **Family**–While David had family members like Absalom who caused him great problems, he did have a godly wife in Abigail (1 Samuel 25:2-42).
6. **People with whom he worked**–After Absalom's death, David mourned deeply. Ahab, commander

jumped to her feet, walked freely, waved her arms and rejoiced ecstatically. Nearly 200 were born again that night, and more than 100 reported being healed. God's healing power flowed there from the very start.

of David's army, encouraged David to see beyond his pain and to his people. As a result David returned to rule Israel (2 Samuel 18:33-19:8). God has often placed coworkers and employees in my life to rightly encourage me.

7. **Himself**—When the Amalekites burned and looted Ziklag, David's own men were about to stone him. In the midst of that difficulty "David strengthened [or encouraged] himself in the LORD his God" (1 Samuel 30:6b). There have been times when there is no one to encourage me; it is then that I honestly repent of any sins and wrongdoing on my part, remind myself of God's past faithfulness and of the promises in His Word, and thus encourage myself.

Encourage by Giving Priority to Another's Ideas and God-Given Gifts

At first I served as the senior pastor of the new church, with Cho as my associate. We did this because Cho was only licensed, and a minister had to be ordained in the Korean Assemblies of God in order to pastor a church. Because I was not fluent in the language, Cho did the bulk of the ministry, assisted by Jashil.

At first we called ourselves the Full Gospel Revival Center, and we soon added a balcony to hold another 500 people. We conducted worship services much like the tent revival meetings, but transplanted into a more permanent building. Usually either Cho or I spoke, but we also invited various outside speakers, always praying to attract an increasing crowd.

After a few months, many of the regular attendees pressed us to make the "Revival Center" a genuine church. Not only that, but the young Cho also informed me, "I want to appoint deacons and deaconesses."

I was hesitant. On occasion American deacon boards became power platforms to command pastors and congregations to do their bidding. Some of the deacons I knew had keen business sense, but little true spirituality. Problems had resulted, and I did not want the same thing to happen to us.

Cho understood my hesitancy and asked me to come to a meeting with our growing group of lay workers. I watched as Cho taught them about servanthood, thanked them for their faithfulness in ministry and encouraged them to continue to minister to others.

Those gathered were the men and women who faithfully helped to usher, to teach the children and youth, and to spend untold hours visiting the homes of recent converts and the sick. As I sat there I began to see things from a different perspective. These were the people Cho wanted to appoint as deacons and deaconesses—faithful individuals, active in ministry to others, unlike some of the deacons I had known. Sitting in the midst of that faithful group, I became convinced that Cho was right.

I then understood that my role with Cho was not to direct him, but rather to encourage him in what God called him to do. Not long after I agreed, Cho appointed deacons

SCRIPTURES THAT ENCOURAGE

When I listen to a person talk, the Holy Spirit will often remind me of a specific scripture or thought to share to encourage that person. While there are many, some of my favorite encouraging scriptures are:

- **Genesis 28:15a**–Behold, I am with you and will keep you wherever you go.
- **Joshua 1:9**–Be strong and of good courage; do not be afraid, nor be dismayed, for the LORD your God is with you wherever you go.
- **Psalm 91:9–11**–Because you have made the LORD, who is my refuge, even the Most High, your dwelling place, no evil shall befall you, nor shall any plague come near your dwelling; for He shall give His angels charge over you, to keep you in all your ways.
- **Isaiah 40:31**–Those who wait on the LORD shall renew their strength; they shall mount up with wings like eagles, they shall run and not be weary, they shall walk and not faint.
- **Jeremiah 29:11**–For I know the thoughts I think toward you, says the LORD, thoughts of peace and not of evil, to give you a future and a hope.
- **Matthew 11:28–30**–Come to Me, all you who labor and are heavy laden, and I will give you rest. Take My yoke upon you and learn from Me, for I am gentle and lowly in heart, and you will find rest for your souls. For My yoke is easy and My burden is light.
- **Romans 8:31, 38–39**–What then shall we say to these things? If God is for us, who can be against us?...For I am persuaded that neither death nor life, nor angels nor principalities nor powers, nor things present nor things to come, nor height nor

depth, nor any other created thing, shall be able to separate us from the love of God which is in Christ Jesus our Lord.

- **Philippians 1:6**–He who has begun a good work in you will complete it until the day of Jesus Christ.
- **Philippians 4:6**–Be anxious for nothing, but in everything by prayer and supplication, with thanksgiving, let your requests be made known to God; and the peace of God, which surpasses all understanding, will guard your hearts and minds through Christ Jesus.
- **Hebrews 13:5b**–He Himself has said, "I will never leave you nor forsake you."

and deaconesses. We no longer had a continuous parade of evangelists and speakers to attract a crowd. Instead we focused on teaching and motivating believers to minister and reach out to others.

I knew that Cho would soon be senior pastor, so I gave priority to his God-given gifts. Cho's sermons were direct and anointed. God had gifted him both in leading people to salvation and in praying for the sick, so we started a pattern that we continued for many years. On Sunday mornings Cho preached on salvation and healing, and on Sunday evenings I preached on the baptism of the Holy Spirit.

When Cho preached during Sunday morning services, people so crowded the building that he could not call the sick forward or have healing lines, so he initiated a practice that continues today. Cho had mass prayer for the sick; then God would often show him specific healings that had occurred. As he mentioned each one, that person would stand with hands raised in praise to God.

We soon developed a weekly pattern. Sunday we would preach, and Monday would be a family day of rest. On Tuesday and Wednesday we counseled in the church office and Cho prepared his sermon for the Wednesday evening service. On Thursday and Friday, Cho and I visited people in their homes.

By 1962, nearly 1,200 people filled our church building every Sunday. In April of that year, the Korean Assemblies of God ordained Cho. I stepped down as senior pastor to become what I termed "missionary advisor." I did not want a regular staff position. My job had changed to one of honoring Cho, and my new role gave me the opportunity to

SEVEN WAYS TO ENCOURAGE OTHERS

I use seven ways to encourage another person. Above all, my goal in encouraging a person is to help him have God's perspective.

1. **I look and listen**—James taught that "every man be swift to hear, slow to speak" (1:19). I begin by observing the person I want to encourage, asking questions and listening with my head and heart to his responses. Sometimes the best way to encourage a person is to genuinely listen to him and let him know that someone believes in him.
2. **I pray and thank God for him**—Paul wrote "I thank God upon every remembrance of you, always in every prayer of mine making request for all of you with joy" (Philippians 1:3-4). Pray fervently for the person you want to encourage, thanking God for what He is doing in that person's life.
3. **I pray with him**—If that person is open, I pray with him about his concerns. I pray the solution, not the problem, and highlight God's love, power and care.
4. **I use my spoken words wisely**—I am to "let no corrupt word proceed out of [my] mouth, but [rather] what is good for necessary edification, that it may impart grace" (Ephesians 4:29). I speak words of encouragement during casual conversation, a personal visit, a telephone call, or on voice mail or a message machine. When I am with that person in public, I say positive things about him.
5. **I use my written words constructively**—I write notes, letters and cards with words that build up and encourage. I often include a scripture of hope, an encouraging word and even an appropriate personal story or testimony.

encourage even more young ministers.

On many weekdays I took a core of Bible school students to other cities, held a revival and left one or two students to nurture the newly planted church. Other weekdays I would respond to invitations to help fledging, newly planted churches, sometimes holding a revival in a home or other location to help a planted church grow.

On May 13 of 1962, we officially changed our name to Full Gospel Central Church, thus highlighting the church's central downtown location and our change in philosophy of ministry. The growing crowd soon became a vibrant congregation.

YOU REAP WHAT YOU SOW

Scripture is right: you do reap what you sow.[141] I honored Cho, and he expressed acts of kindness to honor me. Cho was mindful of my

6. **I serve him**—I try to appropriately meet a genuine need. I take that person on an "encouraging activity," such as a meal or doing something he enjoys. I give that person a meaningful gift that communicates God's care and acknowledges his worth.
7. **I guard my attitudes**—Even though I don't intend to, I often have unspoken expectations of the person I am trying to encourage. When he does not respond in a certain way, I can be disappointed. I must guard my attitudes and "rejoice with those who rejoice…weep with those who weep…[and] owe no man anything except…love" (Romans 12:15; 13:8).

family, and he and Jashil often checked on Maxine and Karen when I was on preaching trips in rural areas.

Cho stopped by once when Karen was in distress. She had a dog named Happy, an attentive and playful golden cocker spaniel with whom she loved to play. But Happy began to lose his sight as he grew older, and a white glaze covered his eyes. In the cold of winter, we brought Happy into the warmth of our small silver trailer, but it wasn't easy for him. Karen's heart almost broke as Happy banged his head on furniture he could not clearly see.

Cho's response was direct. He bent over, placed his hands on Happy's eyes and prayed for the dog's sight. The next day there was no longer a white glaze over Happy's eyes. Happy and Karen played together joyfully after that day, no longer hindered by Happy's blindness. My daughter, like many others in the growing church, learned two important lessons: God is indeed a healing God, and He is concerned with every detail of our daily lives.

Cho encouraged us in other ways as well. Not long before we left Liberia, Maxine had miscarried our son in her fourth month of pregnancy. We buried his small body in a shoebox in our backyard in Africa. Even though we already had Karen, the grief never totally left us. When we went to Korea, the only person we had told about Maxine's miscarriage was Cho.

One day Cho came to see us and excitedly reported what a woman in the church had seen. She explained, "Last night I dreamed that I went to heaven, Pastor Cho. It was so beautiful. But there was a young boy there who said he was John Hurston's son. What does that mean?"

The age at which she described the young boy was the age our son would have been had he lived. For the first time we fully felt the Holy Spirit's comfort in our loss. We would one day see our son again. The man I had once encouraged was now encouraging me.

ABOUT YOU

Remember when Paul (then called Saul) first tried to join the apostles in Jerusalem? They were afraid of the former killer of Christians. What made the difference for Paul? Consider the first two words of one verse, "*But Barnabas.*" Those two words have stirred my imagination ever since, for they point to pivotal actions that changed Paul's life. "But Barnabas took him, and brought him to the apostles. And he declared to them how he had seen the Lord on the road, and that He had spoken to him, and how he had preached boldly at Damascus in the name of Jesus."[142]

Even though Paul later became skilled at encouraging others, there was a time when Paul needed someone to encourage him. Because of Barnabas, the apostles finally received Paul. Later those in Jerusalem heard that many Greeks in Antioch were turning to the Lord, so they

> "sent out Barnabas to go as far as Antioch. When he came and had seen the grace of God, he was glad, and encouraged them all…Then Barnabas departed for Tarsus to seek Saul. And when he had found him, he brought him to Antioch. So it was that for a whole year they assembled with the church and taught a great many people. And the disciples were first called Christians in Antioch."[143]

"But Barnabas…" He later went with Paul on his first missionary journey.[144] The only reason Barnabas left Paul was because Paul would not continue to encourage John Mark.[145]

"But Barnabas…" Barnabas encouraged Paul, and Paul wrote more than half of the books in our New Testament. God used Barnabas to include Paul, to believe in Paul and to give Paul a realm of ministry when others held Paul in suspicion. Except for Barnabas, Paul would never have been the man of God we know him as today. Later Paul encouraged Timothy, Titus and others.

"But Barnabas…" It took a Barnabas to make a Paul, and a Paul to make a Timothy. None of us fulfills God's destiny and purposes in isolation. If you want to fulfill your God-given destiny, one of the best ways is to actively and consistently encourage others.

Who has God put in your path that He wants you to build up and support? From time to time we all grow discouraged. From time to time we all wonder whether it's worth it. You need encouragement and support—and so do those around you.

I learned to be slow to criticize and correct. With our positive words we can build, and with our critical words we can bring destruction.[146]

Prayerfully discern the people into whom God would have you pour your life. If you rightly focus on encouraging others, that focus will transform your life and your attitudes. It certainly transformed mine.

God did amazing things because I chose to encourage Cho and others. Encourage others and God will do the same for you.

Cho and I baptize a new convert in a nearby river in the earlier days.

THE BARNABAS FACTOR: DEVOTIONAL AND DISCUSSION QUESTIONS

Sharing Question

Name one or two specific things someone has done to encourage you. What impact did that have on you?

> *Remember the three guidelines to a sharing question: 1) no one is to take more than one minute in response; 2) go around the circle—if in a small group—and give each person an opportunity to respond; and 3) don't ask other questions at this point, for that stretches out the minute.*

Discussion Questions

1. What one incident or portion of this chapter impressed you? Why?
2. Scan the "Seven Sources of Encouragement in David's Life" on pages 156–157. Which sources did God use to encourage Yonggi Cho? Which one or two of these sources has God most often used to encourage you?
3. Review "Four Benefits in Encouraging Others" on page 154. Share about the benefit that means the most to you, and tell why that benefit is important to you.
4. Which of the "Seven Ways to Encourage Others" on pages 160–161 have you used most often? Would you add any others to this list?

Application

1. Is there a particular person—whether family member, friend, acquaintance or coworker—who you sense God would have you encourage? What one or two specific things could you do this week to encourage that person?

2. Choose one or two of the "Scriptures That Encourage" on pages 158–159. Pair with your spouse (or, in a small group, with someone of the same gender). Share those one or two verses with that person to speak encouragement into his or her life.
3. Conclude by praying for each other and for the salvation of one lost person in your area.

Cho and I stand in the middle of the construction of the Sodaemoon building.

I speak at the dedication of the Full Gospel Revival Center while Cho interprets.

Maxine and I pose with Cho, his father and Jashil on the day Cho was ordained.

Full Gospel Central Church at Sodaemoon after the five-story front with the radio station was added.

The interior of the Sodaemoon (West Gate) Full Gospel Church, about 1963.

Insight Ten

Partner or Perish

Deepen your partnership with the Holy Spirit as you partner with others

ON A HOT Sunday in the summer of 1963, Cho preached to a packed sanctuary in two morning services. He always preached well, but that day he looked especially tired.

That afternoon he was to water baptize 300 new converts. Cho was trying hard to prove himself as a senior pastor, but I was concerned and offered to help. "No," Cho protested. "I'm all right. I'm strong. Besides, it's my responsibility." So three hundred times Cho lowered thin and plump bodies into the water, baptizing them "in the name of the Father, the Son and the Holy Spirit."

Later the same afternoon, Cho was to go the airport to meet a visiting American evangelist, and still later he was to interpret for him during the evening service. Cho was taking his role as senior pastor seriously, but because I did not want to see him overwork himself, I again offered to help: "I can meet the evangelist at the airport for you and bring him to the hotel. That way you can take time to eat and get some rest."

Cho refused again, "No. He's expecting me."

So Cho went to the airport, took the visiting evangelist to the hotel and then brought him to church with him in time for the evening service. Cho had not even had a chance to eat.

When the evening service started, I was sitting in a chair on the platform. As missionary advisor, I usually spoke on Sunday evenings; when there were guest speakers, I was there to help.

I saw Maxine and Karen in their usual pew, and I listened as the choir sang. When it was time for the sermon, Cho walked slowly to the pulpit and stood shakily to the left side of the guest American evangelist. For a few minutes everything seemed fine. A tired Cho interpreted each phrase of the fiery minister's sermon, even trying to gesture and move exactly the way the evangelist did.

Then Cho's legs began to quiver. Suddenly he collapsed and dropped to the floor, his lean body limp on the wooden platform. I rushed from my chair and knelt at Cho's side. "John," he called faintly, "I'm dying."

The deacons quickly rushed Cho to a nearby hospital. I took Maxine and Karen, and we followed closely behind, leaving a startled guest evangelist with a different interpreter to preach to a now somber congregation.

Much of that night still remains a blur in my memory. I do remember the antiseptic smell of the green and white emergency room, and Cho's body lying so still on a hospital pallet. They told us that his heart was beating more than 200 times a minute and that he could barely breathe.

A nurse in a white uniform entered, holding a large syringe with a long needle to draw a sample of Cho's blood for tests. We sat with our heads bowed, praying for God to heal our young pastor.

A doctor finally came to examine Cho's still body. The doctor spent several minutes looking over the test results. Then he turned to us. "This man is physically exhausted. His health has been broken and his heart is weak. To recover, he will require total bed rest." The doctor paused, then continued, "After that, it would be my suggestion that he find another line of work. It would be better if he never preached or pastored again. The strain could kill him."

This crisis needed a quick solution. Temporarily, Jashil and I divided the pastoral duties. Cho would need all the rest he could get.

God's Biblical Plan

I visited Cho often during his weeks of recuperation. He had only limited participation in the church services, and he spent most of his time in bed—praying, resting and reading his Bible.

Cho knew that he could no longer shoulder the entire burden of the church. Even Jashil and I were struggling to carry the load together. Yes, the church had been effective. But if we were to grow more, Cho knew it would be physically impossible for him—or even for Jashil and me—to continue in this way. So he read the Bible to search for solutions.

As Cho read the Book of Acts, he noted the growth and ministry pattern in the early church. On the day of Pentecost, 3,000 people received Jesus Christ. By the fourth chapter of Acts, the number had grown to 5,000. By chapter five, multitudes were coming to Christ. And the Holy Spirit added to their number daily.

Those believers went to synagogues or to the temple, but they did not have a single, large gathering place. And those multitudes of believers only had nineteen leaders: twelve apostles and seven deacons. Cho wondered how the early church in Jerusalem had cared for such large numbers. He couldn't even care adequately for his growing congregation of 3,000.

Cho told me he had read the Scriptures again, and he noted that the Christians met from "house to house," breaking bread, and sharing apostolic teaching.[147] Those thousands of believers broke apart into smaller groups for home meetings. Not only did they visit homes, but they also held worship services in homes. Later Priscilla and Aquila held worship services in their home, as did Nymphas, and Philemon and his family.[148]

Even when Cho's earlier church had met under the tent in Taechodong, they had divided the community into four areas. They had appointed a contact person for each area, and they sometimes held services in the different areas. But the pattern from Acts seemed even better.

Cho also read parts of the Old Testament, and he was struck by the story of Jethro and Moses.[149] He felt that he was overburdened like Moses, so he carefully read Jethro's advice. When Cho prayed, his mandate seemed firm: he was to use his deacons as leaders of home services—the biblical "church in the home"—to meet during the week throughout the city. Cho would still preach in the Sunday morning and Wednesday evening worship services and the church would continue growing. It seemed such a wonderful, biblical plan. Both Jashil and I encouraged Cho in this. We felt that God had spoken to our tired friend.

USE WOMEN AS LEADERS

Cho finally gathered enough strength to go to a meeting of his deacons and male lay leaders. He shared with them how God had been dealing with him about appointing lay leaders to have home meetings, but they were not receptive.

One deacon said that he was too tired at the end of the day to lead a meeting. Another insisted that some groups would get proud, break away and start their own churches. A third lay leader remarked that it sounded biblical, but that they had not been trained for anything like this—it was not part of traditional church activity. "Besides," he informed Cho, "that's what we pay you for." The meeting ended with the leaders' suggestion: "Why don't you go away and take a long vacation?"

Cho returned home discouraged. His first attempt at getting home groups started had been unsuccessful. Traditional thinking was too strong among his male lay leaders.

Jashil often joined with a group of women who effectively made home visits that sometimes resulted in spontaneous home meetings. These ladies talked to Cho about using women as home group leaders, but he was reluctant. Korean cultural bias toward men, and certain Scripture passages, added to his hesitancy. But as he studied the Bible more, his own objections lessened. When he prayed, the Lord reminded him of how often God had used women in ministry.

Cho sensed God asking him, "Who gave birth to Jesus?"

"Mary, a woman," Cho responded.

"Who nurtured Jesus?" came a second question.

"Mary, a woman," Cho responded a second time.

"Who surrounded Jesus' ministry and supplied His needs?" came a third question.

"A group of women," was Cho's reply.

"Who remained until the last moment of His passion on the cross?"

"Women."

"Who came on the first day of Jesus' resurrection and saw His empty tomb?"

"Women."

"To whom did Christ first speak after rising from the dead so that the message of His resurrection would be given to the apostles?"

"A woman."

While Christ was on earth, women supported His ministry. The Church was now Christ's body. Why not let women minister?

So Cho turned to the deaconesses in the Women's Fellowship. When he spoke to them about his physical weakness, several cried. When he explained that the only way he could continue to pastor was to follow the biblical pattern of lay leaders having home meetings throughout the city, they listened with interest. Then they responded: "Pastor, tell us to do anything, and we will obey. We will do the work."

Five Famous Pairs of Bible Partners

1. **Moses and Aaron**—God gave Aaron to Moses as his mouthpiece (Exodus 4:14-16, 27-31). That partnership resulted in the Israelites being delivered from Egyptian bondage.
2. **Deborah and Barak**—Deborah was a married prophetess who judged Israel. She sent for Barak to deploy troops and they defeated Sisera, the commander of Jabin's army. Israel then had peace for forty years (Judges 4:4-24).
3. **Joash and Jehoiada**—Joash was only seven years old when he became the king of Judah. As long as the priest Jehoiada was alive, Joash followed his counsel, and even repaired the temple of the Lord (2 Kings 11:21-12:16).
4. **Paul and Barnabas**—were prayerfully appointed by the church in Antioch and were sent on a missionary journey that resulted in the spread of the Gospel to many Gentiles, as well as the establishment of several churches (Acts 13:1-14:28). Paul later paired with Silas in his second missionary journey (Acts 15:40-18:22).
5. **Priscilla and Aquila**—were a husband and wife team who traveled with Paul, explained God's way to Apollos and started a church in their home (Acts 18:2-3, 18, 24-26; Romans 16:3-5).

But when Cho announced to the deacons that he was going to use women as leaders for groups of other women, they balked. Some banded together and stated that they would leave the church if women were used. He reasoned with the disgruntled deacons: "All right, if that is what you have decided, go ahead and leave. When I asked you deacons to have home meetings, you refused. But I am still sick, and I have no alternative.

I feel that God has cornered me in this situation and has left me no other choice. I have to use the women."

PERSIST PAST PROBLEMS

The first groups soon formed. Since Cho was still struggling with chronic weakness, Jashil took charge of organization. Twenty women in different areas throughout the city were selected as the first leaders.

Only two guidelines were given. First, each leader was to gather and care for the believing Christian women in her area, teach the Bible and pray with them. Second, each leader was to go out and win her neighbors to Jesus Christ and then invite them to her home meetings and to church.

Each leader could choose what she wanted to share in the group. Some played audio cassettes, some tried to teach themselves and others invited outside speakers to share. Several women from the church attended, with twenty to thirty in most groups.

Even though Cho clearly explained to the congregation how God had led him, only a portion of the congregation participated. Their response was disappointing, but Cho and I talked about it often. Cho knew that God had spoken to him and, for a time, things seemed to go fairly well.

However, problems soon surfaced. A new Christian in one group asked the leader what the word *trinity* meant. The ignorant but sincere leader stated, "Well, I think it means our God has one body, but three heads."

Other leaders invited speakers to their meetings who taught a theological position that was different from that held by the church. As a result, a man came into one group and stopped the meeting. Another man became so upset about his wife leading a group and praying for people that he physically hit her.

With few exceptions, those first groups collapsed. Several men in the church were pleased. When Cho turned to the Lord in prayer, he sensed God encouraging him to persist past the problems and to try again.

STARTING AGAIN

When Cho announced that he was going to start the groups again, some of the men thought he was crazy. A few effective female leaders came to his office. They encouraged him but said, "Pastor, we do not know how to preach a sermon. Teach us what we are to say and then let us carry your message to our groups. We need more of your help to know how to have a home meeting."

So every Wednesday before the evening service, Cho met with willing female group leaders. He taught and distributed mimeographed lessons to them, including an outline of what they should share at the next weekly home meeting. At this stage the leaders were "carrier teachers"—"carrying" the material Cho shared to their groups. He also gave them a general outline for how the home meetings should run.

For a short time, all seemed well. Then new problems emerged. The group meetings rotated to a different home each week, and competition developed as hostesses tried to serve refreshments that were better or more plentiful than in the previous home. Some meetings deteriorated into long "religious parties," keeping wives from doing housework and irritating time-conscious husbands. One group's geographical area was so large that some leaders complained about the lengthy bus rides necessary to visit and minister to group members.

Some leaders still invited outside speakers who taught conflicting doctrine. Members of other groups started borrowing money from each other, and members of one group even pooled their money together in what would later prove to be a bad investment. At least one leader pilfered money from the offerings the group leaders took each week. A few groups grew as large as fifty people, more than could be given adequate care by one leader. Older leaders grew weary with the problems and dropped out.

Cho responded by setting clear guidelines. Refreshments should be simple and inexpensive, served at the end of a one-hour meeting that consistently followed a set format. No outside speakers would be allowed without prior approval. Money would not be borrowed or invested with anyone else in the group. Both the leader and an appointed group treasurer would count the offering, after which a designated treasurer was to take it to the church.

Cho recruited younger and stronger female lay leaders. By the time a group reached fifteen in attendance, an assistant was to be appointed. Then they planted a new group, with the assistant sometimes taking up to half the members for the new group plant. After each meeting, leaders completed a written report for the church.

MORE SUMMER CAMPAIGNS

THREE REASONS I NEED TO PARTNER WITH OTHERS

There are many benefits in becoming a partner with others, but Scripture is clear on the following three reasons:

1. **I accomplish more**—"Five of you shall chase a hundred, and a hundred of you shall put ten thousand to flight"...One can "chase a thousand," and two "put ten thousand to flight" (Leviticus 26:8; Deuteronomy 32:30). I can accomplish a multiplied portion *when I partner with others.* Partnering is a force multiplier.
2. **I receive better support**—"Two are better than one, because they have a good reward for their labor. For if they fall, one will lift up his companion. But woe to him who is alone when he falls, for he has no one to help him up...though one may be overpowered by another, two can withstand him. And a threefold cord is not quickly broken" (Ecclesiastes 4:9-10, 12).
3. **God has crafted us to need each other**—"For as the body is one and has many members, but all the members of that one body, being many, are one body, so also is Christ...for in fact the body is not one member but many...there should be no schism in the body, but that the members should have the same care for one another. And if one member suffers, all the members suffer with it; or if one member is honored, all the members rejoice with it. Now you are the body of Christ, and members individually (1 Corinthians 12:12, 14, 25-27).

The summer of 1964, a year after Cho's collapse, Ralph Byrd returned to South Korea to hold six tent revival campaigns. I knew God was leading Cho, so I took two weeks to be with my old mentor. Since I had already been made both president of the denominational Bible college and chairman of the literature committee, I mobilized the students from Seoul to fill the streets before each daytime meeting to distribute literature and share the Gospel. The students were anxious to help, and they gave out more than 500,000 tracts, 200,000 Gospel portions, 1,000 Bibles and 40,000 copies of a Korean Pentecostal magazine.[150]

Once more God demonstrated His power. The crowds in each revival service ranged from 2,000 in the smaller cities to 4,000 in Seoul. Thousands were born again, hundreds were healed and dozens were filled with the Holy Spirit.

A Deeper Partnership With the Holy Spirit

Cho had already developed what I term as "partnership preaching." While Cho's Wednesday evening sermons were expository and aimed at the believer, his Sunday morning sermons were on need-meeting topics, filled with biblical and personal illustrations that any guest unbeliever would find relevant and interesting. Cho thus "partnered" with any believer who wanted to bring an unbeliever to church with him. Many believers came to multiple Sunday morning services, each time bringing a different guest unbeliever. They knew Cho's sermons would touch their friend's mind and heart and would always conclude with an invitation for the unbeliever to repent of his sins and receive Jesus Christ as his Lord and Savior.

By the time I returned from those campaigns with Byrd, the women's groups were doing much better. I also began to see another truth emerge: the more Cho partnered with his members, the more he deepened his partnership with the Holy Spirit. When Cho released one of his members to lead a group, Cho also had to deepen his trust in the Holy Spirit to guide and to protect.

As I continued to ponder about how God led Cho in forming the cell groups, I observed five additional ways the Holy Spirit was leading Cho to partner with others:

1. **Partner by changing your view of roles.** The Spirit first used the groups to help Cho reshape his understanding of roles in the local church. Cho already knew the importance of honoring lay leaders; he had done that when he gave the faithful the titles "deacon" and "deaconess." But at that point Cho only recognized those who were helping maintain existing church services by ushering, singing in the choir, teaching children's Sunday School, preparing monthly communion and visiting the sick. It was good, but it was an Old Testament model, with the "prophet" or pastor as the man of God and everyone around him as his "helps" ministry.

   The Spirit was taking Cho deeper. Even though he did not clearly realize it until later, God was helping him to gain the crucial New Testament perspective of the priesthood of every believer.[151] Each believer has a calling, and every saint has a sphere of influence to reach. The groups became some of the most efficient vehicles for the believer to use to fulfill more of his calling as he reached those in his arena of influence.

The Spirit also helped Cho change his view of his own role. He had once served as the provider of all significant ministry. As the group system expanded, Cho instead saw himself as an equipper of leaders.[152] He never once mandated that everyone get involved; he simply created opportunities, taught biblical principles, inspired, ministered, motivated and provided needed resources.

Every Sunday in the West Gate church, at least a dozen people made decisions to serve Jesus Christ. The Spirit used the groups as vehicles by which many could minister to each other. Each time I visited a group or talked to a group leader, I could sense how the Spirit delighted in His children ministering to one another and reaching new people.

2. **Partner by listening well to others.** While Cho looked to God to give him general direction about the groups, he also listened to others and relied on the Holy Spirit inside his people to help him detail the specifics. It was never Cho's idea to have a common curriculum in the groups, or even to have any curriculum at all—that was what his leaders requested. He didn't even plan to give initial or ongoing teaching or training to his leaders; that was what they wanted of him.

   Cho had no model or current example from which to draw, so he relied on listening well to his people, especially his leaders. Through the years that group system has been reshaped and remolded to be as need-meeting as possible. If the Holy Spirit is anything, He is creative.

3. **Partner by empowering and releasing even the unlikely.** At that time, Korean women were considered second-rate citizens, never the equal of their husbands. More than 70 percent of married women were full-time homemakers, with access to more free time to minister to others than were those who had jobs outside the home.

Initially Cho hadn't even thought about using women in leadership. Then the Spirit dealt with him about empowering and releasing the unlikely. Soon women were leading women's groups. Even though there was failure in the beginning, in time those women's groups met with phenomenal success. Not only did the typical leader hold a weekly home meeting, but she also took two to three hours each week to make visits to the homes of female members in need of additional prayer and care. The Spirit had led Cho to unleash an overlooked resource that still helps fuel that church to this day.

4. **Partner primarily with leaders who are baptized in the Holy Spirit and live consistent, Spirit-led lives.** Through the years one trend has stayed the same: our most effective leaders are baptized in the Holy Spirit, pray daily in tongues, and daily read and meditate on God's Word. Cho and I both found that no matter how extensive the knowledge of the leader, the ones who had healthier groups were Spirit-filled, prayerful and Word-washed.

   There were occasions when we allowed people to become leaders who were not baptized in the Holy Spirit, but were full of prayer and the Word. Our logic was simple—when a person enters leadership, he soon discovers his inadequacy and starts crying out to God—and God often responds by baptizing that person in His Spirit. The Spirit teaches the new leader how to walk in daily dependence on Him.

5. **Partner by creating homogeneous groups around your preferred ministry activity.** From the start, our preferred ministry activity outside pulpit preaching was to make home prayer visits. Often these visits were brief, with the focus on praying for the person or family in that home. It was for this reason that the groups were geographically based—we wanted to make it easier for the leader to make home visits to those in his or her area.

   The Spirit also led Cho to have homogeneous groups, where the people involved were similar to each other. In our case those groups were gender-based, with women meeting with women and men meeting with men. We later found that communication flow is easier in an all-female or all-male group, with clearer focus on whom one should reach—another woman or another man—something not as clear in a mixed group.

WATCH THE SPIRIT PARTNER THROUGH HIS SERVANTS

By the time the groups were doing better in 1964, I left missionary couple Henry and Lydia Swain in our place, and Maxine, Karen and I left for more than two years of furlough in the States. Cho wrote often to update us about what the Holy Spirit was doing in and through him and the church.

By November of 1964, Cho wrote, "Every Sunday we add 20 to 30 new families to our congregation...Now about my upcoming marriage...we are expecting about two to three thousand guests...as soon as we finish the ceremony we will fly down to Pusan...Once again I and Sunghae [his fiancée, also called 'Grace'] miss you very, very much."

I wrote and watched from a distance as the Spirit partnered with His servant Cho, and rejoiced in what God was doing. God was interested not only in what Cho could do for Him, but also in Cho's personal happiness. Even as the church consistently grew, God expanded Cho's personal life. His fiancée Grace was a lovely young woman. A capable musician, she had been well trained in ministry by her mother, Jashil.

In April of 1965, after their marriage, I heard from Cho again. His main focus in that letter was on the growth of the church: "Even our two Sunday morning services cannot hold the crowds; we will start to have a third service from the first week of May...recently God helped me have a very good revival meeting in the city of Taegu. So many tried to get into the building that policemen were sent to control the crowds...Grace and I are now building our own western-style house. When you return we will gladly welcome you to our new home!...Every morning I do not forget you and your family before the throne of grace."

Even from a distance, I could see that the Spirit had rewarded Cho for being diligent in prayer. More than a year after they married, Cho and Grace had their first son. In the midst of all that the Spirit was doing in the church, Cho sometimes still struggled with what his calling truly was. I was grateful in February of 1966 when Cho wrote that "our attendance is almost 5,000 in our three morning services...God has definitely called me to be a pastor and teacher...My son is now quite big. He smiles and talks with me...My wife gives her sincere hello to you. We all wait eagerly for your return."

Even while we were absent, the Spirit worked mightily through His servant Cho and through the small group leaders. We continued praying daily for Cho and his family, and we delighted in how the Spirit was using them.

Maxine and I remained busy with fund-raising during that furlough, and we were also able to build our future retirement home. Karen was then in junior high, a faithful member of Brownsville Assembly of God.

The missions department no longer talked to us about returning to Liberia. The church in Seoul had grown to be one of the largest in Asia; God has a way of defending us when we follow Him in obedience.

Shortly before we ended our furlough and returned to Seoul in 1967, Cho thanked us "for your hard work to raise funds for radio work in Korea." About the church he said, "We have been able to build a fourth floor on the front. Right now we use the fourth floor for Sunday School classes and the young people...We started a church library and literature program. I have started our monthly church magazine...Our work here is growing tremendously, and we need your hands of cooperation very much. All the tears of sowing have passed away, and right now I am having the full joy of wonderful reaping. Come quickly and join us for this victory and great harvest! Only you and we know how many tears we have shed to see this day."

Partners Again

It was good to be back with my friend Cho. In 1967, when we returned from our furlough three years after the groups had started, we found 126 home groups serving the 7,750-member congregation. Growth came even more quickly after that. By 1968, the groups increased to 145.

Spurred by the growing success of the women's groups, and concerned about the men of the church, Chulik Lee began the first men's home group in the spacious living room of a man named Changshick Ahn. Only five men attended the first meeting, but twenty to thirty attended later meetings. They planted another group, and Lee announced their success. Soon men throughout the church started home groups.

We returned to our former weekly pattern. Cho preached in three consecutive morning services each Sunday on salvation and healing, and I preached in two Sunday evening services on the Holy Spirit.

Monday was "family day," when even the church secretaries stayed home. Many Monday's Cho and I slipped away for an hour or two to go to a sauna together, a relaxing Korean tradition that had developed before the days of indoor plumbing. As the hot steam whirled around us, we talked and laughed together. Since it was Cho's custom to outline his sermon on Monday for the upcoming Sunday, we often discussed his sermon points and the scriptures he intended to use.

As before, during weekdays I would take a core of Bible school students to other cities or rural areas, hold a revival and leave one or two students to nurture the newly planted church. When I was in Seoul, Cho and I spent time in the office on Tuesday and Wednesday, counseling and preparing for the Wednesday night service. Thursday and Friday we went on prayer visits to minister to people in their homes and businesses.

PARTNER IN VISITATION

The Spirit continued to show us the importance of making home visits. My strongest memory of one of those visits was on a cold autumn day. Cho and I walked near the top of a mountain to find the shanty of a poor family who attended our church. We sat on the dirt floor of their one-room home, prayed and ministered to them. Just then we heard the distant cries of a baby.

After our visit ended, we looked for the source of the crying. Cho and I hurried through the brisk wind and found a tiny, roofless pasteboard structure, where a mother huddled with her crying toddler. It was so cold, and the cardboard walls did little to keep out the piercing wind. The mother's face was streaked with tears.

Cho and I walked in quietly and talked with her. Her husband had been killed in the Korean War, leaving her with three children. She was only thirty years old, but hard work and the lack of food had already taken their toll. She looked like an old woman, sick and no longer able to work and support her family. Cho stooped down and picked up that crying, dirty toddler and held her close against him until she got warm and stopped crying.

That scene touched my soul. Cho was not just maturing into a pastor of faith and vision—he had also become a man of deep compassion. Cho and I returned to the church to send others back to minister to the widow on the mountain. Men built her a roof, and women brought clothes and food for her and her children. That widow was so touched that she came to church and gave her life to Jesus Christ. After she was physically healed, she returned to work as a street vendor, able to support her three children.

Not long after our earlier visit to the mountain, we hired another staff pastor. By then we had already seen the benefits of making home prayer visits, and we put this new pastor in charge of making prayer visits to segments of our growing congregation that we no longer had the time to visit. In 1970, when the number of men's groups alone passed the 150 mark, the church hired three more staff pastors, each overseeing fifty to 100 groups, each making daily prayer visits, often accompanied by the group leader of that area.

About You

Jesus' apostles had it right. So did Jethro, Moses' father-in-law.

Many in the Jerusalem church complained because the apostles had overlooked some of the widows in the daily food distribution.[153] The apostles found that they needed help, so they appointed seven men who were full of the Spirit and wisdom. After the apostles partnered with those seven, "the word of God spread, and the number of the disciples multiplied greatly in Jerusalem."[154]

Jethro had joined Moses for a family reunion.[155] But when he saw Moses sitting all day long to judge individual cases, Jethro knew that the work was too heavy for Moses. Moses didn't have enough time to spend with God nor with his family; he was going to wear out both himself and the people before he could make it to the Promised Land.

So Jethro gave his classic advice that Moses should choose able, God-fearing men and set them over groups of thousands, hundreds, fifties and tens.[156] Jethro told Moses that he should share his load and partner with others. Moses followed Jethro's advice, and he finally had time to go to the mountain and spend time with God.[157] It was only after Moses had learned to partner with others that God gave him the Ten Commandments.

FOUR AREAS IN WHICH I CAN PARTNER WITH OTHERS

I can partner with another person, group, or my local church in one or more of these four basic areas:

1. **Upreach**–involves prayer, praise and God's Word. I can join another person as his prayer partner; I can join a prayer group; I can lead a Bible study.
2. **Inreach**–involves follow-up and care and any form of service to others. I can follow up on new converts or struggling believers. I might be part of a visitation team, or a ministry that gives pastoral care.
3. **Outreach**–is evangelism. I can be part of an evangelistic team or group; I can serve in a shelter for the homeless or an outreach to a nursing home.
4. **Leadership development**–I can become an intern or apprentice in a group of which I am a part. If I am leading that group or ministry, I can help develop others as leaders by having an intern or apprentice in my group or ministry.

I had often wondered about two things: If the apostles had not partnered with the seven, would the Word of God have spread the way it did in Jerusalem? If Moses had not taken Jethro's advice and partnered with others, would God ever have had time alone with Moses to give him the Ten Commandments?

God never intends for ministry to be a solo performance. The more one partners rightly with others, the more impact one will have.

How does this apply to you? If you've been ministering by yourself, it's time to share and partner with others. You may already be feeling weary. Consider how you might use one or more groups to partner with other members in your congregation, empowering them to minister to each other and to reach out to new people.

You might not be a pastor or a leader in your local church, but your pastor needs your involvement. If you are not already involved in your local church, it's time for you to partner with your pastor and others to do kingdom work.

Remember this: God has a destiny for your life. He wants you to reach those in your sphere of influence—your receptive coworkers, relatives, friends, acquaintances and neighbors. He also wants you to be an instrument to more mightily influence your circle of friends and acquaintances at church.

Just as we often need some sort of vehicle to transport us to different places, God will often provide the vehicle of a group to help us achieve His objectives through us. That vehicle of a group might meet in a home in your community, on your job site, on your school campus or even on the church grounds. You don't need to be the leader, but you do need to invite and include those in your sphere of influence.

You might feel inadequate and unlikely to achieve anything great for God and His kingdom. Join the crowd! God is in the business of empowering and releasing the unlikely. Realize how valuable you are to God. If you are baptized with the Holy Spirit, remember whose power resides within you! Realize how much hidden influence He gives you with others, and be wise. When your pastor, church staff members or leaders ask you questions and want your feedback, respond quickly and honestly.

Whatever your situation, if you don't partner with others the way God directs, you will eventually perish before fulfilling your God-given destiny. Cho had to decide whether he would partner or perish. You have the same choice.

We first called the church the "Revival Center," then "Sodaemoon Full Gospel Church." Jashil Choi is to the right of Maxine; I am to her left. Karen is eight, sitting on the young Cho's lap, surrounded by the ladies who visited more than 1,000 homes, to invite them to come to our church.

Pastor Cho and I would sometimes work together in radio broadcasts.

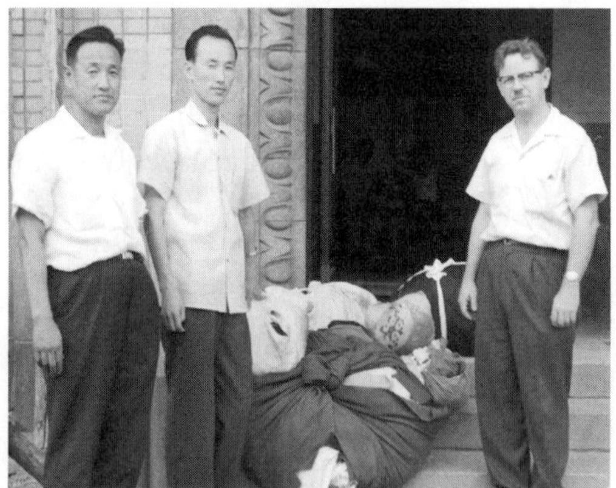

Pastor Cho and I are ready to distribute clothes to the needy.

Pastor Cho asked me to lead in prayer at one point of the ground-breaking ceremony for the land purchased at Yoido Island for the newly planned sanctuary.

Partner or Perish: Devotional and Discussion Questions

Sharing Questions

Have you (like Pastor Cho) ever learned a biblical truth the "hard way" (through a difficult situation)? If so, how did that happen, and what difference did that truth make in your life?

> *Be brief. Remember the three guidelines to a sharing question: 1) no one is to take more than one minute in response; 2) go around the circle—if in a small group—and give each person an opportunity to respond; and 3) don't ask other questions at this point, for that stretches out the minute.*

Discussion Questions

1. Consider Pastor Cho's journey to deepen his partnership with his members and with the Holy Spirit. Which portion of that story did you find most interesting? Why?
2. Have a different person read each of three passages: Exodus 18:13–27; Acts 2:42–47; Romans 16:1–16. After you read each one, ask: What does this passage show about partnership?
3. Which of the "Five Famous Pairs of Bible Partners" on page 171 is your favorite? Why?
4. On pages 175–178, I mention five ways that the Holy Spirit led Pastor Cho to deepen his partnership with others. Which of these ways did you find most significant?

Application

1. Pair with your spouse (or, in a small group, with someone of the same gender). Review "Four Areas in Which I Can

Partner With Others" on page 182. In which of these areas do you feel God is calling you to enter into a greater partnership?

2. Evaluate your current involvements and responsibilities. Is there a specific way you can partner more with those in your family? With coworkers on your job? In an area of ministry?
3. Conclude by praying for each other and for the salvation of one lost person in your area.

We sit here with both the Cho and Choi families, near the front steps of the Sodaemoon church, shortly before leaving for the States and serving in South Vietnam. I sit on the far right of the first row as Pastor Cho's oldest son, Hee Jun, sits in his lap, and Maxine sits between Grace and her mother, Jashil Choi. Karen is the teenager in the back row.

Insight Eleven

FIND THE RIGHT DOORWAY TO THE HEART

How caring for practical needs opens hearts to Jesus

"YOU DON'T KNOW where we're going next," I announced to Maxine, trying to arouse her curiosity.

Maxine's response surprised me: "Yes, I do. We're going to Vietnam. While you were gone, I was praying for you, and God spoke that to my heart."

I had just returned from a trip to plant a church in a rural area in South Korea. While praying before a service, I had sensed God's voice: "Now I want you to go as a missionary to Vietnam." His directive had been so clear that I knew better than to resist.

God clearly confirmed His directive with Maxine's response. Yet we had never even visited Vietnam, nor did we know anything about the culture. I did know that American military aid to South Vietnam had started in the early 1960s. By 1968 the U.S. had half a million troops in Vietnam, many responding to the large-scale offensive the Communists had launched throughout the South during Tet, the Vietnamese Lunar New Year holiday. But soon the war in Vietnam came to be unpopular with Americans back home; troop withdrawals began in the summer of 1969, shortly before God called us there.

When I told Cho that God was leading Maxine and me to serve in Vietnam, he was not happy. We'd made great progress, and attendance in our five Sunday services was nearly 10,000. We had even broken ground for new facilities on Seoul's Yoido Island. But Cho knew me, and he finally gave his blessing to my new assignment.

I wrote a letter to our missions department to explain how I felt God was leading me. I also asked permission to visit Saigon on our return trip to the States for our scheduled furlough. They responded quickly; they already wanted to establish a mission in Vietnam.

A DIFFERENT APPROACH

We left Seoul for our furlough in the summer of 1970, and Maxine, Karen and I stopped in Saigon. The city had been developed during the previous hundred years of French domination while Vietnam was still part of French Indochina. Many called Saigon "the pearl of the Orient" because of its picturesque, well-manicured boulevards, busy shopping centers and elegant, large public buildings.

But by the time we arrived, the Vietnam conflict had devastated Saigon's beauty. The remains of bombed buildings stood as symbols of the terror of war. Young and slightly built South Vietnamese soldiers stood on every corner, large machine guns strapped to their backs. Orphans roamed the streets looking for a kind face and a few loose coins. Poverty forced lovely young women to prostitute their bodies in exchange for money; many were the sole support of parents and siblings.

During our visit, we stayed in the home of missionaries who were serving with the Christian and Missionary Alliance. There we talked about Vietnam late into the night. When we finally went to bed, we slept beneath thick mosquito netting. But we could not sleep well, for the bombing on the other side of Saigon occupied our thoughts and troubled our hearts.

As I lay in bed, I thought of all we had seen. I had thought that the needs were great in war-torn Korea, but I had never before witnessed such devastation as I saw in Vietnam. The Vietnamese were not responsive to the Gospel like the Koreans had been; the demonic clutch of ancestor worship and Buddhism had a much stronger hold in Vietnam, and many Christian churches had only a handful of believers. The Vietnamese desperately needed Jesus as Savior and Healer, but they also had practical needs that were nearly overwhelming. Cho and his elders had often been involved in distribution of clothing and food to the poor in Korea, but the needs there were not as great as they were in Vietnam.

Ministry in Vietnam was going to require a different approach.

Focus on Spiritual Needs

When we finally arrived in the States for furlough, the missions department appointed me head of the newly proposed mission to Vietnam. We were soon busy raising funds for Christian literature, for church planting and for personal support.

I had to make a second trip to Vietnam, leaving Maxine and Karen in the States, for we first had to secure a charter from the minister of the interior to formally register the new work as a mission. The government welcomed us, but they also asked that we help them with some of the pressing social problems that had developed because of the war.

We started to raise funds for relief work, and we officially opened our mission in South Vietnam in 1972. Maxine and I finally left to live in Saigon, leaving Karen behind in college. Maxine quickly fit into the culture, sometimes wearing the native dress and following many of the cultural patterns. Later she would often say, "I went to Africa because I loved God. I went to Korea because I loved John. I went to Vietnam because I loved God and John."

Within a short time there were several missionaries under my oversight, not only from America, but also from the Philippines and France. Later Cho even sent a missionary couple from Korea to help us—Nam Soo Kim and his wife, Esther.

There was constant tension in Vietnam, and all the missionaries who served on our team knew the conditions before they joined us. They were a devoted breed, committed to Paul's principle that the enemy cannot kill us until God is through with us.

We did many things to open hearts to receive the Gospel. We held what we termed "Good News Crusades," where we preached and handed out tracts and saw hundreds turn to Christ. Some of our missionaries planted churches in several cities, because our primary focus was to meet spiritual needs. We organized our first church in Vung Tau together with a missionary who had started a servicemen's home and a foster home for children. Before long that church had 67 members. A Vietnamese businessman even donated land for a church in the city of Dalat. That year alone, because of the strong desire of the Vietnamese to read and learn, we gave out over one million Gospel tracts and distributed Christian literature as fast as we could print it.

NEW TESTAMENT SYMBOLS OF THE HOLY SPIRIT

The symbols the New Testament uses for the Holy Spirit tell us about His nature:

- **Fire**–Matthew 3:11; Luke 3:16b. He convicts, brings righteousness and judges (John 16:7-14).
- **Water**–John 4:14. He quenches the thirst of our souls (John 7:37-39).
- **Seal**–Ephesians 1:13-14. His seal on our lives shows that we belong to God (2 Corinthians 1:21-22).
- **Dove**–Matthew 3:16; Mark 1:10; Luke 3:22; John 1:32. He is pure, tender and gentle.
- **Wind**–John 3:8. He moves where and when He desires.

THE CATHOLIC CONNECTION

Before I left the States, a friend had given me a book entitled *Catholic Pentecostalism.* While reading that book in Saigon, I felt the Holy Spirit direct me to contact the archbishop of the Catholic Church in Vietnam. When I arrived at his office, there were two Catholic priests in the waiting room and we began to talk. They had just returned from the States and, while there, had discovered that there were one million Catholic charismatics in America.

I invited the two priests to join me in my appointment with the archbishop and allowed them to share before I began. I then gave the archbishop my copy of *Catholic Pentecostalism,* and we talked for nearly an hour about the Catholic charismatic renewal movement.

The archbishop's keen interest in the Holy Spirit and the charismatic renewal did not end with our discussion. He appointed Father Galenas, a French-Canadian Jesuit priest, to continue our talks and to report back to him on the contents of our interchange. During our first encounter, I bombarded Galenas with scriptures and biblical proof of the Spirit's workings. But after three hours of explanation, I didn't feel I'd made any impact. I had not been able to touch Father Galenas's tender heart and mind by means of my factual approach.

That night Maxine and I knelt and prayed about the next meeting. When I woke early the next morning, the Holy Spirit impressed me to simply share my personal story of what the Holy Spirit meant in my life. During our next meeting, I told Father Galenas how much the Holy Spirit had helped me with a new dimension in my prayer life, how I was more effective in sharing the Gospel, how much closer I now felt to Christ and the difference His baptism made in my ministry.

The Works of the Holy Spirit in the Old Testament

The Holy Spirit was present with the Jews in the times of the Old Testament, but would come upon a selected individual, or individuals, for a designated period of time–often to perform a specific task. In the Old Testament, the Holy Spirit:

- **Created the world** in which we live (Genesis 1:2).
- **Empowered some people to prophesy or to utter an oracle**–including the seventy elders chosen by Moses (Numbers 11:25), Balaam (Numbers 24:2), Saul (1Samuel 10:10), Saul's messengers (1 Samuel 19:20) and Azariah (2 Chronicles 15:1).
- **Gave wisdom** to Othniel, who judged Israel and won important battles (Judges 3:10); David, when he was anointed king (1 Samuel 16:13); and Solomon (1 Kings 3:28).
- **Granted favor** to Gideon and an army of men gathered around him (Judges 6:34).
- **Gave strength** to Samson, who tore a lion apart, killed 30 men and destroyed the temple to Dagon (Judges 14;6, 19; 16:28-30).

The now enthusiastic priest interrupted me saying, "Today you have made the Holy Spirit alive to me because you have shared something of yourself. Please pray that I, too, will receive this power of the Holy Spirit."

Father Galenas soon brought other priests into our talks, and I prayed for them to receive the baptism of the Holy Spirit. Not long after that, two of the priests visited me in my office in Saigon. "We taught other people what you taught us," they informed me. "Then they fell down and started speaking in tongues just like we did."

I couldn't help but smile. Those two priests were among the most excited people I had seen in a long time. Soon a growing charismatic movement emerged in several segments of the Catholic Church throughout South Vietnam.

FOCUS ON MEETING PRACTICAL NEEDS

But our delight about the Catholic priests was soon dampened by unpleasant news. Different military factions signed the Paris Peace Accord in January of 1973, and the U.S. withdrew the last of its troops in March of that same year. By then an estimated 47,000 American troops had been killed; two million Vietnamese were dead, four million were wounded and more than half of the population was homeless. The war had devastated large areas of cultivated land, and little of the beleaguered nation's infrastructure remained intact. Fighting continued, however, as the North and the South accused each other of truce violations. A second cease-fire was signed in June, but the hostilities continued.

By June of 1973, we had leased the former USO in downtown Saigon and officially started church services on the fifteenth of that same month. Karen even joined us for a few weeks and opened a Christian coffee shop to reach the young people. But no matter what we did, we could not escape the fact that our beautiful Vietnam had endured thirty years of continuous war. Large numbers of Communist Viet Cong guerrillas infiltrated the border and, by way of Laos, joined forces with bands of native Communist terrorists in the south. The chief objective of these rebels was to disrupt South Vietnamese social and economic programs.

Millions of refugees continued to flee from the Communists in the North. The war in the rural countryside produced a continuous mortar barrage that devastated countless numbers of homes. In several areas, ruthless Viet Cong destroyed entire villages. Every time the South Vietnamese rebuilt a village, the Communists would shell it; every time they rebuilt a bridge, the Communists would blow it up.

The South Vietnamese government tried to move many dislocated villagers to safer relocation camps where they could start life again. Many went without proper nutrition because of the constant competition for food and supplies between the North and the South.

The government asked for our help. It was no longer enough to meet spiritual needs; we also had to meet practical needs. We soon came in contact with some ministers in the Swedish Free Pentecostal denomination who had an active interest in Vietnam. When we told them of the need, they said they wanted to help us build entire refugee resettlement villages, and they were soon busy raising money back home in Sweden.

By the end of 1973, we had four mature Vietnamese men who had received Bible training and were qualified to become licensed ministers. There were 6,000 students enrolled in our Bible study courses through the mail. Most importantly, our Swedish brethren had raised $500,000 to help build homes and relocate refugees to rich farming areas. We worked with them, as well as with many of our Catholic friends, to help in these resettlement villages.

We assisted the refugees primarily by providing materials to build simple cement-block houses. We also donated $25 to each family to provide building and gardening tools and to purchase seed to help them start a modest farm. Relocation gave many a new hope for the future. In each

The Works of the Holy Spirit in the New Testament

The Holy Spirit's works greatly expanded in the New Testament, for God then poured out His Spirit "on all flesh," and no longer limited His workings to the Jews (Joel 2:28; Acts 2:1-17, 39). In addition to the types of works He did in the Old Testament, He now does the following:

- **Gives glory to Jesus and continues His work on earth:** John 16:7-14
- **Interprets Scripture:** John 16:12-15. He is later shown to be the ultimate author of Scripture (1 Peter 1:21).
- **Is the instrument of our new birth in God:** John 3:3; 1 Corinthians 12:13
- **Adopts the believer as a son of God:** Galatians 4:4-7
- **Teaches:** John 14:26
- **Fulfills prophesy:** Joel 2:28-29; Acts 2:14-18
- **Fills and baptizes:** Acts 2:1-4; 4:23-31; 8:14-17; 10:44-48; 19:1-6
- **Helps us to pray:** Romans 8:26-27
- **Leads and guides:** John 16:13; Romans 8:14
- **Bears fruit:** Galatians 5:22-23
- **Gives spiritual gifts:** 1 Corinthians 12:7-10

relocation village where we followed this plan, the government gave us land on which to build a church. We soon started construction of churches in three refugee villages.

OPENING DOORWAYS TO THE HEART

When a person saw that we cared enough to minister to his practical needs, that care often opened the doorway to his heart to receive Jesus. Our churches in the refugee villages reached formerly homeless people who had never before heard the Gospel, and others who had never before considered Christianity a viable alternative to Buddhism and ancestor worship.

But the needs in Vietnam were not limited to the homeless. Before the U.S. troops left, a serious drug problem had developed among the American soldiers. Planes from Laos had regularly smuggled in opium and other drugs, with dealers touting their wares as a welcome diversion from an unjust war. We were told that anywhere from 10 to 25 percent of our enlisted soldiers used heroin—the highest addiction rate for any population in the history of opiate drugs.

Our denomination's drug rehabilitation program, Teen Challenge, had taken volunteer addicts through a long-term program of spiritual therapy and daily discipline, coupled with Bible study. Through this program, hundreds of soldiers who were addicts had already been brought back into society's mainstream.

But once the U.S. troops left in March of 1973, the pushers turned to the Vietnamese young people. By the fall of that same year, there were more than 50,000 heroin addicts from every level of Vietnamese society. Hospitals received daily calls from concerned parents who wondered what to do about their children who were hooked on heroin.

The government made appeals to nearly thirty religious and social organizations to help with the drug problem, but there was little response.

THE PRESIDENT'S WIFE

Those problems opened the door for me to have an appointment with Madame Thieu, the president's wife, who was also the head of a major women's social organization. During that Thursday appointment in September, I told Madame Thieu that Teen Challenge had good results in helping solve drug problems.

Other South Vietnamese government officials who had heard of Teen Challenge's earlier work wanted us to establish such an operation in Saigon. Even before our appointment ended, Madame Thieu told me that they would give us a choice piece of property in downtown Saigon to use for a rehabilitation center.

The following Monday, Madame Thieu and I signed the agreement that would allow us the use of a 60,000-square-foot piece of property in downtown Saigon, as long as we used it for social and religious purposes. In return we were to build a fifty-bed drug rehabilitation center with a chapel. At the signing, I explained to Madame Thieu and the officials present that man's spiritual side was most important in solving the drug problem. Our plans were to build the drug rehabilitation center in Saigon and then to establish similar centers and churches in four other leading cities. God was continuing to work on our behalf.

Gaining Access to the Family

Family ties in Vietnam were deeply rooted in the Buddhist religion, and ancestor worship was highly valued. It was not easy for an individual to break away from such bondage. When we helped free a Vietnamese young person from the snare of drugs, we also gained access to his family. We found that it was easier to reach an entire family than just one individual. What better medium for direct evangelism than for God to work miracles by solving drug problems in families?

Soon we built a 200-seat spiritual renewal center on the complex that was to be for all of the people, including the families of problem youth. We used existing facilities on that property to house a handful of volunteer addicts who wanted to go through our first drug rehabilitation program cycle in Saigon.

We conducted church services in the renewal center. In combination with the drug rehabilitation program, we soon had a strong church where God's power was constantly being shown, with many born again and baptized with the Holy Spirit. Those demonstrations of His power caused many Vietnamese to throw off the religious traditions that had held them captive for centuries. God used our care for practical needs to open hearts to receive Jesus.

THE SPIRIT'S OUTPOURING

FOUR DOORWAYS GOD USES TO OPEN THE HEART TO RECEIVE JESUS

1. **The spoken word**–Jesus taught as "one having authority," and multitudes opened their hearts to hear Him (Matthew 7:29; Mark 1:22; 2:13). When Jewish believers were scattered from Jerusalem because of the persecution, they preached the Lord Jesus "and a great number believed and turned to the Lord" (Acts 11:21b). God can touch an unbeliever through your pastor's sermon on Sunday morning, a teaching or an anointed song on a Christian television program or in a Sunday School class, as well as the words you speak in casual conversation.
2. **The written word**–After Paul and Silas taught in the synagogue, the Bereans searched the word daily and "received the word with all readiness" (Acts 17:11). When I served as head of literature committees and of correspondence courses, I repeatedly saw how powerfully the Holy Spirit uses the written word to open peoples' hearts. Give Bible portions, well-written tracts, Christian books and Christian articles to unbelievers who show interest.
3. **Actions that show God's power**–After Jesus restored sight to the man blind from birth, he believed in Jesus and worshiped him (John 9:1–7, 35–38). When Peter raised Tabitha (also translated "Dorcas") to life, "many believed on the Lord" (Acts 9:36–42). When you sense the Holy Spirit's prompting, be quick to pray for an unbeliever to be healed or to experience God's power.
4. **Actions that reflect God's love and care**–Jesus appointed Judas to keep a money bag in order to give to the poor (John 12:3–6), and He

In 1974 one of our missionary couples started a Bible school in Vung Tau, and it soon had thirty full-time students. Near the middle of April 1975, we held a conference for all of our pastors, students and missionaries. Joining us were two Catholic priests and three nuns. We had four days of meetings, with three services each day.

During those meetings we had the greatest outpouring of the Holy Spirit that we'd ever seen in Vietnam. During one service I looked around and listened carefully; with few exceptions, each one present—including the Catholic priests and nuns—was praising God in tongues.

Nearly 120 gathered for the closing communion service, and there was a strong sense of the Spirit's presence. It was then that we heard the unwelcome news that the Communists were again bombing in the distance. Large concentrations of North Vietnamese Communist soldiers had broken through the demilitarized line and were rapidly moving south to capture Saigon.

After we closed our meeting, there was still some time before we could return to Saigon. As the bombing continued in the distance, Maxine went down to the beach to pray and think. Several women from the conference followed her, crying as they spoke. They knew that freedom would soon come to an end in South Vietnam.

instructed us to minister to others in practical ways (Matthew 25:34-40). This ministry may range from a hand extended in genuine friendship, to caring acts that meet small or significant needs.

Sometimes God combines two or more doorways in a single incident. When Jesus told the woman at the well that she'd had five husbands, He used both the spoken word and an action that showed God's power to reveal. As a result, she and "many of the Samaritans of that city believed in Him" (John 4:39a). I often pray that God will do the same when I am interacting with an unbeliever.

THE BEGINNING OF THE END

We also knew that it was the beginning of the end of the mission as we had known it. We took all thirty Bible school students to Saigon with us. There the American Embassy advised us to get our missionaries out of the country as quickly as possible. I wanted Maxine and myself to stay, because I felt that even the Communists would welcome humanitarian relief work. But, since I was head of the mission, it was my responsibility to get the other missionaries out.

We began working twenty-hour days, for there was so much to be done. While I found a seat for each missionary on evacuation planes, Maxine taught the Bible school students in the chapel of the drug rehabilitation center.

Even during those difficult days, the Holy Spirit worked powerfully. In one of her classes, Maxine prophesied over several of the students. She was especially drawn to Tran Dinh Ai (pronounced "I"), who had once been a Buddhist monk. Disillusioned with Buddhism, he then turned to witchcraft. Later Ai became a Roman Catholic and then an atheist. God powerfully saved Ai, even while he was mocking Christianity. When Ai became born again, his Buddhist parents rejected him from the family; at that point he had come to our Bible school.

As Maxine laid hands on Ai, the Lord gave her a clear word for him: "Son, I have called you and chosen you to serve Me. Be faithful, even though you will face difficulty and trials. If you continue to be faithful to Me, I will be faithful to you. I will raise you up to be the leader of the church in this nation. I will even send you around the world to prepare my church. So be faithful."[158]

CLOSING DAYS

I didn't want to leave Vietnam. Although our mission had officially started in Vietnam in 1972, it was the Holy Spirit's outpouring in our conference in mid-April of 1975 that really birthed us into a mighty spiritual dynamic. Why would any parent abandon a newly born baby? It just didn't seem right.

But as wonderful as the conference had been, the realities around us were harsh. Because we had only been in Vietnam a few years, our mission infrastructure had been built around the missionaries; now we had to quickly reassign responsibilities and positions to the Vietnamese pastors and even to some of the Bible school students. We hurriedly made one pastor our general superintendent and another pastor head of our Bible school; we even put Bible school student Tran Dinh Ai in charge of our Bible correspondence courses.

The American Embassy told us that the evacuation of American and foreign citizens would soon come to an end. They said we were to keep our radio tuned to the American military network station. When a certain song played, that was to be our signal that it was the final day of evacuation.

I was able to help all the missionaries evacuate except one visiting missionary, but I was determined that Maxine and I would stay. Maxine felt differently, though. Already many South Vietnamese people were angry that the American military had pulled out in 1973. When they saw the evacuation of American citizens from Saigon that April, their anger changed to hatred.

We started receiving reports that several Americans had been killed as they tried to make their escape. At Maxine's insistence, we packed many of our belongings and shipped them to the States, keeping only enough to sustain ourselves.

The Last Day

On a warm morning in late April, Maxine was kneeling at our bed while I was about to get up. "Honey," she began her plea, "we need to leave. I feel such an urgency that we must evacuate today. I understand how you feel, but we won't be able to do anything after the Communists gain control. At best they will probably kill us, and that would discourage our Vietnamese brethren more than anything."

I was firm. "You're wrong, Maxine. We will be able to work here. We should stay. The brethren here need us."

In the background our radio began to play the song the American Embassy had told us would be our signal for the last day of evacuation. Maxine continued to kneel beside the bed, praying. As the song played, I remembered what little I had heard about Communism in North Korea: food was used as a weapon against opposition, and Christians were starved to death or brutally persecuted. Women were sexually abused, and young children were forced into labor.

The Communists in North Vietnam had not proven any kinder; a member of the Viet Cong had even broken into the apartment of one of our young missionary couples. The intruder had held a gun to the man's head, forcing him to watch as he raped his wife in front of him.

I wanted to stay and protect as many of the believers as I could, but I also needed to honor how my wife felt God was leading us. I finally agreed to go. Maxine and I picked up a few belongings, as well as a large amount of cash that I had drawn from the bank the day before; we wanted to leave our pastors and believers with as many resources as possible.

We went down to the basement to get into our car. When we got there, I remembered that I had left our camera back in the apartment. I left Maxine in the car and walked quickly to the elevator for a return trip.

While I was gone, a man on a motorcycle approached Maxine and the car, carrying something that looked like a gun. Maxine was concerned that he might try to get into the car and take the stash of cash in the back, so she got out of the car, locked it and stood to one side. As the man started toward Maxine, another Vietnamese man saw what was happening and loudly revved his motorcycle engine so the first man would hear that there was someone else present. When the first man heard the noise of the other engine, he sped away.

As Maxine unlocked the car door to get back in, a third man seemed to come out of nowhere. He pointed a pistol at Maxine's head.

Just then I came back down with the camera and walked out of the elevator. My presence must have frightened the man with the pistol, because he saw me and ran away. Maxine and I quickly got into the car. We first drove to pick up the one other remaining missionary, there on a short-term visit to Vietnam. Like me, he had wanted to stay. The three of us then drove to the mission to say farewell to a group of our pastors and Bible school students and to give them money to help to sustain them through the difficult days ahead.

Even after we arrived at the airport, my missionary friend and I still wanted to return to Saigon, but Maxine prevailed. Before long the airport representatives officially closed the gates; no one else could leave or enter. Maxine was relieved; by that time she was so weary that she lay down on the sidewalk and went to sleep while we waited for one of the last evacuation planes.

Instead of sleeping, I pondered the state of our mission. The Spirit-filled Catholic priests had told me that God had used them mightily and that there were already one thousand Catholic charismatics in Vietnam. Our mission brethren had reported about 2,500 Spirit-filled believers, some of whom had been touched by our relief work or by our drug rehabilitation efforts. We had more than 20,000 in our Bible correspondence course.

Within a few hours I was brought back to the present as we were herded into the belly of an army transport plane. There were no seats; we sat in rows on the floor, with a giant cargo belt strapped across each row of passengers. As the plane took off for a military base in the Philippines, the rays of the sun pierced through the small windows. I could hardly believe what was happening, but I knew that God had used us in Vietnam. He had helped us find the right doorway to open hearts to receive Him.

About You

What about you? What doorway did God use to open your heart to receive Him?

It's fascinating to see which doorway God uses to open a person's heart to receive Jesus. I remember watching the face of one man who had just seen a crippled woman healed in Liberia. God used that healing to open his heart; he was one of the first to respond to the altar call.

I watched many in the West Gate church when Cho preached. Cho was a man of prayer and had a powerful anointing as he used compelling illustrations in his Word-based sermons. God used Cho's sermons to open thousands of hearts, and each Sunday dozens repented of their sins and received Jesus Christ as their Lord and Savior.

I remember looking on as many poor people in the West Gate church started to tithe and prosper. God used their testimonies to open the hearts of those struggling just to make a living. Many who watched God

How to Discern Which Doorway to Take

Each person is unique. I use three guidelines as I decide which doorway God would have me use in leading an unbeliever to Him:

- **Observe that person's interests and needs**—Paul observed that the Athenians had an altar in the Areopagus inscribed "TO THE UNKNOWN GOD" (Acts 17:22-23) and used that starting point to speak about God, even quoting their poets (17:28). As a result, several came to believe in Jesus (17:34). I observe an unbeliever's specific interests and needs in order to better relate the Gospel to him.
- **Listen to the clues in that person's conversation**—Philip heard the Ethiopian eunuch reading Isaiah, and he used that circumstance to start a conversation that resulted in the eunuch's salvation (Acts 8:30-38). As I listen to what an unbeliever says, it helps me to know which doorway God would have me use.
- **Pray and ask God for wisdom**—It is no mistake that the *word of wisdom* is listed first in the spiritual gifts (1 Corinthians 12:8), for I need wisdom whenever I minister to others, especially when I am reaching out to an unbeliever. James's instructions were clear: "If any of you lacks wisdom, let him ask of God, who gives to all liberally and without reproach, and it will be given to him" (James 1:5).

prosper tithers, later turned to faith in Jesus Christ, who provides for our needs.

I found that God allows each of us to find the right "doorway" to open the heart of the unbeliever. We are to minister not only to the spiritual and emotional needs of others, but also in practical physical ways.

God uses many doorways to open the human heart, but we often need to enter the process with Him. Consider someone you might now be trying to bring to a saving relationship with the Lord. Maybe you've even tried using the same doorway God used to reach you, but it hasn't been effective. Maybe that person, like many of the Vietnamese, is bound by ways of thinking that require a different doorway.

Consider practical acts of kindness. When the Lord speaks about the kingdom of heaven, He gives us a glimpse into the future. When Jesus returns in His glory, He says that He will use a specific criterion to separate the sheep from the goats: those He chooses to be with Him will be those who have fed the hungry, given water to the thirsty, clothed the poor, looked after the sick, given hospitality to strangers and ministered to those in prison.[159]

The apostle James later connected genuine faith with acts of generosity to the needy:

> What good is it, my brothers, if a man claims to have faith but has no deeds? Can such faith save him? Suppose a brother or sister is without clothes and daily food. If one of you says to him, "Go, I wish you well; keep warm and well fed," but does nothing about his physical needs, what good is it? In the same way, faith by itself, if it is not accompanied by action, is dead ...Pure and undefiled religion before God and the Father is this: to visit orphans and widows in their trouble, and to keep oneself unspotted from the world.[160]

Sometimes one of the best ways to win someone to the Lord is to show Jesus' love in practical ways that meet tangible needs, yet confirm the person's dignity and worth. That might involve filling a bag with groceries, buying a new outfit of clothes or simply offering a listening ear. May God give us wisdom from above in knowing which doorways to take to open hearts to receive our precious Jesus!

Find the Right Doorway to the Heart: Devotional and Discussion Questions

Sharing Questions

Have you ever heard God speak to you—whether in a still small voice, in a Bible verse that "jumped" out at you, or in another way? If so, what did He say? How did that impact you?

Be brief. Remember the three guidelines to a sharing question: 1) no one is to take more than one minute in response; 2) go around the circle—if in a small group—and give each person an opportunity to respond; and 3) don't ask other questions at this point, for that stretches out the minute.

Discussion Questions

1. Briefly share what you knew about the war in Vietnam before you read this chapter. Did this chapter change your perspective? If so, how?
2. How did God use the difficult situation in Vietnam to bring people to Himself? Has God ever used a difficult situation in your life to draw you closer to Him? If so, how? (Remember to be concise in your answer.)
3. Review the "New Testament Symbols of the Holy Spirit" on page 190. Which of these symbols do you personally relate to as the Holy Spirit's dealings in your life? Why?
4. Which of the "Four Doorways God Uses to Open the Heart to Receive Jesus" on pages 196–197 did God use to bring you to faith in the Lord? Would you add any other doorway(s) to this list?

Application

1. Think of someone in the area that you want to see come to faith in Jesus. Review "How to Discern Which Doorway to Take" on page 201. Consider that person's "clues," interests and needs. What might be a good doorway through which to reach that person for Jesus?
2. What could you do specifically this week to help open that person's heart to receive Jesus?
3. Conclude by praying for each other and for the salvation of one lost person in your area.

My initial interview with Madame Thieu regarding our mission's desire to work with the young drug addicts in South Vietnam.

I sign the agreement with Madame Thieu to start drug rehabilitation work in Saigon.

Madame Thieu, the president's wife, and I officially shake hands after signing a written agreement for the government to give us prime land in Saigon for our mission's promised drug rehabilitation work.

Insight Twelve

Loose Ends

How God ties together the "loose ends" of disappointment and defeat to fulfill His sovereign purposes

I WAS DEVASTATED. Two months after we left Saigon and finally arrived home in the States, I received heartrending news. All of our mission's pastors and Bible school students had fled Vietnam in a boat bound for freedom. They feared that the Communists would punish them severely, especially because they had worked with a mission that had been related to Americans.

We were happy to be reunited with Karen, and we even saw her graduate with honors from Bethany College in California. But there was a pain in my soul that would not leave. If I had remained in Saigon, our pastors and Bible school students might also have had the resolve to stay. I had instead abandoned my responsibility, and I believed that my example had caused them to do the same.

Nothing seemed right. My being away from Vietnam seemed wrong, as did Karen's situation. Maxine and Karen often talked about Karen's upcoming entry into a doctoral program in clinical psychology in a seminary in southern California. Karen didn't want to be in full-time church ministry, but instead wanted to be a respected professional. I felt that God had different plans for her, but I also knew that she had to make her own way in life, so I was silent on the subject.

Two months later I received a letter from the Vietnamese pastor I had left as the superintendent of our denomination in Vietnam. He wrote me about their boat trip to freedom, and he told me that they had finally arrived in the States. Before that letter came, I had hoped that perhaps the news about their leaving was incorrect. Now I felt that we had abandoned the infant move of evangelism and of the Spirit that God had helped us birth in South Vietnam.

MY SOUL'S DISTRESS

My thoughts often drifted to the believers our mission had led to the Lord in Vietnam. I agonized in a state of silent distress. What would those believers do with no one from our mission to care for their souls? If their own pastors had fled, how could they be expected to endure the Communist persecution? Would the Catholic priests we had influenced take care of our believers?

I did not want to burden Maxine, so I shared only a few comments about my feelings. Maxine continued to believe that we would have been killed if we had stayed, but I was never convinced of that. Still, there was nothing I could do to change the situation.

Karen started her doctoral program, and Maxine and I served temporarily on the staff of a nearby church, awaiting our next assignment. We thought we might ask to go to Thailand, which, after all, was near Vietnam.

Karen's first year of graduate school left her with excellent grades, but miserable. I knew the basic problem. Karen and I had both made choices that seemed good, but that were not in God's best plan. She was fighting God's call on her life, and I felt I had shirked my responsibility.

CHURCH GROWTH INTERNATIONAL

By now Cho had two honorary doctorates and was affectionately called "Dr. Cho." Donald McGavran—a missionary statesman and seminary professor whom many called the "father" of the church growth movement—visited Dr. Cho's church in early 1976. The church had a membership of nearly 35,000 at that time, with more than 1,600 cell groups, and McGavran claimed that it was "the best organized church in the world." He suggested that Dr. Cho begin an organization to encourage and teach the many pastors who were visiting his church to see the explosive growth first hand.

While on a plane to California, Dr. Cho sensed God's confirmation of McGavran's suggestion. When he found us in southern California, Dr. Cho asked Maxine and me to return to Seoul to help him establish just such a ministry to train visiting pastors. I knew at once that God was directing our next step.

Soon after, Karen joined us for lunch. After telling her that Dr. Cho had invited us to return to Seoul, I invited her to join us and help me in the formative stages of the new organization. Karen smiled and said, "I don't even need to pray about this one." God was still at work in our lives.

By November of 1976, Maxine, Karen and I were back in Seoul, starting an organization we named "Church Growth International," holding seminars for pastors and church leaders in Seoul and abroad. Dr. Cho was president, and I was executive director. Karen and I were kept busy, but my thoughts kept turning to Vietnam. My quick departure from there still seemed a loose end, tied only to regret and disappointment.

At Church Growth International (CGI), we held three types of seminars: one in Seoul for pastors and leaders who came to study the church up close; a second abroad for those unable to come to Korea; and, in the early years, a third in Seoul for our own church's leadership.

I will never forget the electric sense of excitement as we hosted the church's first international pastors' seminar in June of 1977: there were nearly 600 participants—including more than 200 American pastors and about 120 Thai pastors and church leaders. By 1978, CGI was firmly established; we held more than nineteen seminars at home and abroad with more than 6,000 pastors and leaders participating. That same year we also started the CGI advisory board, comprised of leading pastors from around the world, most of whom led churches with congregations of 1,000 or more. Dr. Cho and I would teach at the various seminars, often aided by one or more pastors from our advisory board.

In late January of 1978, we held our first overseas seminar in Jakarta,

FIVE TEACHINGS WE SHARED THROUGH CGI

Primary to church growth is the need to give consistent priority to evangelism. We taught several other principles and practices in CGI, including these five:

1. **Recognize and honor the Holy Spirit**–Jesus asked the Father to send His Holy Spirit to be our Helper (John 14:16, 26; 16:7-14). We therefore need to value the Holy Spirit as the third member of the trinity and recognize and honor His work among us. Dr. Cho taught that we also need to spend time fellowshipping with the Holy Spirit and that we should expect His signs, wonders and healings among us.
2. **Develop God-directed visions and goals**–As God gave Abram a vision of his future (Genesis 15:1-7), each of us needs to pray and seek God for a specific vision for our future. It is especially important that a pastor have a clear sense of God-given direction. God will also often give us specific numerical goals for things He wants us to prayerfully accomplish. Whether that goal is for the number of people God wants us to reach for Jesus, or the size of our church's membership, a specific numerical goal helps us to target our prayers and efforts and aids us in evaluating our Christian walk and service.
3. **Let faith-filled prayer and fasting permeate your life and ministry to others**–We cannot accomplish anything of significance without God's help. This includes our prayer lives, the time we spend in fellowship with God, our ministry to others and, at times, even spiritual warfare and binding the enemy. Dr. Cho's church provides a Prayer Mountain for those serious in seeking God, and, except for Sunday nights, his church holds daily all-night prayer services.

Indonesia. In spite of the state of national emergency in Jakarta, more than a thousand pastors and lay church leaders attended the sessions. Up to 5,000 attended the evening "miracle rallies," featuring Dr. Cho preaching on salvation and healing and praying for the sick.

One Monday in 1978, Dr. Cho and I were at the sauna. We talked about the children from the church in Seoul. Some parents were not bringing their children to Sunday School because of the long bus ride, and we knew we had to do something innovative. At Dr. Cho's direction, Karen and I developed a plan to establish children's cell groups; these later became some of the most evangelistic cells of the church, with 70 percent of the children coming from homes where parents were not believers. The Sunday School department also started regional Sunday School chapels in various areas of the growing city of Seoul, making children's Sunday School as accessible as possible.

4. **Preach anointed, Word-based sermons that bring hope in Jesus and meet peoples' needs**—I often heard Dr. Cho say that "We are not to preach from Mt. Sinai, where thunder and lightening flashed as people were condemned. Instead, we are to preach from the pulpit of Mount Calvary, giving people faith and hope in the cross and in the finished work of Jesus Christ."
5. **Release and empower others in ministry**—Moses and the early church released and empowered others in ministry (Exodus 18:13-26; Acts 6:1-7), and we must do the same. One of the best ways to do this is through a good, working home cell system, with small groups that provide opportunity for evangelism, fellowship and spiritual growth.

The Same Pattern

In late April we took CGI on a European tour with daytime seminars and evening rallies in six cities in Germany, Sweden, France and Switzerland. The Stockholm seminar saw 1,200 pastors from twenty countries, including Yugoslavia and Poland. In Karlsruhe, Germany, 4,000 attended nightly miracle rallies. During these meetings, several people were healed of cancer.

Dr. Cho continued to be a mighty man of prayer, believing God to work through him with His healing power. I realized that CGI was using the same pattern I had learned to use in the follow-up revival in Liberia. During the day we taught pastors basic principles; in the evening Dr. Cho demonstrated how God's power could flow through a faith-filled pastor.

In July CGI welcomed an Australian group that included 208 pastors and lay leaders. We taught them church growth principles and practices over three weekdays, and we took them on research tours of church departments. They especially enjoyed the Friday night prayer service, joined in a Sunday worship service and visited home cell groups. By the end of that seminar, the Australians had set goals that would eventually result in an average attendance growth of 600 percent in their churches over the following five years.

In September we held an all-Asia seminar at the church, with the largest contingent (330) coming from Indonesia. Among the delegates were former President Sukarno's first wife, Ibu Fatmawati, two of Indonesia's top musical vocalists and three Catholic nuns.

GREAT NEEDS

By that time the church had more than 2,000 cell groups, and pastors wanted even more information on the groups than we were able to give them in the seminar sessions. Together, Karen and I co-wrote a book we titled *Caught in the Web,* taken from the words of a member who stated that he had been "caught in the web" of the church's cell system.

Within a year that book was chosen as "book of the month" in the Church Growth Book Club. The book would eventually go through four printings, and God used it to help many pastors start cell groups in their churches. That same year, with Dr. Cho's permission, Karen began the quarterly English-language magazine *World of Faith* to coordinate with the church's Korean-language magazine of the same name.[161]

The needs were great. In Thailand there were only 600 small churches, as contrasted with 25,000 Buddhist temples. Four out of five Thai churches did not even have a full-time pastor. Instead of going as a missionary as I had considered, I joined Dr. Cho in Bangkok in early 1979 to hold a four-day church growth seminar and evening miracle crusade. More than 600 Thai lay leaders and pastors took part in the seminar. An average of 4000 people packed a downtown Bangkok auditorium nightly. Not only were many saved and filled with the Holy Spirit, more than a hundred were healed of such diseases as deafness, tuberculosis, asthma, back problems, skin allergies and even a leg weakened by polio. Christian leaders hailed the meetings as the greatest yet held in Thailand.

Reverend Somboom, from the town of Roiet, wrote about the dual impact of the daytime seminars and evening miracle crusade: "During those meetings I not only learned much, but was also healed of pain in my back and leg. I now work with ten churches in the northeast part of Thailand. We are starting to have early morning prayer meetings, as well as teaching people about fasting and prayer. This year we are believing God to give us 300 new people. We praise God for what we have learned!"

In April of 1979 we held a three-day church growth seminar in southern Australia with nearly 1,500 pastors and leaders from all over Australia, Tasmania and New Zealand. They came to learn how to increase their personal faith, how to draw more non-Christians to their churches and how to nurture members in home groups. Delegates included Pentecostals, Baptists, Catholics, Lutherans and representatives from The Salvation Army and the Uniting Church.

At night the delegates, along with an additional 3,000 local citizens, attended the evening miracle rallies. Dr. Cho spoke and invited people to salvation, then asked each sick person to lay hands on the diseased part of his or her body and agree with friends and relatives in prayer. God often gave Dr. Cho words of knowledge concerning the illnesses being healed. Two sisters, who had traveled nearly 800 miles to the evening services, were healed of chest pains. Another woman was healed of a goiter that had plagued her for thirty years.

A woman named Cath Laverick had been hospitalized with bone cancer so painful that she was on doses of morphine every three hours. She left the hospital, came to an evening service and, during prayer for the sick, felt a warm sensation in her body. When Dr. Cho said that God was healing someone's bones, she realized that her intense pain was entirely gone. When her doctor later tested her and saw the marked improvement in her test results he said, "Let me know next time there's something like that service. I want to go, too!"

A pastor from a Uniting Church wrote, "This church growth seminar has been one of the most exciting and challenging experiences of my life ...I need a vision of faith; Jesus Christ created the Church to grow, and this depends on the power of the Holy Spirit...We need to minister to the needs of the people, and to rediscover the importance of prayer and the authority of Scripture. We must...feel an urgency to share our faith with others...[and] develop the intimacy of Christian fellowship in cell groups." Another pastor wrote, "God cannot build His Church any bigger than He builds the leadership. God has worked through this seminar to enlarge the minds and spirits of Christian leaders throughout Australia."

Our Greatest Impact

We continued to find our impact greatest overseas when we combined church growth seminars with evening miracle rallies. There were always reports of healings, and the healings seemed to intensify with each passing meeting. One highlight came in a crusade in San Jose, Costa Rica,

FIVE TYPES OF "LOOSE ENDS" IN THE NEW TESTAMENT

1. **Mistakes**–Peter made the greatest mistake of his life when he denied Jesus three times (Luke 22:31-34; 54-62). But Jesus saw beyond Peter's sinful mistakes, restored him and used Peter to preach a powerful sermon on the day of Pentecost that resulted in 3,000 coming to faith in Jesus (John 21:7-19; Acts 2:14-41).
2. **Disappointments and unmet expectations**–Two disciples on the road to Emmaus were deeply disappointed when the Romans crucified Jesus, for they thought that meant He was not the Messiah they expected. Then Jesus walked beside them as a stranger, rightly explained the Scriptures to them and restored to them God's perspective and hope (Luke 24:13-35).
3. **Puzzling circumstances**–The apostle Thomas was totally confused. First the Romans crucified Jesus, then the disciples said that Jesus had supernaturally appeared to them when they were behind closed doors. Thomas doubted and needed proof. Jesus again appeared behind closed doors, this time to show Thomas His scars. Thomas then made one of the most moving confessions of faith in the New Testament, saying to Jesus, "My Lord and my God." (John 20:24-28). Even in the midst of puzzling situations, we need to proclaim His Lordship (Habakkuk 3:17-18).
4. **Difficult or failed relationships**–When Mark deserted Paul and Barnabas in Pamphylia, Paul no longer wanted to take Mark with them, and even parted from Barnabas (Acts 15:36-40).

when a man in a wheel chair was healed and started walking.

In 1979 we began another tour of Europe, this time with seminars and evening rallies in cities in Portugal, France, Switzerland and Finland. More than 3,000 pastors and leaders participated in four church growth seminars, and, in places like Lisbon, Portugal, up to 8,000 nightly flocked to the miracle rallies.

Several pastors and leaders sent letters to the coordinating office of the Nimes, France, seminar, attended by more than a thousand pastors, evangelists and lay leaders from a wide variety of denominations. The president of the International Evangelical Mission wrote, "I have been strengthened, refreshed, and renewed in my ministry and in my faith." Several Baptist leaders wrote, "We are now determined to enter into the vision the Lord has opened to us." One charismatic leader wrote, "All participants discovered or rediscovered deeper dimensions of God's greatness in an objective, positive, and effective manner. It is about time we learn that God cannot build His Church any larger than the vision of His servants."

While we never hear that Paul and Barnabas were restored in relationship, Paul later wrote Timothy and asked him to bring Mark to him, "for he is useful to me for ministry" (2 Timothy 4:11). We also will have some difficult or failed relationships that God will help us restore, and others—for a variety of reasons—that might never be fully mended.

5. **Unfulfilled promises, hopes and dreams**—No one understands dealing with as-yet-unfulfilled promises and hopes better than Jesus: "I will come again and receive you to Myself" (John 14:3). One day, with a shout, the trumpet of God and the voice of an archangel, He is coming back for us (1 Thessalonians 4:16).

By November of 1979, our own church in Seoul celebrated a membership of more than 100,000. Pat Robertson, founder and host of the "700 Club" spoke at the celebration service. The church continued to strengthen its bustling 7,000 home groups and sent out 92 missionaries who built 82 churches in 16 different countries. The church also added youth cell groups, aimed primarily at young adult singles who worked in Seoul's factories.

We held our first All-Chinese Church Growth Seminar in Seoul in 1980. More than 300 delegates from Singapore, Hong Kong and Taiwan gathered to learn church growth principles. Many returned to Taiwan to be part of "Target '80," aimed at helping 2,000 churches in Taiwan equip and utilize their lay leaders.

By 1980, Dr. Cho realized that there must be changes if the cell system was to grow more in his own church. He started "middle management" lay leadership by appointing "section leaders" from among the best of his 10,000 cell leaders. Each section leader was to minister to and oversee five to ten group leaders in his or her section of responsibility.

This additional level of leadership had a great impact. In the first six months of 1981, the church averaged one new member every seven minutes and one new cell group every hour and a half. By the middle of 1981, there were 13,387 women's, men's, youth and children's cell groups; and by the end of that year the church had 200,970 members.

By this time, Maxine's old Bible school had moved to Lakeland, Florida, and had become Southeastern College. In recognition of my contributions to the ministry, they conferred an honorary doctorate on me, and I was soon called "Dr. Hurston."

CONTINUED GROWTH

By November of 1981, we had directed CGI for five years; we had held 115 seminars for nearly 50,000 pastors and church leaders. We had also watched the Seoul church grow from a membership of 40,000 to more than 200,000 and had seen the cell groups climb to a total of more than 13,000. Dr. Cho was an internationally recognized pastor, influencing thousands of pastors and churches around the world. His church was considered a divine phenomenon.

But I knew it was time for us to return to the States. We had developed an efficient staff, and there were many capable Koreans who could carry on the work of CGI.

In the meantime, Maxine and I were delighted at Karen's change of direction. Through her work in Korea, she had sensed her own call into ministry and had been ordained in our denomination, sharing with others the principles she had learned in Dr. Cho's church. God had taken the "loose ends" of her earlier choices and, with His loving hand, had woven them into a tapestry reflecting His purposes and destiny.

However, I was still bothered by my decision to leave Vietnam. It was a loose end that still did not seem to tie into God's design.

After our return to the States, I stayed in touch with Dr. Cho. By 1982 I learned that his church had 330,000 members and that Prayer Mountain welcomed an average of 1,500 visitors daily. The year 1984 marked the 100th anniversary of Protestant Christianity in Korea, and the church's name was changed from Full Gospel Central Church to Yoido Full Gospel Church. Billy Graham preached in one of the seven Sunday services held to honor the centennial. Dr. Graham later said, "I felt the presence of the Holy Spirit permeate the main sanctuary. My words flowed freely when I spoke."

On October 1 of that year, church membership topped 400,000. Dr. Cho was in increasing interdenominational demand, speaking at events such as Billy Graham's Itinerant Evangelists' Conference in Amsterdam and the National Religious Broadcasters Convention in Washington, D.C. By the end of 1985, whenever Dr. Cho went on his short speaking trips, he left 342 pastoral staff and nearly 200 administrative staff in charge at home.

Jashil Choi, Dr. Cho's coworker throughout the years, retired in October 1985, thereafter spending her time speaking in Korean churches abroad. The church's overseas work continued to grow. By October of 1988 the church had sent 261 Korean missionaries to 27 countries. The work was also progressing nationally. The year 1980 marked the beginning of Agape Line, a lay counseling telephone ministry to Seoul residents. Dr. Cho established a ten-minute dial-a-sermon program in 1986, and the ministry logged a million calls its first two years.

By the end of 1986, membership had leapt to 510,000; in 1988 it climbed to the 600,000 mark. Throughout this time the lay leadership base of the church expanded steadily. In 1988 alone the church appointed 10,000 new lay leaders. By June 1988 they had completed the multi-million dollar Elim Welfare Town, then the largest facility in Asia for housing elderly homeless persons and for training disadvantaged youth in marketable skills.

During the 1980s, Dr. Cho established branch churches, called "regional sanctuaries," around the sprawling city of Seoul. By 1992, twelve regional sanctuaries welcomed as many as 50,000 people weekly to their Sunday services.

CGI continued holding seminars for foreign pastors, featuring speakers such as Pat Robertson, Robert Schuller and C. Peter Wagner. By 1990, Church Growth International reported a combined total of more than one million participants from 40 countries in its seminars and in Dr. Cho's speaking engagements.

Paul Ai, the "Seed" That Bore Much Fruit

Over the next two decades, I served in the States in a wide variety of ways: as president of a school of theology, as a speaker and church growth consultant, and as a staff member in a number of fine churches.

Then, more than 20 years after we had fled Saigon, I received a letter from Tran Dinh Ai, one of the Bible school students to whom Maxine had prophesied. I was surprised to find that the return address was in Vietnam, for I had assumed that he had fled to the States with the rest of the Vietnamese pastors and students. What surprised me even more was that Ai was inviting me to return to Vietnam to minister to the pastors of the underground churches he had helped to develop.

Over the following months I learned more of Ai's story. He had been appointed as head of the International Correspondence Institute (ICI) and had been ordained and elected as the secretary of the mission just after we left. When the other pastors and leaders decided to leave, Ai had driven the van to the dock, planning to join them on the boat.

But Maxine's prophecy filled Ai's thoughts. He had a keen sense that God would indeed use him as a leader of the church in Vietnam, so Ai decided not to go with the others. Three weeks later, while his fellow church leaders were in the boat drifting to freedom, the police arrested Ai. The Communist authorities claimed that the ICI and CIA were interchangeable terms and that Ai was a spy.

After Ai was put in prison, the authorities sent him to a forced-labor camp. Over the next thirteen years, Ai was in and out of prison and forced-labor camps, sharing the Gospel and leading many fellow prisoners to the Lord. Tran Dinh Ai comforted himself with Paul's example—to the point that he adopted Paul's name as his own.

While Ai was in prison, God gave him an idea of how to develop effective church leaders by using five different levels of training, each level requiring both teaching and specific goals for fieldwork. Ai restarted the Assemblies of God mission in Vietnam in 1988, using those five levels.[162]

Ten years later, at Paul Ai's invitation, Maxine and I again visited Vietnam. We were thrilled at what we saw. The Assemblies of God there had grown to nearly 15,000 born-again members in 175 congregations. Most were house churches, similar to the cell system, and all were vibrant with new life in Jesus.

I felt that I had failed God when Maxine and I fled Vietnam in 1975 because so many other leaders later left as well. But God had used the one "seed" of Paul Ai to bear much fruit, with growth that far surpassed anything I could ever have expected to accomplish.

Loose Ends Tied Together

Dr. Cho invited me to return to Seoul to preach in the opening session of the church's fortieth anniversary celebration services in May of 1998. He further honored me by choosing to be my interpreter and presented me with a plaque of appreciation for my contribution to the church's growth in its earlier days.

I'll never forget one moment as I sat on that platform, soon to speak, looking over a sea of more than 25,000 faces in the main sanctuary that represented just a portion of the more than 800,000-member congregation, knit together by an extensive cell group network. By then Dr. Cho's church was aggressively planting other churches, both in Korea and abroad. Karen sat in the congregation, now ordained, capable and called in her own right, soon to be preaching in the Friday all-night prayer meeting.

As I sat on the platform, I pondered the past and the present—and I finally understood. Paul was right when he wrote that "all things work together for good to those who love God, to those who are the called according to His purpose."[163] God is a Master Weaver. He takes what seem to be the "loose ends" in our lives, and He weaves them together into a magnificent tapestry according to His divine pattern and for His own purposes.

Maxine and I had not failed when we left Vietnam; rather God had orchestrated that move to reposition us to help Dr. Cho start CGI. The change in Maxine's and my lives had resulted in an important change in Karen's life and career path. The loose ends had come together in His capable hands.

Over the following years I would see even more loose ends tied together. We met Ron Cottle, now the son-in-law of Sister Mitchell and the husband of Joanne, the teenager who had played the piano in the first church Maxine and I had pastored together. We discovered that Ron had started an innovative approach to Bible school training with campuses located in churches around America, and I was soon teaching a course on "Growing the World's Largest Church" on several of those campuses.

Jan Crouch, whom God allowed Maxine to lead into the baptism of the Holy Spirit when Jan was just a child, continued to make great strides with her husband, Paul. In 1983, when I was president of a school of

FIVE WAYS JESUS RESPONDS TO "LOOSE ENDS"

Our heavenly Father has promised that Jesus will return again (Matthew 24:36-44; Mark 13:26-27; Acts 1:6-11; 1 Thessalonians 3:13; 5:23; 2 Thessalonians 2:1-8). So Jesus deals with the "loose ends" of His Father's yet unfulfilled promises and plans with five responses we also need:

1. **He prepares**–Jesus has gone "to prepare a place" for us (John 14:2). Even though He does not know the exact timing of the Father's plans, He prepares for them. You and I also must continue to believe in the Father's goodness and prepare in any way we can for the fulfillment of His promises to us.
2. **He prays**–After Jesus ascended into heaven, He did not go into a flurry of activity. Instead, Jesus sat at the right hand of the Father, praying and interceding on our behalf (Romans 8:34). Jesus asked the Father to send the Holy Spirit, who now works with us to continue Jesus' ministry (John 14:16; 16:7-14). Sometimes you and I are quick to work to try to bring about some desired result with our loose ends. But, like Jesus, we instead need to pray to the Father for the Holy Spirit to work on our behalf.
3. **He waits**–The writer of Hebrews gave us this insight: "After He had offered one sacrifice for sins forever, [Jesus] sat down at the right hand of God, from that time **waiting** till His enemies are made His footstool" (10:12-13 [emphasis added]). Instead of trying to manipulate and work for a solution, you and I also need to patiently wait: "Those who wait on the Lord shall renew their strength" (Isaiah 40:31a).

theology in California, we conferred an honorary doctorate on Paul Crouch. I was proud of all God had helped the Crouches to accomplish. Trinity Broadcasting Network is now the world's largest Christian television network. Worldwide by 2003, TBN had more than 4,000 television stations, twenty-six satellites, and could also be seen via the Internet and on thousands of cable systems. TBN now has coverage in every country around our vast world.

On Father's Day of 1995, the Brownsville Assemblies of God, the church in which Karen was born again and the one we attended when we lived in the Pensacola, Florida, area, broke into continuous revival that is still going on through the time of this writing.

Even though Liberia has gone through years of devastating civil war, I received word that the current president helped in a 2002 "March for Jesus" because he was desperate for God's intervention in his nation. God was tying up more loose ends.

4. **He forgives**—Jesus not only died on the cross to forgive sins, but even now He continues to forgive when we confess our sins (1 John 1:9). You and I also need to forgive, even when we do not understand the loose ends of difficult or failed relationships in our lives, and let God bring restoration in His timing.
5. **He keeps focused**—Jesus endured the cross because of His focus on the "joy that was set before Him" (Hebrews 12:2). Jesus now keeps focused on the Father's faithfulness, and you and I need to do the same.

Church Growth International continued to grow and have an impact in countries around the world. Our beloved coworker Jashil Choi died, but she still influences many people through Prayer Mountain. Nam Soo and Esther Kim, who served with us in Vietnam, later became pastors of a church in New York that has grown into one of the largest Korean congregations in our nation. Paul Ai and his family finally came to the States, leaving a staff of strong leaders to continue the work to 250 churches and 35,000 believers in Vietnam, while he focused on planting churches among the Vietnamese in America.

There are still a few loose ends in my life. But our Master Weaver continues to go about His business.

About You

Abraham had a major "loose end." God had promised him descendants that would be as great as the number of the stars in the sky,[164] but Abraham was still childless at the age of eighty-five, and his wife Sarah could no longer conceive.

Remember the loose ends in Joseph's life? God gave Joseph two dreams of greatness, but he soon found himself rejected by his own brothers and torn from a father who loved him.[165] When Joseph did the right thing in Potiphar's house and rejected the advances of Potiphar's wife, an unwitting Potiphar threw Joseph into prison.[166]

Consider Moses' loose end. He felt deeply the Egyptian oppression of the Jews, but his first attempt to bring justice ended with his flight to the backside of the desert.[167]

You might be in the same situation. As He did with Abraham, God might have given you a promise that is still unfulfilled. You might be like Joseph, knowing you have been destined to do greater things, but instead finding yourself in the prison of a difficult situation. Or you might seem like Moses, wanting to bring justice to the oppressed but instead struggling in what seems to be a hopeless situation. You could even be like me, feeling you have made a mistake that has hurt both God and His work. "Loose ends" range from unfulfilled promises, to situations or choices that appear to us as defeat, to disappointments in which you can see no hope.

In the midst of it all, God continues to be the Master Weaver. Abraham was ninety-nine years old when Sarah gave birth to their son Isaac, the forefather of the Jewish nation. After Joseph first learned to rule his own responses to difficult situations, God used Pharaoh to lift him from prison and make him a mighty ruler in the nation. God strategically positioned Joseph to rescue an entire nation, along with his own family, from famine. God called Moses, a broken shepherd on the backside of the desert, from a burning bush. He then used an eighty-year-old Moses to rescue an entire nation from oppressive bondage.

What are your "loose ends"? Do you struggle with a sense of failure or disappointment? Maybe God has given you a promise that is still unfulfilled and that nags you in the night hours. Be patient. He is the Master Weaver, and, in time, He takes the loose ends of our lives and ties them together in a beautiful tapestry of His purposes.

Trust Him. He continues to work out your divine destiny. Above all, remember heaven's perspective. Even now heaven is filled with Christ's longing for His bride. Even now Jesus looks upon us and declares, "Surely I am coming quickly."[168]

I spoke in dozens of daytime CGI seminars, including this one in Indonesia. We concluded with an altar call for pastors who needed God's ministry in their personal lives.

This All-Asia CGI seminar in 1978 impacted a broad range of people.

Dr. Cho and I pray at the church's eighth missions conference.

Dr. Cho interprets for me one last time as I preach in his church's 40th anniversary in 1998.

Dr. Cho embraces me before we begin preaching.

Dr. Cho presents me with a plaque in recognition of my "dedication and commitment to the development and growth of our church" (May 20, 1998)

Loose Ends: Devotional and Discussion Questions

Sharing Question

If you had all the money you needed, and knew you could not fail, what one thing would you want to do for God and His kingdom?

Be brief. Remember the three guidelines to a sharing question: 1) no one is to take more than one minute in response; 2) go around the circle—if in a small group—and give each person an opportunity to respond; and 3) don't ask other questions at this point, for that stretches out the minute.

Discussion Questions

1. Have you ever had a major "loose end" in your life (such as a disappointment, unmet expectation or something you felt was a failure) that was later tied together? If so, briefly tell what it was and how it was resolved.
2. Review the "Five Teachings We Shared through CGI" on pages 210–211. Which of these teachings was of greatest interest to you? Why?
3. Consider the "Five Types of 'Loose Ends' in the New Testament" on pages 214–215. Which one of these do you think the person or persons involved found most challenging? Why?
4. What are one or two "loose ends" you have seen frequently in the lives of those around you?

Application

1. Reread "Five Ways Jesus Responds to 'Loose Ends'" on pages 220–221. Try to list two to five "loose ends" in your life today. Then choose the one "loose end" (or two) that bothers you the most.

2. Pair with your spouse (or, in a small group, with someone of the same gender). Share with that person about the "loose end" that causes you the most concern, as well as how you sense God wants you to respond to it. After each person shares in your pair, pray for each other.

3. If you are in a small group, come back as an entire group. Consider the twelve insights shared in this book. Which insight do you think is most significant at this point in your life?

4. Conclude by praying for each other and for the salvation of one lost person in your area.

Dr. Cho congratulates me after Church Growth International's (CGI's) 100th seminar. Maxine and Karen stand beside me. The woman sitting in the background is Jashil Choi.

I was president of a school of theology that conferred an honorary doctorate to Paul Crouch in 1982. Ralph Wilkerson stands to the right.

Endnotes

1. Deuteronomy 32:10; Psalm 17:8; Zechariah 2:8
2. First stanza of "Must Jesus Bear the Cross Alone," Thomas Shepherd and others, public domain; also see Matthew 16:24; Mark 8:34; 10:21; Luke 9:23; 14:27.
3. See 1 Corinthians 13:12b
4. Acts 7:55–56
5. Acts 12:3–16
6. Revelation 20:2–3
7. John 6:8–13
8. Acts 1:6–7
9. John 20:25–29
10. Genesis 15:2; 24
11. Luke 16:19–26
12. Matthew 23:37, NIV; Luke 13:34
13. John 3:16–17
14. 1 Corinthians 9:22b.
15. Exodus 14:10–31
16. 1 Samuel 18:6–19:1; 22:1–24:22; Psalm 142:1–7
17. Acts 12:1–3
18. Luke 18:7–8a, NIV
19. Ephesians 5:26
20. Romans 8:28
21. 2 Peter 3:9
22. Genesis 12:1–4
23. Exodus 1:1–7, esp. v. 7 with 13:17–22
24. Luke 9:1–6; 10:1–20
25. Matthew 28:19a
26. Titus 3:1
27. John 12:24
28. Acts 1:5
29. Acts 2:4
30. Acts 4:31
31. Acts 8:14–19
32. Acts 8:19
33. Acts 8:20
34. Acts 10:46
35. Acts 19:6
36. Corinthians 14:13, 27–28

37. 1 Corinthians 14:14–15
38. 1 Corinthians 14:18–19 (emphasis added)
39. 1 Corinthians 14:4
40. Jude 20
41. Proverbs 18:21
42. 1 Corinthians 14:39
43. 2 Corinthians 10: 3, 5
44. Romans 12:2; Hebrews 4:12
45. Matthew 12:31–32; John 14:16–17; 16:7–15; Acts 1:4–5, 7–8
46. Luke 11:9–10, 13 (emphasis added)
47. Acts 10:34
48. Psalm 103:1–5
49. John 3:8
50. Ephesians 6:12
51. 2 Timothy 1:7; 1 John 4:4b: Acts 1:8a
52. Mark 1:39 (emphasis added)
53. Mark 1:25
54. Matthew 10:1, 8 (emphasis added)
55. Acts 1:8
56. Acts 3:6
57. Acts 16:18
58. Philippians 2:10a
59. Numbers 14:26–35
60. Matthew 3:13–17; Mark 1:9–11; Luke 3:21–22
61. Matthew 3:17
62. Matthew 4:1; Mark 1:12; Luke 4:1
63. 1 Corinthians 14:13
64. We have changed Amin's name to protect his family.
65. Titus 3:1
66. Acts 1:14
67. Acts 4:24, 31
68. Acts 2:44a, 47b (emphasis added)
69. Acts 4:32a, 33 (emphasis added)
70. 2 Chronicles 20:1–30
71. Esther 3:12–4:3; 4:15–5:8; 8:4–9:10
72. Jonah 3:4–10
73. Glenn Horst, "I Saw Revival in the Philippines," *Pentecostal Evangel*, 31 July 1955, page 6.
74. "Signs Follow Preaching of the Word in the Philippines," *Pentecostal Evangel*, 25 March 1955, page 6.
75. 1 Samuel 1:8–20; 2:21
76. Daniel 10–12
77. Matthew 4:1–2; Luke 4:1–2

78. 1 Corinthians 7:5
79. Matthew 17:17, NIV; Mark 9:19, KJV
80. Matthew 17:21; Mark 9:29
81. Maxine attended Southeastern Bible Institute, which later became Southeastern College (now located in Lakeland, Florida).
82. Matthew 17:14–21
83. Luke 4:38–39
84. Luke 13:10–16
85. Mark 6:5–6
86. John 5:19
87. Matthew 11:12
88. Hebrews 10:38–11:40
89. Mark 16:17a and 18b, KJV
90. The senator's healing was even reported on the front page of the secular newspaper, *The Liberian Age,* on January 13, 1956.
91. Front–page article written by Jacob E. Odugbe in *The Liberian Age,* 12 January 1956, taken from the Glenn Horst archives, courtesy of Joyce Horst.
92. Front–page article in *The Liberian Age,* 13 January 1956.
93. C. Letecia Blaine wrote this in her column "Think of These Things" in *The Liberian Age,* 20 January 1956, page 5.
94. C. Letecia Blaine's column "Think of These Things" in *The Liberian Age,* 27 January 1956, page 6.
95. *The Liberian Age* ran the following articles in 1956: January 12, front page article; January 13, article on page 1 and page 8; January 20, article on page 2 and two articles on page 5; January 27, two articles on page 6; February 3, two articles on page 5; February 10, page 7; February 17, page 3 and page 6.
96. *The Liberian Age,* 20 January 1956, page 2.
97. Acts 10:34–35
98. Quoted from the February 27, 1956, telegram written by Senator James Anderson to President Tubman; taken from the Glenn Horst archives, courtesy of Joyce Horst.
99. Quoted from the March 3 summary report written by Senator James Anderson; taken from the Glenn Horst archives, courtesy of Joyce Horst
100. This interchange was reported by "Aunt Clara" who wrote the "Children's Corner" in the secular newspaper, *The Liberian Age,* 3 February 1956, page 5.
101. Matthew 14:23; 26:36–44; Mark 1:35; 6:46; Luke 5:16; 6:12; 9:28; 22:32; John 17
102. Matthew 5:2–7:29; 13:54; Mark 1:21–22; 2:13; 4:1–33; 10:1; Luke 4:14–15; 5:3; 19:47–48; John 7:14–29; 8:2, 28
103. Matthew 4:24; 8:5–13; 9:20–22, 35; 14:14; 19:1–2; Mark 1:40–42; 2:1–12;

10:46–52; Luke 7:20–23; 13:10–17; John 4:46–5:15; 9:1–7

104. Matthew 8:14–17, 28–34; 9:32–33; 17:14–18; Mark 1:34, 39; 7:24–30; 16:9; Luke 11:14–26
105. Matthew 8:23–27; 9:23–26; 17:24–27; Mark 6:45–51; 8:1–9; 11:12–14, 20–21; Luke 5:4–11; 7:12–15; John 2:1–11; 11:1–44; 21:3–6
106. Matthew 10:1, 8
107. Mark 16:17–18
108. John 14:12
109. John 6:29
110. Quoted in "Rev. Byrd's Work in Bassa," *The Liberian Age,* 2 March 1956, page 9 (no author given).
111. C. Letecia Blaine in "Think on These Things," *The Liberian Age,* 6 April 1956, page 9.
112. These additional articles appeared in *The Liberian Age* in 1956: February 27, front page; March 2, page 9 and page 10; March 9, page 3; March 23, page 2; March 28, pages 3 and pages 11–12; March 26, page 4; April 6, page 9.
113. C. Letecia Blaine in "Think on These Things," *The Liberian Age,* 17 February 1956, page 3.
114. "Rev. Byrd Concludes Most Successful Evangelical Tour," *The Liberian Age,* 23 March 1956, page 3 (no author given).
115. This quote is taken from Glenn Horst's March 20, 1956, journal entry, courtesy of Joyce Horst.
116. This was reported in *The Liberian Age,* 23 March 1956, pages 11–12..
117. Matthew 28:19
118. John 15:16
119. Matthew 13:3–23; Mark 4:3–20; Luke 8:5–15
120. Nwana Obi, "Religious Revival," *The Liberian Age,* 27 August 1956, page 7.
121. "Religious Revival Has Improved Soldiers' Discipline," *The Liberian Age,* 2 November 1956, page 4.
122. 1 Corinthians 4:20
123. 1 Corinthians 2:4b
124. Acts 19:12
125. Acts 14:21–22.
126. Matthew 6:14–15; Mark 11:25
127. Luke 23:34
128. 1 Corinthians 10:13
129. Ephesians 4:31–32
130. Psalm 126:5–6, NIV
131. Matthew 25:14–30
132. James 4:10
133. Genesis 2:15–17
134. John 3:16

135. Genesis 2:6; 6:13–22
136. 1 Kings 18:16–40
137. Luke 1:26–38
138. Proverb 28:1
139. Matthew 14:22–33
140. "Seoul Revival Center Dedicated," *Pentecostal Evangel*. 24 December 1961, pages 8–9.
141. Galatians 6:7
142. Acts 9:27
143. Acts 11:22b–23a, 25–26
144. Acts 13:2–14:28
145. Acts 15:37–39
146. Proverb 18:21
147. Acts 2:42–46
148. Romans 16:3–5; I Corinthians 16:19; Colossians 4:15; Philemon 1–2
149. Exodus 18:5–27
150. *Pentecostal Evangel*, August 8, 1965, page 11.
151. 1 Peter 2:5, 9
152. Ephesians 4:11
153. Acts 6:1–4
154. Acts 6:7
155. Exodus 18:5–27
156. Exodus 18:21–22
157. Exodus 19 and 20
158. See Isaiah 41:9–20
159. Matthew 25:32–40
160. James 2:14–17; 1:27
161. The name of that quarterly magazine later changed to *Church Growth*.
162. The first was the *Caleb soul-winning level*, with one month of teaching in basic Bible doctrine, followed by fieldwork in which each student was to win five people to a saving relationship with Jesus Christ and to read through the entire Bible. After a student met those qualifications, he could come back for the *Joshua cell leader level*, which included three months of teaching in eighteen intensive Bible courses, and three months of fieldwork in which a student was to win fifteen people to the Lord and read through the entire Bible five times. By this time each student would be the equivalent of a cell group or small group leader.

    Those who successfully completed the Joshua level returned for the *Andrew church-planter level*, in which teachers instructed each student in another eighteen Bible courses. By this time the student was to have twenty members in a local church baptized both in water and in the Holy Spirit before he or she would be licensed as a minister. In the *Aaron local pastor level* the student functioned as a licensed minister, sometimes under a local church pastor, and in some cases pastoring a church he started. In the final *Moses trans-local leadership level,* the licensed minister would have to complete 128 credits of Bible study for his or her bachelor's degree, and either plant a new church from his existing church or, if arrested and put in prison, plant a church in prison. Only at that point would the licensed minister be ordained.

163. Romans 8:28, KJV
164. Genesis 15:5
165. Genesis 37:3–36
166. Genesis 39:1–20
167. Exodus 2:11–3:10
168. Revelation 22:20

The church complex on Yoido Island when we left in 1981; by that time the church had a membership of 200,000 with 10,000 cell groups.

Sidebars, Devotional and Discussion Questions